CH00622127

DEDICATION

This book is dedicated to the many
hundreds of participants who have
taught me what I have come to know
about training others in counselling
skills in the introductory workshops
I have led over the last ten years.
To them all thanks.

I hope this goes some way to clarifying
the many dilemmas they have raised
in that time.

Bryce Taylor

CONTENTS

Preface

There is considerable and increasing interest on the part of many people involved in the helping or 'caring' professions in the role that counselling and counselling skills can play in promoting the interpersonal effectiveness of helpers. **Counselling, however, is only one particular form of helping relationship** that can be distinguished from a range of others. The value of counselling as the **appropriate** strategy to employ with any individual or group will depend upon the purpose of the help being offered, the problem under review, and the preferred method and skills of the helper. Most people attending counselling courses are not necessarily looking to become psychological counsellors, working with individuals on a long-term basis to produce therapeutic change. Rather they are aiming to increase the range of their understanding of counselling approaches and the skills employed in counselling and its application to other helping activities in what may be termed their 'guidance role'.

Section I

Helpers & Helping

Chapter One

Helping as an Activity

Many factors influence what goes on when one person helps another or when a group meet and overcome some difficulty. Whatever we would like to believe about our own motives as helpers, the first issue for any helper to acknowledge is **'What's in it for me?'** Helping others serves the helper's needs, whether it be the need to feel satisfied at a job well done, or appreciated by an individual who has succeeded in some task they have previously failed. Helping is not an exclusively altruistic activity and helpers have needs of their own. Unless helpers are clear about their needs, they can suffer from over-work, exhaustion and the phenomenon of 'burn-out', which is indicated by a loss of commitment. Because helping is a very demanding activity, helpers stand in danger of being open to exploitation and manipulation either by clients or by the organisations which employ them. This may not be out of any deliberate or conscious intent but more likely out of the expectation that the helper must respond to anyone at any time. Perhaps the most important skill for helpers is to establish satisfactory personal boundaries to ensure they have time for themselves, time to recuperate, and time to take stock.

What Helpers Need

The desire to help another is no guarantee of success.

All forms of helping, including counselling, are essentially applied activities; mere **knowledge alone is not sufficient to make an effective helper**. The key is the ability to apply knowledge sensitively and appropriately to facilitate an individual or group toward the resolution of some dilemma. Consequently, a helper's main resource for their work is themselves. The more they understand about themselves, and the greater self-awareness they possess, the less likely it is that they will become subject to any of the many pitfalls there are to effective helping. **Self-awareness** is an all embracing term to describe a group of inter-related aspects of self-other understanding. There appear from research (Avila, Combs and

Purkey, 1977) to be six major elements of self-awareness that contribute towards making an effective helper and in developing one's own resource strength. These are set out below. The term used to describe helping activities which rely upon the use of self as the major resource is the **self-as-instrument.**

Knowledge

Helpers need to have a sound understanding of the underpinning rationale for whatever kind of help they are offering. Intuition and playing hunches can sometimes be a potent source of assistance, but are not a sufficient basis for offering systematic, purposeful and aware help to others. For individuals coming into a helping role without prior training, acquiring a sound understanding of the effective limits to their helping role can take a considerable time, and cause much uncertainty and anxiety. It is important for helpers to take time to discuss their views and increase their understanding of how they can help, what help they can legitimately provide, and perhaps most importantly, why they are being seen as a helper in the first place. Experience in such matters is no alternative to training. Opportunities to share issues and concerns with others in a similar role is an essential need for developing in helpers a sound understanding of what they are there to do.

Frame of Reference

All people in a helping role act upon some basic assumptions they have acquired, often unconsciously, about the nature of the world in which they live, the rights and responsibilities of people, and how they regard helping as an activity. If these assumptions are based upon a need for control and direction for their own good, and a need for assistance in making the right choices, then these assumptions will find their way into the helper's way of responding. If, however, the frame of reference of the helper is one that generally regards human beings as essentially trustworthy, able to achieve growth and change and overcome difficulties, they will operate from a different value position. An individual's 'frame of reference' is often not easy to identify, least of all for the person themselves, yet it influences all that they think and do. It provides people with their ready-made view of the world which they bring to any situation they find themselves acting in.

How people behave at any particular moment is a result of how things seem to them. Helping people achieve more satisfying ways of living and being is therefore a matter of **facilitating change in what people think and believe about themselves and their world.** To do this well, effective helpers need to understand the nature of personal meaning and how the individual's view of the world can be widened and enriched.

Views of What People Are Like

Helpers are influenced by their views about what people are really like. An attitude toward others in difficulty that respects the dilemmas they face, and offers support without taking over the problem, will communicate itself to the individuals seeking help. Some assumptions that suggest such an attitude are:

* People are essentially worthy of dignity and respect.
* People can resolve their own predicaments if given support of the right kind, and will do it better than others, since they got themselves into the predicament to start with.
* People can work together positively.
* People have an inherent capacity to work, learn, grow and mature.

Helper's Self-concept

An individual's self-concept is not a 'thing', but an original set of ideas, perceptions and values that attach to an individual's sense of self. It extends to cover one's loved ones and possessions, as when my friend becomes upset when I thoughtlessly put aside a piece of 'junk' which he later tells me is his latest product at his art class. Our sense of self becomes invested in our relationships with others, so that we come to feel keenly the distresses they experience and the satisfactions that accompany their achievement.

Self-concept represents what people perceive themselves to be and what they believe themselves to be. For helpers it is especially important to investigate and understand their own self-concept in order to increase their awareness of the motivations and beliefs influencing them in offering help to others. If helpers have a self-concept which is categorised by low self-esteem, for example, if they believe themselves to have little to offer, then they may be in the helping business to earn the gratitude of those they help.

People who are seeking help are often at their most vulnerable and have to overcome the embarrassment and insecurity of admitting they need outside assistance. This may make them easily dependent on the helper and may lead them to see the helper as some kind of wise and all-powerful mother or father-figure able to make things right. A helper who is looking to earn gratitude from their clients may easily succumb to such appeals, and run round doing things and putting the client's world right in order to secure the praise clients can readily give, never realising, until too late, that such activity only fosters the dependency of the client upon the helper.

A helper's self-concept will influence very considerably how far they set out to encourage a client to move toward a genuine **independence, autonomy and freedom of choice,** and so will affect how successful they are as a helper. Individuals who have examined themselves, who have seen something of the discrepancies **between how they would like to think they are and how they really are,** and **who can accept themselves** with all their imperfections, are likely to be more effective in encouraging others who are struggling with the same process. The more helpers learn to accept themselves, the more, it seems, they are able to accept others, and the more able those people are to accept themselves. Self-acceptance, however, is not to be mistaken for complacency or making a virtue out of any shortcomings.

Purpose

Helpers must take account of their activity in relation to the purpose they set for themselves, in relation to the purpose of the setting in which they find themselves, in relation to the time available and the wider purpose of the society in which they exist, as well as in relation to the purposes the client may have. These can be difficult issues to integrate together harmoniously, and many helpers have to learn to live with **high levels of ambiguity** about what they do and how far the limits of their involvement should extend. Since most people involved in helping do so only as part of some wider role, this issue can be particularly acute. A willingness to do one's best to help another may well begin to reveal dimensions of difficulty that the helper is under-equipped to deal with, and that the organisation is unprepared to accept, with too little time to handle any of it constructively. The results can be distressing, or worse, for all concerned. Training courses where such issues can be explored in the company of others facing similar issues can help inexperienced helpers begin to understand the complexities of their dilemmas and to learn that there are no simple answers.

In acute cases where the ambiguity between the purpose of the organisation and the purpose of the helper is too wide, helpers may well leave to seek a setting to operate within that is more in keeping with their own values and beliefs.

Helping Methods and Techniques

Gerard Egan (1975) says that ineffective help is not something neutral: it can have positively damaging effects. It may reinforce the individual's belief that no-one really will listen, and therefore lead them to avoid looking for help elsewhere, or it may help precipitate an avoidable crises. Helpers, therefore, need to have a repertoire of methods, techniques and skills at their command, and to use them with **deliberate and aware choice.** It is not possible to know the effects of interventions before they are made, but it is important to recognise the likely areas of enquiry which certain skills will open for examination. Skills to help others can be acquired with training and practice.

Chapter Two

Types of Help

Offering help to another may take a number of forms. In practice a particular problem may require elements of several of these forms, but they are distinguishable and each have certain costs and benefits worth noting. Six main types of helping are distinguished here:-

(i) *Taking Action*

The helper initiates a piece of action intended to alleviate the person's predicament - for example, undertakes to represent him or her at a hearing, write a letter on his or her behalf, make a telephone call, etc.

Costs

* The individual may not learn how and why the helper chooses to act in a particular way.

* If the problem recurs, the client may have few extra skills or resources to bring, and may revert automatically to seeking the 'expert' again.

Benefits

* Action is prompt, and the problem is usually dealt with swiftly.

* If the 'expert' is well-chosen and can be relied upon to know the 'best' course of action, the problem is solved.

* The 'helper' recognises the limits of the time, skills, etc. it would require to solve the problem for themself.

(ii) *Advice Giving*

The helper makes a suggestion based on knowledge and understanding of the person and problems, and allows the individual to decide on its appropriateness.

Costs

* If it is considered and rejected, the adviser can come to feel rejected and refuse further help.

* It is difficult to estimate the full consequences to someone else of any course of action recommended.

* The adviser does not have to live with the consequences of any suggestion.

* There is a danger of advice being given prematurely - it may only serve to solve the wrong problem.

* Giving advice is very easy to do badly and very difficult to do well

Benefits

* It can cut through a lot of confusion.

* It can help the individual to see a way forward without forcing them to take the preferred suggestion.

* It can be particularly useful when there is professional expertise involved: for example, over specific issues such as legal and financial matters, housing etc.

(iii) *Changing Systems*

The helper alerts the system, whether it be a group, an office, a factory, school, hospital or other organisation, of issues that individuals are repeatedly encountering. This implies that the predicaments of some individuals are best resolved through changes to the system, or to its procedures, rather than through changing the individual. If 24 students leave a course in two years, this suggests there is something wrong with the course or its selection procedures, and that it is these that should be altered rather than the students.

Costs

* Systems are not easy to confront: who does the helper negotiate with?

* Negative information is often not heard constructively by organisations.

* The role of change agent requires considerable skills and access to sources of influence and ultimately of power.

* Individuals who seek to change systems can sometimes risk that their career in the organisation will be blocked.

* Change agents are often regarded as disrupters and a nuisance to stability.

Benefits

* Improved organisational effectiveness is likely to improve morale.

* Responsiveness by the organisation to the people it serves increases their commitment.

* Change has positive outcomes for all if handled constructively.

(iv) *Teaching*

The helper manages a learning experience or structures a situation in order that the individual might improve his or her knowledge, acquire new skills, or develop insights further.

Costs

* It takes time to establish 'real' learning needs.

* It can be experienced as oppressive to the learner.

* Experts can seem to wish to retain their own sense of separateness and to keep knowledge to themselves.

* Learning skills and transferring them to a new situation is not easy, and teaching often makes it look easier than the individual discovers it is in practice.

Benefits

* It recognises the need to plan for a solution and does not expect it to appear by chance.

* Once a skill has been acquired or information gained, it can be used repeatedly.

* Individuals can be helped to plan their own learning programmes.

* It takes a developmental view of difficulties rather than a crisis approach.

(v) *Information Giving*

The helper provides a piece or pieces of data based on evidence, gives accurate accounts of facts and figures, and generally offers reliable sources of information, without recommending any as having more or less value than another.

Costs

* Not much information can be presented without suggestions being made as to how it should be used, in which case it becomes advice.

* It requires good inter-agency contacts to make the most of information services.

* The relationship with clients is usually of a short span - it is not always possible to diagnose 'real' needs, as opposed to those the client admits to having, in such a short time.

* It can mean the individual has to seek help at another agency and tell their story all over again.

Benefits

* It leaves the client to decide; it is relatively value free.

* Information services can be relatively cheap to run and can cope with large numbers of enquiries.

* It can make the most of helpers who have no great amount of training.

(vi) *Counselling*

* One way of defining counselling is that it consists of 'offering a relationship to another for the purpose of change'.

The helper works with the individual's 'internal dissension' through the relationship offered. Where other types of help rest on making an effective enough relationship with the client to move to the task in hand and solve the problem, counselling is both the means and the method. It is, then, through the relationship itself that the problem becomes identified, acknowledged, worked with and, hopefully resolved. Counselling is therefore a task which requires high levels of commitment to provide appropriate support to those in difficulty, a consistent way of relating, and some measure of internal self-discipline and supervision. Since no-one knows all that goes on between two people, opportunities to review a session are an integral part of monitoring performance and deepening both the skills and the insights of the counsellor. Counselling implies a process of encouraging individuals to confront their dilemmas and difficulties in a supportive framework of trust, safety and acceptance.

Costs

* It is often a lengthy process.

* It is very easy to do badly.

* The predicament has to be one appropriate for counselling.

* Counsellors can be asked to 'save' others from themselves and they can also be asked to 'save' colleagues (or 'difficult' students, customers, staff).

Benefits

* It enables people to 'own' their inner difficulties and overcome them.

* Growth and change are inherently challenging - counselling can provide support to assist such growth and change.

* Some experienced difficulties require a strong, stable and supportive relationship if they are to be resolved.

* It encourages accurate communication at both a content and feelings level.

(vii) *Support*

Support is the least directive form of help offered by one person to another. It is more often associated with the informal interest of friends and neighbours than viewed as a deliberate strategy of a helper. However, non-judgemental support, or the knowledge that there is someone there who will first listen and only listen, can be a vital resource for someone moving towards accepting the reality of a difficult situation.

Costs

* Support can be very demanding if limits and boundaries are not discussed.

* Support can amount to little more than 'collusion', helping the client stay where they are.

* Support can generate a mutual dependency between helper and client.

Benefits

* Support leaves the client in control.

* Support enables a client to have a haven of security where they are not being asked to answer for themselves.

* Support can be a very powerful form of reassurance.

Chapter Three

A Helping Framework

Aim of Helping
To promote increasing self reliance,
choice and personal responsibility
↓

Mediated through a relationship based upon:
*Openness
*Equality of worth
*Trust

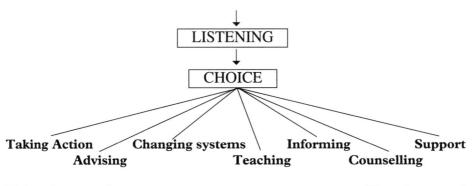

Helping and Control

If you look at the framework reproduced above it becomes apparent that
the further to the left hand side of the spectrum a helper operates from the
more they retain the initiative and the power. As you move towards the
right, control gradually pushes towards the client until with **Support**
control is unilaterally with the client. Helpers would therefore be wise to
ask themselves if they can really deliver the goods if they offer to support

someone because the implication is that it is "OK to be where you are for as long as you want to be there". You, as a helper may feel that way towards the client, but your agency may well have expectations that they will see results. The resulting **role conflict** can put great strain on the helper and the helper-client relationship. Qualified support however, is in almost every case worse since you never know how far it extends or for how long it will last. Better to work out a realistic arrangement of what you can offer one another than pretend time is limitless if it is not.

Helping Styles, Strategies and Problems

With the exception of counselling, the remaining strategies assume that the individual's needs are clearly known and have advanced to a stage where a specific activity is both necessary and appropriate. In practice this may not always prove to be the case: a fact which underlines the importance of taking time to review the situation in order to accurately understand the nature of the real problem before any of the above activities may be undertaken. This is an important and over-riding helping skill. A particular problem may well require elements drawn from a number of activities in order for it to be resolved. For example, in order to leave college, a student may require **counselling** to discover if such is the decision. They may also need information about alternative options, jobs, voluntary work, and so on, and may feel the need to be **taught** new skills to enable them to cope with new situations.

Helping and Counselling

One reason why **counselling skills** as opposed to **counselling training** is widely used in the preparation of a very wide variety of helping professions is because at the heart of counselling are two essential ingredients. Firstly the importance of **effective listening skills**, and secondly the communicating of the core conditions of **respect, empathy, and genuineness**.

All helpers need to learn to listen or they will end up solving the wrong problem! So practice in counselling skills can be a beneficial development in the training of a **first-in-line helper**.

In considering any strategy, as we have already indicated, the nearer the left-hand side of the fan on page 14, the more the helper is in control and directing the way help is provided. The more a helper moves to the right, the more the client is in control of the helping process.

Thus in a counselling relationship the balance is very clearly in favour of the client, who decides: the **level of disclosure**, the **extent of willingness to explore an issue**, and **whether or not to attend future sessions**. Helpers should be very clear in their own mind when they move into such a relationship that they have genuinely accepted the amount of direction offered to the client in counselling.

A further factor influences the helper's choice of approach when dealing with problems, and that is their own preferred style. There are, for example, helpers who have little interest in exploring the nuances and ambiguities of any issue but who are highly effective in mobilising resources and getting things done. Helpers need to recognise their preferred style and to understand something of its strengths and limitations before they find themselves repeatedly and unthinkingly applying a single strategy which may be inappropriate to some situations.

Referral

Referral is not separately distinguished within the range of helping strategies illustrated in the fan on page 14. Rather than being seen as one particular skill, referral is better regarded as an underlying resource which needs to be available irrespective of any particular strategy. For **first-in-line** helpers (as in the following chapter) knowing the extent of their involvement with those in difficulty is only part of the information required to work within their boundaries effectively.

They also need to learn the appropriate referral agencies and the contact persons within these agencies who they are most likely to rely upon. Identifying local agencies alone is rarely enough to make referral an effective step in helping someone. Referral takes place when a client is presenting difficulties or experiencing dilemmas that are **beyond the ability of the agency or its helpers to cope**. There are therefore high levels of insecurity around for everyone. Clients are likely to experience further insecurity at the thought of having to retell their story all over again to someone else. And the thought of being so 'odd' that they need yet another type of help than the one already offered, may discourage them from going to someone else.

Such circumstances are not the best for the staff of one agency to attempt to make contact with those of another for the first time. This is a separate task which requires to be undertaken in preparation for such a crisis and not at the same time. It is very often the informal, personal links between staff from different agencies that make all the difference in effecting the smooth transition of the client from one agency to another.

Opportunities for individuals from different agencies to meet their respective contacts generally receive too little encouragement by the host agencies, and yet the pay-offs can be immense in the improved effectiveness of the help offered and in efficient use of the time and status of the people involved.

Chapter Four

Who Are The Helpers

There are many people who offer help as an incidental part of their work. There are others for whom it is an essential part, nursing, for example. But for a great many people helping is a part of what they do and has to be accommodated into a wider set of constraints and responsibilities.

First-in-line Providers

Helping is an important part of the role of certain specialists - social workers, nurses, teachers, etc., but it is not the exclusive preserve of any. It is open to all of us to offer our help in whatever way we feel right for us throughout our daily lives. Frequently it is the case that the individual with **first-in-line** responsibility for staff in an organisation - the supervisor, the foreman, the teacher, the ward sister or charge nurse - will be the first-in-line point of contact for a member of staff meeting difficulties. This raises immediate problems.

Most such staff with first-in-line responsibilities have a contrasting role to that of helper to their staff. They are also **boundary managers.** They have a function in setting and maintaining clear boundaries of action and conduct. It is often felt that these two aspects of the role are in conflict - as indeed they are - and therefore incompatible, which need not be the case.

Such **role-conflict** is not unique to helpers, but it can be an acute problem for them. It will often be the case that an individual who needs help will be performing below their usual level of competence and may well be presenting problems of attendance or discipline as a symptom of their current difficulties. This places both the client and the first-in-line helper in something of a dilemma unless they are careful. Whenever a person is invited to explore an issue where such role relationships exist, the first-in-line helper should set out from the beginning the nature of the meeting they are to have and leave the client with no room for uncertainty about the purpose they have come together to fulfil. If the meeting is a fact-finding exploratory discussion, this should be made clear and it should stay in that territory. If it is really a means to challenge an individual to improve their performance, it should equally be made clear, and if it is to offer a person a genuine opportunity to begin to unburden themselves of the concerns that are influencing their performance, this again should be made clear.

Specialists

Some organisations have already convinced themselves of the need to have specialist helpers on hand, and view them not as a non-productive use of resources, but as valuable contributors to maintaining the overall effectiveness and morale of the staff.

Clearly, if the tasks of the first-in-line provider are to be performed skilfully, then there will be a need for some form of support. This is an important role for specialists, who may themselves not have direct contact with clients throughout their working time, but who may act in a consultancy, advisory and support role to first-in-line providers and undertake a proportion of internal referrals. Such specialists are also in key positions to negotiate not only across the internal boundaries of the organisation in which they work, but also across external boundaries with other agencies. This makes them well placed for coordinating helping activities within their organisation and between their organisation and relevant referral agencies.

Confidentiality

Clarity of purpose must be accompanied by the discipline of maintaining confidentiality of information given. Information gained in a counselling session should not be made available to other staff without a clear and aware decision and a willingness to give an account of oneself to the client first as to why the information should be shared. Nor should such information be used by the same individual in other aspects of their role. If you invite people to confide in you, you need to be able to respect that it may bring you problems but should not add to theirs. Confidentiality is a complex question and is returned to later in this manual.

Chapter Five

Helpers and Their Settings

In addition to the personal limitations of helpers themselves and the limitations that arise from lack of experience, training and skills, there is a further set of constraints which can have great influence upon the effectiveness and involvement of potential helpers. These are the constraints imposed by the organisation, the setting and the role within which the helper has to practise.

Organisations and Boundaries

All organisations operate within some set of boundaries or limits which determines the extent of their willingness and ability to respond. Many helpers operate from within organisations whose primary purpose is not the giving of help itself or the solving of individual problems. For example, most industries are established to satisfy needs via products or services. This may mean that the helper is regarded as an essentially non-contributing member of the organisation, and individuals with problems as potential labour operating at less than optimum efficiency. Such a view 'marginalises' the importance of the helper's activities. On the other hand, an organisation that recognises a willingness to respond to the wider needs of its members, as a way of improving the overall working climate, is likely to respect its helpers and offer them access to those who formulate policy. Most organisations come between these two positions and may constantly re-examine how far they are willing to respond to individuals in difficulty according to a variety of internal pressures. Helpers who ignore the purposes of the organisation and who operate in an unsupportive climate may experience loss of interest, commitment and motivation. Trying to help in ways not acceptable to the organisation is a recipe for conflict.

The Setting

Where the helper is located in the organisational environment - whether they are in suitable premises, and are a visible member of the organisation

- will influence how accessible others find them. The time available and the place in which helper and 'client' meet will have great influence upon what can be accomplished. Many helpers operate in settings that are not conducive to full-scale counselling, and therefore need to 'manage' their contacts with people in difficulties so that they can arrange to make themselves available for the time required. Over-hasty counselling can be worse than no counselling. If it can't be done, do not attempt it. The important thing is to offer real help, not to demonstrate how compassionate you are if it does nothing to help the client.

The Role

The role an individual plays within an organisation will have a great impact upon the helping activities he or she undertakes. Some people occupy roles of considerable ambiguity: on the one hand, they are in a managerial role with all that implies; on the other, they are somehow supposed to act as a supporter to their staff. Sometimes this role conflict is 'resolved' by the individual emphasising one part of the role at the expense of the other, but this is rarely satisfactory. An important helping skill is making clear to those who need to know what boundaries and limits are in operation and what the consequences are of ignoring or disregarding them. Such limit-setting need not be punitive, but helps to create the structure clearly in the minds of those involved.

There are other **role influences** which affect the way in which helpers can operate. **Status and rank** will make the work of some helpers seem more 'un-sympathetic' and so on by others. Helpers can become **'role-stereotyped'** just as other groups can.

Chapter Six

Problems in Helping

Problems for the Helper

The wish to help is not sufficient to ensure success. There are a number of 'blocks' to effective helping, and some of them are related to lack of skill, confidence or awareness on the part of helpers themselves. There are three important ways in which help can become degenerate rather than productive as a result of the helper's behaviour. They are: **unsolicited** interventions, **manipulative** help, and **compulsive** efforts on the part of the helper.

Unsolicited Help

Here the helper begins to intervene without first clarifying whether help is being sought and whether they can supply it adequately. This can be a subtle form of interference and can remove from the client important areas of personal decision-making. It is often very difficult to challenge such help out of fear of appearing ungrateful or being accused of being arrogant. Fear of rejection can also play its part in someone going along with this process. Unsolicited help can encourage passivity and dependence and leave the problem little improved.

Manipulative Help

Help that is motivated primarily out of the self-interest of the helper is manipulative. In its extreme, it is the clear, conscious and deliberate making use of others to fulfil our own needs or personal ends.

Compulsive Help

Help that is narrowly restricted to the same set of suggestions or formulas that have been well tried already would suggest compulsive help. Similarly, repeatedly 'fishing' over areas of the client's life that may have abiding interest to the helper but no crucial relevance to the problem is another example of the same process.

Problems for Those Being Helped

It can be a very difficult and painful admission to recognise you can no longer manage your difficulties and need the assistance of someone else. It can be made worse if you feel you really ought to "pull yourself together and get on with it". Other difficulties that many of us experience include being told that we somehow ought not to have the problems we have now admitted to having.

Help v 'Rescuing'

We have so far seen that there are three major influences acting upon helpers. Rarely do these three influences act harmoniously together. Most of the time we are 'helping', there is at least some degree of 'dissonance' or tension between the conflicting demands placed upon the person in the helper role. These three sources of pressure are: **the setting**; **the role**; and **the level of skill** a helper possesses.

Frequently helpers confront dilemmas about the legitimacy of their involvement. How far should they get involved? Have they the skills required? How far do you go in offering support? How do you challenge clients to take some measure of responsibility for what is happening to them? How do you offer support in such a way that it can be rejected if it is not the right time for them and without appearing casual in your concern? How do you approach issues when there might well be a catalogue of painful experiences behind them? And not least; how do you cope with the fact that some clients are dealing with lives that are far more emotionally distressing than anything you have ever experienced yourself?

There are no easy answers to such questions. Establishing appropriate limits which will lead to a satisfactory involvement for all concerned - client, helper and setting - is not easy. In part, the answer lies in the level of skill possessed by the helper. But skills are only the starting-point.

Assuming the role of helper immediately places an individual in a position in which difficult choices still remain to be made about the role appropriate to those skills and to the setting. Designated helpers often feel a tremendous obligation to be doing something because they believe it is expected of them. Equally, the feeling that it is their task to 'solve' all problems places an unrealistic burden of responsibility and later of guilt when problems do not get solved as neatly or as easily as the helper would like. Burn-out amongst helpers is high for these reasons.

It is useful for helpers, therefore, to distinguish between **'Rescuing' or inappropriate attempts to help**, and 'helping' which is a legitimate response to assist another person in difficulty. For those employed in a caring or helping role, the 'Rescuer' position comes all too easily available as a response to the feeling of pressure to be seen to be doing something at the first sign of someone in difficulty. Over time, it can become a patterned response that may well not meet the needs of the situation. 'Rescuing' of this kind has a compulsive quality about it. The client comes to be seen as a 'Victim' and is inadvertently encouraged to become dependent on their 'Rescuer', who gets the things done for them that they cannot do themselves. Far from encouraging self-reliance, such **'Rescuing' perpetuates dependence and exploits the difficulties of the client in order to enable the helper to meet their own needs** - perhaps the need to be seen as a dedicated concerned helper or as skilful problem-solver.

The important question to get straight is to find out if your help is appropriate in the first place. Four questions can help to clarify a decision:

* Is this person able to do without my help?

* Will what I am doing contribute towards their independence?

* Did this person ask for help or accept my offer of help?

* Is there a clear understanding between us about the nature of my help?

Just as **help offered too soon is as ineffective as help offered too late**, so too 'Rescuing' for the helpers' own need to feel they are doing their job has the consequence of removing choice away from the client being helped, when increasing choices is the purpose behind offering helping in the first place.

Once a client senses that they are being 'Rescued' the way lies open for deception, manipulation and exploitation of the helper. Deception can take the form of pretending the problem is solved to get out of the stifling clutches of someone who may take over your life; manipulation can take the form of praising the helper for being so wonderful so far that "Here's an even bigger problem for you now"; and exploitation can take the form of generating new crises to maintain the helper's involvement in the life of the client whenever the helper suggests it is time to consider terminating the relationship.

Chapter Seven

Conditions for Effective Help

All person-centred approaches are most effective when the individual offering help is able to establish a sound relationship based on **trust** with the person they are helping. Evidence from research points to there being three core conditions for the establishment of such a relationship. These are **genuineness, empathy and warmth**, described by Truax and Carkhuff (1967) as follows:-

Genuineness

'Genuineness' represents the helper's successful avoidance of posturing with the client, playing a role, or erecting a facade or barrier between themself and their client. This quality has sometimes been called 'transparency' or 'congruence'. The congruence is between what the helper is in reality and what they appear to be to the client: they allow themself to be known as a real and authentic person. This calls upon resources of honesty and courage on the part of the helper.

Empathy

'Empathy' represents the helper's successful attempt to comprehend their client's thoughts and feelings in the way in which they are comprehended by the client, and to communicate that comprehension. It means to know and to say what it is like to be this other person. It seems to require considerable powers of mental flexibility on the part of the helper. It should be carefully distinguished from sympathy.

Warmth

'Warmth' represents the helper's communication of their willingness to accept and respect the client. It is a non-threatening, non-evaluating acknowledgement of the reality and integrity of the client as a person. It needs to be carefully distinguished from a dependent wish to be 'nice' to people or to 'make excuses' for people. It is a realistic, not a sentimental, posture.

Communication

For helpers it is not enough to possess the qualities above: it is equally important to communicate them effectively to those seeking help. It is possible to improve the skills of communicating such qualities with training. No amount of training, however, will create what is not basically there.

Chapter Eight

Stages of Helping

All the forms of help that have been examined above have a place to play in the overall aim of helping another to achieve constructive change. **Helping is a person-centred activity**. The first priority is to establish accurately the type of help that will most appropriately aid the client: that is, to accurately understand the nature of the predicament. Any type of help is likely to pass through a number of steps in moving toward the solution of the dilemma.

The Essential Steps

Initiating contact: establishing a good working rapport.

Exploration of themes/issues.

Identifying options.

Assisting towards choice and decision.

Such a simple four-stage model of the helping process identifies the importance of **establishing an effective working relationship**, something which takes precedence over everything else. Once it has been established, then an elaboration of the themes and issues can begin. This in turn leads toward the identification of options: a consideration, say, of the types of help available and the cost and benefits of each. Finally, the stage of choice and decision-making brings the process towards some closure: a decision to meet to review progress might form part of such a phase.

A Model of Helping

Brammer's model of the helping process breaks down the four stages above into greater detail to give a more precise formulation to the sequence effective help takes. The model is reproduced below, in relation to the four stages discussed here.

A FOUR STAGE HELPING MODEL

The Meeting Phase

* Initiating satisfactory contact.

* Clarifying   : exploring the apparent cause of coming together.

* Constructing   : devising a suitable structure to work in.

* Contracting   : agreeing the boundaries of working together.

* Relating   : developing the helping relationship.

Exploring of Themes and Issues

* Exploring   : outlining the range of the problems.
                      : identifying related issues.
                      : clarifying implications.

* Consolidating   : focusing on areas to work on together.
                      : developing a theme.

* Challenging   : confronting the incongruities.
                      : challenging restrictions and self-imposed limitations.

Identifying Options

* Reviewing   : understanding the ground covered.
                      : reviewing progress.
                      : identifying learning and implication for change.

Assisting Towards Choice and Decision

* Decision-making : outlining options, considering alternatives, devising strategies.

* Implementing   : agreeing action plans.
* Concluding   : closure - drawing the session and ultimately the relationship to an appropriate close.

Section II

Listening and the
Core Conditions of Helping

Chapter Nine

Listening

"A good listening is soothing to the heart". The experience of being really and fully listened to is not as common as most people believe. Most conversations, even with those we know well, do not take place with the full attention of those taking part, and are always open to one or other of the parties changing the subject at any time. Listening is an essential precondition for any type of effective help, and follows quite different ground-rules from normal conversation.

Aspects of Listening

First of all, there is an expectation that the listener will not change the subject, but instead will assist the client to focus more closely on the issues that concern them. There is also an expectation that the helper will give more than superficial attention to what is being said and will not be subject to internal personal distractions of their own. In a very real sense such listening is a self-denying activity and one which requires full attention and concentration.

A critical part of the role of listening in a helping relationship is to create a climate of freedom and openness in which the other person can feel able to disclose to the fullest extent of the problems which they are confronting. **Self-disclosure** - the giving away of personally important information - **is a risky activity**, and can touch off concerns about an individual's self-image and worries that they may be being judged for admitting to inadequacies or defects.

Listening in a helping relationship is very closely linked with the ability to establish the core conditions for effective help that have already been identified: genuineness, empathy and warmth. These conditions will be re-examined in some detail later.

Elements of Listening

"If I do not listen well, then I do none of the rest that I am supposed to be doing", said one college counsellor. Accurately hearing what is being described, hearing 'the music behind the words', is an active process which involves overcoming many of our habitual ways of responding when others are talking.

The major barrier to better mutual inter-personal communication is the natural tendency to judge or criticise, to approve or disapprove, what the other person is saying. A good deal of communication resembles a game between those involved. The speaker assumes they are being listened to, and the listener conveys the impression that they are listening and reacting even though, for the most part, they may have 'tuned out'. Such listening has no place in a helping relationship.

The most complete form of listening is not listening to, but listening with another person in an **active and involved way**. This means that we are no longer observers but become active experiencers of what we are being told. Research in communication reveals that listening is a complex form of behaviour involving many skills - skills which can be identified and improved. How well a person **can** listen and how well they do listen are not the same thing. There are numerous factors which influence the quality of the communication between individuals or groups. **The situation itself**, how and **who organised it**, the **intended purpose of the occasion**, and the **eventual outcome** of the meeting, will all influence the involvement of those taking part.

The relationship between a talker and listener is open to mismanagement and manipulation. Information gained in a helping session can be inappropriately used outside such a meeting, with loss of confidence on the part of the client, who may decide never to trust the helper again. The limits of information-sharing should be decided with the client, so that if information is to be taken elsewhere, then they know clearly who it will be shared with and for what purpose.

Messages can be broken up in several ways: in particular, they have a **content** - a meaning - and they also have an **emotional component** - which tells us something of how the speaker feels about what they are saying. This second part, the **affective component**, is conveyed through the non-verbal signals accompanying the message: through the use of such things as tone of voice, facial expression, gestures and so on. Recognising and using such non-verbal cues in order to help the client express fully their concerns is an important part of effective counselling.

Difficulties in Listening

How an individual feels about what they are saying is often more important in establishing what they really mean than what they actually say (content). People who do not know each other well, or who have some reason to be wary or apprehensive of one another, may find it difficult to 'hear' clearly what is being said to them. Anxiety in a listener increases defensiveness and the propensity to misinterpret statements, and the tendency to find unintended threats and challenges increases. Supportive encouragement from the listener, with the use of gestures and expressions of encouragement, can help to reduce anxiety and to lead the way to a more open form of communication. Such encouragement indicates to the speaker that they are being listened to and that what they say is being valued. The more space to talk that they are given, in an encouraging way, the more they will be able to explore what they think and feel.

Listening is an active skill which can be learned, changed and developed like any other behaviour.

We all experience the world differently, and our concepts of things rarely match exactly those of anyone else. This may lead to difficulties when listening because we assume that the speaker's meaning matches the one we have. Often this will not be so: their own personal experience of events may have given them a different shade of meaning from that which we possess.

Internal States and Attitudes

How we feel and look upon what we are being told affects profoundly how we respond to it. **What we decide to select out as important**, what we choose to screen out and overlook, influence the way we feel about what happens to us. Being aware of our own prejudices and biases can help us to listen better, but strongly-held attitudes have a pervasive effect upon how we respond. All of us tend to evaluate what we hear far too soon, and once we have made our evaluation, it takes us a long time to give it up. **We become attached to our ideas as much as to anything else, even when they are inaccurate**. There is some evidence to suggest that there are differences in the listening skills of men and women, differences which are in line with our role-stereotypes for each of the sexes. How far this is innately true and how far a matter of cultural conditioning is not clear. Women are regarded as having a more finely developed intuitive grasp of things, whilst men are said to be more rational, logical and so on. Perhaps the most important thing to be gained from such studies is to remind us that we are all inadequate as listeners and all have skills which are in need of development.

The capacity to listen varies from one person to another, and from one day to another, but listening concerns the individual's ability to select and structure what is being presented and to remember it. This will be influenced by such things as intelligence, motivation, familiarity with the subject, and so on.

The willingness to listen is probably as important as the capacity to listen. Some people seem never to listen; others seem to distort whatever they hear. An ability to listen that is never put to use is no good to anyone. Poor listening habits cause many of us to listen much less well than we could. Listening well is an essential skill in any helping relationship.

Most communication is used to influence an individual or an outcome. Therefore defensiveness is always possible on behalf of those involved, and this may make it difficult for them to 'hear' accurately what is being said. Deliberate attempts to coerce, exploit or manipulate the listener will be counter-productive in the long run and will lead to a deterioration in the quality of the relationship. Even with good will assured on both sides, successful communication cannot be guaranteed.

Modes of Listening

Most people use the time during which others are talking to prepare what it is they are going to say. Although we like to believe that talking and listening goes something like:

YOU SPEAK   I LISTEN
YOU LISTEN   I SPEAK

In truth it is much more like:

YOU SPEAK   I LISTEN
I LISTEN - EVALUATE - LISTEN - PLAN - LISTEN - REHEARSE - SPEAK

(at the first opportunity I find to stop you)

Even 'good' listeners are often guilty of evaluating critically what is being said before attempting to understand what the speaker is trying to convey. The result is that they often jump to premature conclusions about what the speaker is driving at. This, rather than assisting the flow of communication, only disturbs it. The speaker has to try to explain what he means a second time.

Problems of Listening

We tend to listen least well to the middle of a statement.

Our previous knowledge and expectations may lead to our hearing only what we expect to hear.

Similarly, because of previous knowledge and existing attitudes, we frequently reduce a message by eliminating detail - **in other words, we listen selectively**.

Before the speaker has finished delivering their message, we are already formulating an answer. This means we do not listen to the end of the message, and may even finish off the sentence for them.

Problems for Listeners

There are a number of interventions which do not encourage the talker, but which many listeners find themselves using. Among the most frequent are:-

Inappropriate probing	-'Why exactly do you feel this way?'
Excessive reassurance	-'Everything is going to be O.K.'
Evasion	-'Please don't be upset.'
Evaluation/Judgement	-'You feel upset, but just think how your wife feels.'
Hostility/Judgement	-'Your behaviour is stupid and foolish.'

The aim of effective listening, then, is to allow the client to explore their own feelings in more depth. Only by coming to terms with their own emotions will they be able to cope with and understand new information, or to formulate a policy of action.

Blocks to Listening

There are a number of commonly experienced blocks to effective listening. We have
 difficulty in hearing the words of another when any of these factors are present:-

-When different value systems exist between helper and client, or when differences in education, experience and class background are present.

-When the vocabulary used by the two parties is very different.

-When either of the parties has an accent or appearance that is extreme in some way.

-When the content is shocking.

-When the helper gets out of their depth.

-When the information offered is not what the helper wants to hear.

-When the helper is distracted by their own internal pre-occupations.

-When judgements of liking or approval are not forthcoming but are being sought or expected.

-When the environment is unsuitable.

Chapter Ten

Core Conditions

Respect or acceptance, **genuineness** or authenticity, **empathy** or appreciation are regarded as the core conditions necessary for effective counselling to be possible.

Respect

In order for someone to enter fully into their dilemma, they have to come to feel that they themselves are not going to be judged as failures. To admit failings is one thing, but many people when they seek help do not believe that they are going to be accepted by the person in whom they are about to confide. 'Respect' is the term used to convey the quality of non-judgemental acceptance offered by a helper to the other person. It is the quality of expressing a genuine regard for the other and a warm dispassionate interest in what the client is attempting to disclose and understand. Rogers (1961) uses the term 'unconditional positive regard' to convey his understanding of this essential component of the helping relationship. It means holding to the belief that the client has the potential to move beyond their current difficulties in a positive and life- enhancing way. Rogers explains "It means there are no **conditions** of acceptance, no feelings of 'I like you only if you are thus and so'." Egan (1975) also stresses the importance of regarding the client as unique - another element in the quality of respect - and says that "although they are committed to helping the client change, this does not mean that the helper is determined to make the client over in his own image and likeness". This may mean that ultimately the client will choose a course other than that the counsellor would choose or one which the counsellor thinks is below the most effective available to the client. But the helper will unequivocally respect such choices.

Respect for others forms part of the underlying core of beliefs that effective counsellors and helpers hold. In this sense it is not something simply acquired once and for all, but something to be striven for and developed **both as a belief and as a communicated act** toward those the helper works with.

Genuineness

Genuineness is about risking being real. "It indicates an openness in dealing with others and behaviour that is truly reflective of the core of the being." (Pietrofesa *et al*; 1978). Genuineness is therefore about being at one with oneself, not employing facades. Another term often used in this respect, is 'congruence', and refers to 'transparency' or internal consistency.

These elements are linked to the capacity for **appropriate self-disclosure**: the willingness of the counsellor to display and take responsibility for personal values, ideals, feelings and experiences. Spontaneity also seems linked to this same area of activity, i.e. behaving freely and without constraint.

Such behaviour has the effect of offering a model to the client that such openness to self can be risked without loss of self-acceptance or risking the necessary condemnation of others. But these qualities require a certain level of mature and genuine non-defensiveness in their expression; otherwise they might become little more than the outpourings of the counsellor's own unresolved difficulties. Such 'genuineness' would be likely to offer little therapeutic benefit to the client.

"If the 'counsellor' spontaneously and honestly conveys his thoughts and reactions, I believe they are not only communicating his concern but they are in effect both eliciting and reinforcing kindred uncontrived behaviour." (Jourard, 1964).

When counsellors withhold their 'real selves' some measure of energy is required in order to maintain the deception which this takes away from the therapeutic task. 'Certainly the aim is not for the therapist to express or talk about his own feelings, but primarily that he should not be deceiving the client as to himself. At times he may need to talk about some of his own feelings (either to the client, or to a colleague or superior) if they are standing in the way' (Rogers, 1961).

Avila *et al* writes (1977) "We suggest a major problem of poor helpers is the fact that their methods are inauthentic, that is, they tend to be put on, contrived. As such they can only be utilised so long as the helper keeps their mind on them. That, of course, is likely to be disastrous on two counts. In the first place it separates them from their client or student, and the message conveyed is likely to be that they are not 'with it', are not really interested, or are a phoney. Second, it is almost never possible to maintain attention to the 'right' method for very long. As a consequence, the poor helper relapses frequently into what they believe his previous experience has taught them. So the method they are trying to use fails because of the tenuous, interrupted character of their use of it."

Authentic and Inauthentic Behaviour

Inauthenticity is unhealthy and removes people from experiencing themselves truly.

Inauthentic behaviour makes it very difficult to know 'what's going on' in situations for two reasons. First, it is likely to be assumed that everyone else is as inauthentic as you are, therefore making any accurate interpretation impossible. And second, it is difficult to make even tentative assessments of atmosphere and dynamics if you are out of touch with the instrument you rely upon, i.e. yourself.

Authentic behaviour encourages others to take risks and offers a model of how it might be done.

Spontaneity and self-disclosure are indicators of genuineness.

Genuineness indicates a 'being at home with oneself': an important quality for anyone helping others to experience the same unity.

Self-concealing takes time and energy away from the opportunity of fully relationships with others.

Techniques are much less important than the ability to experience and convey genuineness to the client.

Genuineness of itself is not necessarily therapeutic, but without it the therapeutic process is not likely to succeed.

Empathy

In helping others it is not only important to understand what it is the client is saying; it is just as important to communicate such understanding effectively. This is the area of counselling and helping covered by the word 'empathy'. Empathy is not only the ability to listen to and understand the experiences, feelings and beliefs of others: it is also the ability to communicate the understanding and appreciation of these experiences, feelings and beliefs accurately back to the client. Communication at this level helps the client feel understood and therefore freer to express more of their own inner life.

Everyone experiences the world differently and builds up an individual frame of reference. Empathy in counselling is indicated by the counsellor suspending their own frame of reference in order to enter that of the client, attempting to make sense of what the client discusses in the same way that the client does, and making the client aware that this is what the counsellor is doing.

It does seem from studies (Carkhuff, 1971) that people from similar backgrounds are more likely to be empathic to one another than people from widely different backgrounds: blacks, for example, will have more empathy with other blacks, and so on. This might be especially the case on occasions when the counsellor is using their own experience of what a situation is like to guide them toward understanding the effect it has upon a client. The danger of such use of self is that it can be wide of the mark.

Another basis for an empathic response is to offer a 'normative response': to offer a reaction that would be 'typical' of 'most' people in that situation. Here again the danger lies in generalising that what most people might feel, this person actually **does** feel.

To build an empathic relationship, counsellors need to attend very carefully to the variety of clues from the client, both verbal and non-verbal. To make such detailed attention available, the counsellor must be **free from internal preoccupations, external distractions, or defensiveness toward the client.**

The Importance of Empathy

Fielder's work (1950), supported by other research since, indicated that it was the quality of empathy and acceptance communicated to and experienced by the client which had most influence in promoting positive change for the clients, irrespective of the particular theoretical orientation offered. It was not what they knew that made the helpers effective, but how fully they could indicate real understanding for their clients and their difficulties.

In the last four or five years, the work of Bandler and Grinder (1978) has explored these issues in more detail, and has helped to devise strategies to enable therapists and counsellors greatly to increase their effectiveness through Neuro-Linguistic Programming (NLP). NLP encourages helpers to establish much more effective levels of contact by alerting helpers to the way in which people make sense of the world through different channels of communication, i.e. visual, auditory, or kinaesthetic (feeling). The ability to recognise which channel a client uses and to respond back in that same channel is a highly effective way of indicating empathy.

Empathy in Practice

An empathic relationship is one in which a counsellor is attempting to explore the client's understanding, rather than the client trying to explore the counsellor's suggestions or advice. The counsellor is not 'taking over' the problem or solving it on their own behalf, but is offering a mutuality of understanding. **The counsellor thus remains outside the dilemma but inside the understandings**, and 'stays with' the pace and tone of the client. The counsellor helps things to emerge -they do not drag them forth or discourage them from appearing. Following on from this, it is clear than an evaluative or judgemental attitude to a client will undermine any empathic building which has taken place.

Empathic responses place a value on the person and give recognition that the individual in difficulty is worthy of care and attention. They help individuals to experience themselves more deeply and therefore more completely. To give this kind of **permission** can have swift and liberating effect. To encourage, for example, a bereaved relative to find, experience and express the accompanying anger at the loss of loved one, as well as the sadness and longing, can provide an important realisation that such feelings are part of the total process of grieving, though a part that is often overlooked.

Levels of Empathy

There are different degrees of empathy, from simply understanding the content of what someone says, to entering into the complexities of the emotional tone of an experience. The ability to respond accurately to the emotional component of a response requires considerable skills and attentiveness. Depending on the relationship, empathy may be conceived as having four different levels, each one more difficult to model successfully.

Can you tell the client what they just told you?
Can you repeat what is said?

Can you tell the client what they are trying to tell you?
Can you infer what is meant?

Can you tell the client what they would really like to tell you.
Can you infer what the client wants to approach?

Can you tell the client what they are scared to tell you?
Can you pick up the clues and identify the area of experience the client wishes to talk through but feels too scared to begin, and encourage them sensitively to talk?

Suggestions for Indicating Empathy

Be attentive, physically and mentally, to what is happening.
Listen carefully and note the key words.
Respond encouragingly to these core messages - but be willing to move in new ways if indicated.

Be flexible. If what you are doing is not working, try something else.
Give permission for the emotional tone to find expression as well as the content.
Look carefully for cues that you are on target.
Be aware of signs that you are not together and be prepared to change. It is not clients that are resistant, but counsellors who are not effective in finding the right strategy.

Section III

Aspects of Counselling

Chapter Eleven

Counselling as a Helping Relationship

What is Counselling?

Counselling is a word with different meanings for different groups of people who are engaged in a helping or supervisory role with others. Some of the different definitions offered seem to bear little relation to one another. For example, it is not uncommon in the Health Service to find the term 'counselling' associated in many people's minds with part of a disciplinary process as well with the supportive relationship that a nurse offers a patient! Such incompatible definitions exemplify the very real difficulty in striving to find a satisfactory definition of the extremely complex activity which occurs when two or more people enter a counselling relationship. This is not surprising when you consider that the term can be used to describe a range of activities from giving informal advice to professional consultations. The dictionary is little help either, since the word is linked there with activities including advising and recommending which have more of a prescriptive flavour to them than counselling itself usually implies.

Another factor complicating matters even further arises out of the different backgrounds and training of the various professional groups who employ counselling skills as a part of their working role and who therefore come to associate the core skills and approach of counselling with their own particular style. When professionals from different groups come together to discuss 'What is counselling?' it is not unusual to find competing definitions and claims from each group that their particular approach or their particular method is **the** one which is most representative.

Youth workers, for example, operate in an informal and semi-structured way which allows counselling skills to arise from the activities they stimulate. Not unnaturally they prize the equality of the relationship they offer to young people and the way in which counselling forms part of that relationship. By contrast, probation officers, social workers, and others often have highly structured guidelines in which to operate. This in turn restricts how counselling skills can be employed. Such workers will often emphasise the value of the formal element of counselling for this reason.

Perhaps the most important point to be learned by all concerned is that the setting bears a great influence upon the way that counselling skills are employed and that the structuring of the relationship in which counselling is established is a topic of particular importance (see below).

Defining Counselling

There are two definitions of counselling offered here. The first and simplest reflects the central importance of the **relationship** that makes counselling possible at all. The second is taken from the British Association for Counselling and is used because it attempts to include a range of underlying features held in common by a variety of professional helpers.

Sometimes 'counselling' is used almost synonymously with 'psychotherapy'. The boundary where one ends and the other begins is ultimately almost a matter of nicety of distinction. Long-term counselling might well be indistinguishable **from** some types of psychotherapy, but for most people using this manual this issue is not likely to arise. If it does, then they would need to consult and read other more advanced texts than the present one.

Definitions

"Counselling is offering a relationship to another for the purposes of change."

"People are engaged in counselling when a person occupying regularly or temporarily the role of counsellor offers or agrees explicitly to offer time, attention and respect to another person or persons temporarily in the role of client." (BAC)

Within this definition counsellors are seen as undertaking to meet a number of professional responsibilities.

Chapter Twelve

Helping The Client: An Overview

Counselling as a Helping Process

Carl Rogers (1961) defines a helping relationship as one in which "one of the participants intends there should come about in one or both parties more appreciation of, more expression of, more functional use of the latent, inner resources of the individual". Such a definition can therefore extend beyond the counsellor-client relationship to include the relationship of parent to child, of doctor to patient, of teacher to student, in fact any relationship which promotes human flourishing.

If counselling works through the medium of the relationship established between those involved, certain implications follow.

A Positive Relationship

Effective help depends upon the ability of the counsellor to establish a positive relationship with the client. (Research indicates that warm egalitarian attitudes by parents towards their children have positive influence in promoting such things as emotional stability and feelings of security, and that therapists achieve better results when viewed as being 'caring' by their clients.)

Responsiveness

In order to facilitate the client through their difficulties, the counsellor must be responsive to the client in difficulties. (Dittes, quoted by Carl Rogers (1961), found that any sign of a reduction in acceptance by therapists towards their client was sufficient to lead to an immediate increase in anxiety symptoms, increased heart rate, etc., and to the display of stress signals. One study found a strong relationship between success in therapy and the degree of liking and respect felt between client and their therapist, rather than the particular school of therapy the therapist had been trained to use.)

Responsibility

The counsellor accepts responsibility for providing focus, direction and structure to the sessions. The counsellor offers the client certain skills to help bring meaning out of the apparent chaos of their feelings and to assist them towards a clearer understanding of their own world. (Fielder (1950), quoted by Rogers (1961), found that what appeared to be most important to successful therapy was the therapist's ability to demonstrate a genuine desire to understand the client's feelings and meanings.)

The Client

The client is someone whose world is in turbulence or whose emotions are in conflict. The client experiences the world in which they live as 'Not being as I would like it to be'. They come to the counsellor in the hope or belief that the situation can be changed towards becoming 'More like I want it to be'.

It is not often possible (or desirable) to change the world in which the client lives, but it may well be possible to help the client change the way they experience the world and how they feel about it, not by providing solutions to the client's difficulties but by helping them find their own.

Counselling Groundrules

Counselling works through the medium of the relationship that develops between the client and the counsellor. The fewer obstacles the counsellor puts in the way, the fewer personal concerns they have and the more open and free the attention they offer, the more the client is able to make a real opportunity of the situation in order to explore their fears, concerns or dilemma.

A number of ground rules and suggestions follow from these assumptions:

*The counsellor needs to establish rapport easily and swiftly.

*The counsellor needs to know which behaviours help deepen and extend rapport and **to be willing to use them.**

*The counsellor's task is to enable the client to feel safe enough to talk about those things they wish at a level that is productive.

The qualities that best describe these abilities are:

Acceptance, or Respect: for the client in difficulty.

Appreciation, or Empathy: a willingness to attempt to understand the client from the client's own point of view.

Authenticity, or Genuineness: for the counsellor not to adopt a distancing pose, but to allow for there to be genuine meeting.

Having such qualities is not in itself sufficient to establish the counselling relationship. **It is important to communicate these qualities by behaving in ways that illustrate to the client that you have them.**

Acceptance is indicated by such things as:

*basic courtesy.

*attending and listening carefully.

*creating time and space free from distraction.

*not supplying ready made solutions.

Appreciation is indicated by such things as:

*sharing your understanding of the client's story as it unfolds.

*not jumping to conclusions.

*allowing the client to clarify their understanding through asking questions, seeking information and feelings.

Authenticity is indicated by such things as:

*a readiness to share such aspects of your own life and experiences as are appropriate and relevant to the client's needs.

*withholding from seeking to make use of the relationship for your own needs, but recognising that they exist.

*a willingness to be sensitive to the full that some things people tell you will disturb and upset you and there is no reason to let such reactions get in the way of you being there for the client.

Counselling is a learning process and the client will learn a number of things from the time they spend with you that may seem incidental but will have an impact upon their life. For example:

*the way you help someone solve 'this' problem will help them learn a process they will probably go on to apply to every other problem that has the same structure. **Make sure you teach them well.**

A Model of Counselling

An individual enters the counselling relationship to make sense of some dilemma or to move towards the resolution of some problem, and look to the counsellor to bring their experience and expertise to bear to facilitate that process in a way which combines specific skills and strategies.

Contact and Relationship Building

Rapport is about developing a satisfactory relationship in order for change or development to take place. Behaviour which promotes effective rapport includes:

Matching: using language similar to that of the client in non-patronising ways.

Mirroring: offering similar body movements and allying one's body posture towards that of the client.

Pacing: working at the client's speed and being willing to suspend one's own belief system for long enough to help the client identify their own.

A further element in **Rapport** which begins to move the client forward is **leading.**

The counsellor helps the client move from a position where the world "is not as I would like" toward a place where the world is "more like I would like". It is essentially a problem-solving process. It has a pattern and a sequence which can be broadly identified.

Frame of Reference

The problem exists for the client within themself and their own world. This makes it unique. However much it sounds like another example of something commonplace, to the client, it makes sense only in relation to their own internal frame of reference, the values they hold and the difficulties they have already worked with. It takes a long time (rather than a short one) to establish enough of a sense of the client's **frame of reference** to make confident guesses as to what they feel or think. Time spent unravelling and exploring is well spent because you too will be aware of the implications of the options the client is considering.

Clarifying and Listening

The skills the counsellor relies on most frequently are various forms of questioning to fulfil a number of purposes to:

* **gather information.**
* **test understanding.**
* **seek feelings.**
* **summarise.**
* **challenge implications.**
* **encourage action.**

Many of these skills are designed to help the client **clarify** their understanding and to provide a richly detailed description of the internal experiences that are limiting their choices.

Problem Solving and Questioning

The counsellor needs to help the client define the situation and circumstances, to work through the implications and dilemmas and to define the options clearly as well as to act responsibly.

Challenge and Change

Counselling is not always a linear process that follows a simple beginning, middle and end to a session. There are important periods of apparent diversion, moments of insight, times of rambling and scouting around the issue. However there needs to be a **sense of some progression** in any session and a development for both counsellor and client, if they are to feel they have achieved something worthwhile.

Progress and Change

Progress can be defined as change or movement in one of the four following areas:

(i)   *An Increase in Understanding of the Situation*

As a result of counselling, the client may feel little different. The situation may still be as intractable as ever, but the process of speaking out loud has enabled them to discern a thread of meaning which make the circumstances more tolerable. Such growth in **insight** does not necessarily lead to change, but is almost always a precursor to any successful change.

Counselling may help the client come to a greater understanding or appreciation of the complexity of an issue which appeared to be relatively insignificant but incapacitating. Difficulties in relationship with close colleagues, friends or partners are often triggered by what appear to be almost trivial differences. Through counselling, a client may well gain insight into the patterns of interaction and the different interpretations of the same event that are possible and which lead to situations of conflict. **Like changes in feeling, increased insight does not necessarily make things any different, but the additional knowledge may enable a client to tolerate higher levels of uncertainty** about a situation through which they are passing - for example, separation or bereavement.

(ii)   *A Change of Feeling*

Having talked through an issue or dilemma, the client encounters deeper layers of feeling. This the counsellor acknowledges and helps encourage the client to release. Following such an **emotional discharge** or **catharsis**, the client recovers a greater degree of "free attention" or increased awareness of the room for manoeuvre within the situation.

Expression of feeling is often in contrast to a long-standing pattern of holding back, a feeling of pretending that "things will get better if only I hold myself together". Many clients need encouragement, or 'permission' to allow themselves to feel their feelings fully. This is often painful because it has built up over a long period. If a client is allowed to discharge old hurts freely (each time they surface) they recover greater freedom of action and autonomy to go on to make more effective and life enhancing decisions. Discharge of feelings is another preliminary for the client before they go on to changing parts of their world.

As a result of counselling, an individual's life circumstances may appear no different than before, but they may feel very different about those circumstances. Much counselling is centred in this area of enabling the client to more freely express and 'own' their feelings, acknowledging their internal contradictions and thereby increasing their self acceptance. Such expressions of feeling may be important first steps in assisting clients to mobilise their energy toward doing something, but a change of feeling about something is a quite separate result from doing something about it.

(iii)   *Making a Decision*

As a result of changing both their understanding (seeing things differently) and emotional release (feeling differently about the situation) a client can then move towards a readiness to make a new decision. This is a stage of **contemplation** and not action: a time of consideration of options and implications and deciding upon the **right course of action.** This is not the same thing as **taking action**. It may well take some time to work through this phase, and may well include trial - learning, rehearsal or further information gathering. At this stage however the client is working towards change and the focus is on the 'how' and not 'whether' to change or not.

Only when a decision is made does counselling move into activity outside the session. Over issues of concern and at times of crisis it is very often the case that the client becomes embroiled in a whole welter of competing demands and expectations which reduce an individual's power to initiate any decision. Counselling can help an individual to sort out the options, to assess their relative effect, and to consider their implications in a safe environment.

(iv)   *Implementing a Decision*

It is **only when the client acts differently** and only when they do it out in the world **that counselling begins to make a difference to the client's day to day life**. Implementing decisions is often a very risky business. A lot is invested in a proposed change; fear of failure may produce crippling anxieties, sudden and unanticipated objections may begin to appear. The counsellor must be available to help the client choose the what, the how and the when and help them refine it to a **workable, achievable result.**

Once a decision is made, it remains to be put into effect. In short, **the client has to take responsibility for actually doing something**. Counselling can help the process by preparing the client for coping with its possible effects and for anticipating some of the likely blocks to success.

Counselling can stop at any point in this process but the counsellor needs to ask if the client's best interests are being served if they only gain insights, only discharge feelings or only ever contemplate change.

Becoming A Client

Many people find the admission that they may need the help of someone outside their personal network of support an admission of failure, somehow an indication that they are inadequate. Our society places a high value on people 'getting on' by themselves, and not needing help and looks upon activities like counselling as a service for social 'casualties'. Whilst this attitude prevails many people will put off seeking help for as long as they possibly can, often adding to their difficulties in the process. All too often they will seek to find reasons why they do not need it now, or that the four sessions they have had are 'enough'. This makes it all too easy for the client to discontinue counselling before the full benefits have been achieved.

Things To Attend To In Oneself

*   If you are not interested in the client it will 'leak out' sooner or later. Appropriately pointing out a lack of interest in what the client is saying about their own life may be a step towards helping them understand why it is difficult for others to be interested. Being 'there' for the client includes pointing out how far you can remain engaged with what they have to say.

* Equally if you are over-committed to the client's dilemmas, you will show it and it will get in the way of the client's freedom of action.

* If you over-identify with the client you will be in danger of feeling what it is like for them all too well, and not being of much further use.

Chapter Thirteen

Structuring Counselling: Boundaries and Responsibilities

Counsellors have obligations to at least five sources: **themselves, their colleagues, their clients, their organisation**, and **their professional group.**

Counsellor and Client

It is important when counselling is taking place that the counsellor makes explicit, to themself at least, that this is what they are doing. This includes enabling the conditions to arise which promote open communication between client and counsellor. Also important is identifying any boundaries which may influence the amount of contact and time available to offer to the client.

The counsellor owes it to **the client**, who may be inexperienced in seeking help, to let them know something about 'what they are in for'. This may mean only a supportive comment, or it may mean outlining in some detail the methods the counsellor uses, the frequency of meetings, the expectations the counsellor has of the client for work outside the sessions and so on. In short, the counsellor is responsible for establishing the effective conditions for counselling to take place.

If the counsellor knows their role then they can help the client to learn theirs. Since most people are not 'natural' clients, they do have things to learn, and may have questions they are shy of asking. Attempting to ignore such issues by superficial displays of 'chattiness' can do much to prevent counselling reaching the quality of disclosure and challenge necessary to help the individual in difficulty.

The counsellor is responsible for making clear:

*   Time - the length and frequency of sessions.
*   Space - the location and providing of sufficient freedom from interference and distraction.

* Interventions - the range of ways of working with the client.
* Structure - overall clarity so that the client cannot misconstrue the situation or the reason for the meeting.

The purpose of counselling is the increase of personal responsibility in the client and/or the diminution of dependency. Clear guidelines given at the appropriate time can positively assist this process.

Contracts

The counsellor may work with formal contracts, i.e. with agreed and shared goals formulated by the client in an explicit way, or they may not. But the counsellor offers an implied contract of responsibility and dependability to his client. In addition, the counsellor has contracts with their organisation and professional colleagues.

The Organisation

Organisations will place differing role expectations upon those they recognise in the helping role. Some of these will be explicit - like turning up on time, being in a certain place, operating within certain agreed boundaries, and so on; others will be much less so. **Role conflict** is inevitable for counsellors at some stage, though it does need to be kept to a minimum: otherwise it can serve to discredit even the most positive work, or can be used by either side - counsellor or administration - as a way of avoiding dealing with important issues of practice which 'ultimately' have wider repercussions. Supervision or regular opportunities to consider such issues and to review practice in the light of changing circumstances is an essential requirement. Such regular exchanges of information help to minimise misunderstandings and to reduce the possibility for manipulative or mischievous clients creating unhealthy dramas that everyone is better without.

The Profession of Counselling

The helper in a counselling role has professional standards to uphold and promote. Association with others working in similar or related fields is not only an important source of mutual support and general professional development, but also an area in which to raise issues of concern and uncertainty that come to everyone involved in counselling. Standards of competence and consideration of ethical issues are a continuing feature of professional life, not matters to be sorted once and for all. Sometimes, too, a client brings forth an unexpected personal dilemma for the counsellor which requires the counsellor to call upon the skills of colleagues outside the situation.

Increasingly people involved in counselling are realising the importance of some form of peer support for themselves. This is reflected at the professional end of the helping continuum with considerable current discussion about the ethics of counselling and the accreditation of counsellors.

Chapter Fourteen

Working with Clients

The importance of early experience in the development of personality cannot be over-estimated. Such experience lays the foundations for the ways in which people interact in their wider world as they move through life. There is not space here to discuss this at any length, except to note its bearing upon the relationship that is to develop between the counsellor and the client. Though therapy is not being suggested here, what is important to realise is that clients in difficulty arrive with wide differences in the personal resources they can call upon to meet the challenges of their inner lives. How successfully or otherwise someone has coped with life changes in the past will affect how far and how freely they can respond to the one they are experiencing at the time they come for counselling.

Clients are always individual and their dilemmas are always unique. Nevertheless, three broad categories of client are worth noting. For convenience I am terming them the 'temporary' client, the 'problematic' client and the 'serious' client.

The Temporary Client

There are times in almost everyone's life when a crisis or problem emerges beyond our resources to deal with it effectively. Such individuals who come into counselling will usually have a personal history that has enabled them to establish effective and valuable relationships. They will have a measure of internal **personal security** (however much it may be off-balance at the moment) and a sense of **personal responsibility** for bringing about the changes they are seeking from counselling, and they will not have excessive illusions about the value of the counsellor or seek to foster an unrealistic dependence upon them. They will come to resolve a specific dilemma, will appreciate the help they get, and will leave the relationship once they have made the gains they are seeking. Often their difficulties will be focused upon inter-personal issues - specific crises to do with jobs, study and so on - or with enquiries into a particular dilemma they confront. Such clients are often those who offer the counsellor relatively early signs of change and development. The relationship is more nearly that of peers in which one party is temporarily drawing upon the resources of the other.

The Problematic Client

This second group of clients often enter into counselling for reasons similar to those above. Some current dilemma, an important relationship or a life crisis stimulates the search for help and assistance: a need to talk it through with someone outside the situation. But such clients differ from the temporary client described in the previous section, in that they have **much less in the way of personal resources** to enable them to overcome their current concern. **Their essential wholeness cannot be taken for granted.** There may be past experiences, not consciously recalled, which have significant influence upon how the individual relates to themselves and others. There may be long-standing and underlying problems of moodiness and depression, for example, or a long history of repeatedly unhappy experiences in certain areas of life.

Involvement in counselling thus only begins to indicate a more serious state of affairs and a past history of incomplete or unhappy experiences. Sometimes the very relationships that counselling offers - the exclusive time and attention of another - is itself something which may complicate matters. Such care and attention can come to be seen as an expression of 'friendship' in its widest sense, leading to an expectation that the counsellor will somehow become involved in the life of the client and is someone available to the client as and when the need might arise. Initially such appreciation may be gratifying and, inadvertently, the counsellor can come to reinforce such false assumptions, taking a readier role in the life of the client than is either desirable or useful. Such 'boundary' problems then become a matter of concern, and lead to circular arguments about how the counsellor is failing the client. These have sufficient validity in them for the counsellor to feel unable to put them aside. The scene is set for poor helping of any kind.

Not all such clients end up attempting to engage their counsellors in this way. They are more likely to present **the counsellor** with a sense of almost hopeless expectation that nothing they attempt together will really change anything significantly. Being prepared to work with commitment when the client displays signs of passivity, reluctance or even hostility is a demanding role for any counsellor and the temptation to make comments or challenges that come from frustration and anger, rather than concern, are not always easy to avoid. It is just because these issues only emerge as contact increases that makes working with such clients so difficult. Often referral only gets thought of when the situation is practically uncontainable - a time long past when it can be most effective. Guilt, frustration and the sheer sense of impotence are not uncommon outcomes for counsellors dealing with such difficult clients.

The Serious Client

The serious client is the client most in need of help, for whom counselling will often change little in their lives, and who are often easiest to identify
These are people who for all manner of reasons are psychologically damaged, who have aspects of their lives that are seriously impaired, or who function in certain situations with tortuous inadequacy. They will often come to counselling as part of an organisational response to attempt to enable them to integrate more successfully within the culture of the group to which they belong. Such clients have more serious difficulties than most counsellors can expect to cope with. What counsellors can do, however, is something which is far more constructive than inadequate psychic explorations, is to become a reliable source of safety and support - an anchor point for the individual to seek out at times of acute stress or challenge. Such long-term support can make all the difference to such individuals and **can help them to make progress with dignity and success through a placement or work experience that otherwise might simply collapse** from the unsympathetic and unskilled efforts of others who are unused to providing such a role. It is not always the case that

individuals with serious difficulties **must** be moved on elsewhere by being referred to another agency. Often they can be very positively helped with the appropriate support and caring attention of specialist helpers on-site who are themselves in touch with appropriate referral agencies.

Chapter Fifteen

Types of Counselling

There are two principal types of counselling offered by most helpers: **remedial** counselling and **developmental** counselling. Most helpers see the need for working in a developmental way and not simply in a remedial capacity. But most organisations are unable and/or unwilling to release the resources required to introduce a developmental programme.

Remedial Counselling

Remedial counselling begins when an individual group or system experiences some difficulty. The time-scale is typically short-term, the theme is one of seriousness or crisis, and the request of the client is likely to be one of 'make this go away'. Suicide attempts, broken relationships, abrupt redundancy, are all examples of issues that require a remedial approach. The helper's role is usually seen as one of bringing things back to the familiar and reassuring pattern of the past before the crisis began. Sometimes a client will acknowledge that the crisis is part of an accumulating pattern, the latest in a series of similar events, and will seek to look beyond the alleviation of discomfort and begin to 'unscramble' the elements that contribute to the difficulty. 'Acute' stress is one of the times when most of us are prepared to take the necessary risk to do something to 'sort it out'. Chronic pain, however, is something most people learn to live with and accept. Only when there is some disturbance to the familiar pattern is there enough motivation to change.

It can be a source of frustration to many helpers that they could spend a majority of their time and effort in remedial counselling, in patching up emotional wounds and watching the individual return to a situation with nothing changed. It can be just as frustrating to give time, care and attention to **someone** in a crisis, only to realise that in three months time you will be doing exactly the same thing again, i.e. they will again be saying how much they now know about what's been happening and how it will not happen again. Usually they are right: they don't do it in the same way; instead they do it even more dramatically!

Acknowledging this is important for helpers if they are not to become demotivated and cynical. This is not to say that there are not many individuals for whom remedial counselling over a specific issue is not only appropriate but also successful.

Developmental Counselling

Most helping professions originally came into being for rehabilitative or remedial reasons. Guidance for schools students, for example, often came into being to help those students who for one reason or another failed to fit existing institutional arrangements and demands. "Even the oldest professions like teaching and the clergy, evolved out of a major desire to 'save' their subjects - in one case from stupidity, in the other from sin."

Our social world is characterised by the ever-increasing awareness of the rapidity of change. To **cope with change successfully requires flexibility, openness and the ability to let go of things left behind**. Patterns of work and leisure, sex-role expectations, etc. all challenge our traditional assumptions and are indicators that new patterns of demands are being made upon all of us.

Developmental counselling is based upon the assumption that individuals can develop and flourish when they are in healthy interaction with their surrounding world and not paralysed into passivity or reacting through fear. Developmental counselling assists that process of helping individuals increase their choices, enabling them to make use of their opportunities and take increasing responsibility for their actions and their consequences. An individual therefore does not have to be in a 'crisis' to benefit from the attention and careful listening of another. Developmental counselling can be seen as a strategy to enable things to continue to be fulfilling, and follows the maxim "You don't have to be sick to want to get better". An individual does not have to have poor relationships to want to improve on the skills they already possess for relating to others.

By preparing individuals for change through focusing on issues before they appear, developmental counselling can enable individuals to pass through a 'crisis' with greater ease, and can enable them to make fuller use of all the opportunities there may be, instead of becoming overladen with anxiety.

Much developmental counselling can be done through thematic groups. 'Life planning', 'decision-making' and 'weight control' are a few illustrations. Individual sessions may arise out of contact with a helper in order to overcome a crisis. Developmental counselling is an area of increasing growth.

Chapter Sixteen

Counselling Strategies

Defining The Outcome

The first and crucial step in resolving an issue is to **define** precisely and correctly **the desired outcome** the client is working toward. The counsellor's role is that of **clarifier** and **challenger**. Clarification is required to assist the client in assessing the realism of their desire. Challenge is frequently a necessary part of this process.

Often people define their outcomes negatively. They state what they want to stop happening: 'I don't want to get angry', 'I want to stop always being late'. **Negative outcomes are unsatisfactory** as aims for two principal reasons. Firstly, they give no clue as to what might need to happen instead, leaving the way open for other problems to come into being. Secondly, they do not acknowledge that the behaviour in question actually serves some purpose. Until a better way of serving this purpose, or a way of replacing it can be found, both counsellor and client can expect the behaviour to continue.

Defining the outcome positively in terms of 'I want...' enhances motivation and transferability of any learning, and helps to switch the **client's** attention into drawing behaviours and feelings from their situations, behaviours and feelings with which **they** wish to replace the negative pattern. Defining the outcome is not an easy process and is not something to work with in the early stages of a session, but it is something the counsellor needs to have in mind - that they are both there to **do** something.

Selecting Skills

The counsellor is responsible for identifying which skills will best enable them to help the client move towards the objective they have agreed together. It may be a question of helping the expression of blocked feeling, as in the case of loss; or of action planning, as in the case of deciding whether to apply for a new job.

Goal-Setting

Once the outcome has been defined, the skills, knowledge or behaviour required of the client to achieve it has to be considered. Not always will the counsellor share this information immediately with the client. However, the counsellor needs to consider the intermediate steps in the process: how to arrange the change process so that behaviours are 'in-step' with the client's increasing confidence, how to encourage attempts at rehearsal leading to trial efforts in the real situation, and how to enable the client to assess the consequences of such attempts both on themself and on others in a realistic way.

Consider the Constraints

A client lives within a network of surrounding lives. They live within a set of expectations and demands which are both limiting and supporting in their effects when it comes to change.

Clients may express a strong conviction about their wish to change, but find themselves handicapped by the network of relationships that they live amongst. The counsellor needs to pay attention to this issue and to help clients to clarify their understanding of the implications any change may have upon this network. It may be that expressing my irritation to my boss will enable me to feel better, but there may be other consequences that will follow.

Establish the Sequence

The counsellor is responsible for helping to identify the pattern and timing of the sequence of change with the client and for assisting in getting the process under way.

Monitoring

Over the sequence of meetings, an important feature is reviewing the results of any changes in the client's awareness or circumstances. Helping clients to appreciate the importance of monitoring their own behaviour encourages self-responsibility.

Section IV

The Counselling Process

Chapter Seventeen

Principles of Counselling

Counselling is based upon a belief in the fundamental impulse towards growth and maturity in individuals, and their capacity to take increased charge over their own lives. One view of the client's problem is to regard it as an attempt towards resolving that which has been unsuccessfully resolved in the past, this may mean that the client has to regress to earlier experiences and feelings to discover how the present conflict originates before they are able to move forward.

All behaviour is emotionally conditioned. It arises out of some experience (however distant) and is directed towards the future. However strange or bizarre, behaviour has meaning for the client.

Changes in behaviour result from changes in the emotional life of the client. To help bring about change it is necessary to understand the feelings which precipitate the behaviour.

Movement towards the resolution of conflict or an increase in effectiveness is only achieved when the client is involved in working out their own problems and defining their own solutions.

The counsellor offers the client time, space and skills to see the nature of their difficulties more clearly and to gain self-direction. Counsellors do not impose their own solutions, values, or judgements.

"The underlying common faith is the development of the relationship between the client and the therapist. It is through the strength and acceptance of the relationship that the client begins to achieve self-acceptance for those parts of themselves which are difficult to acknowledge or integrate."

One definition of counselling: Counselling is offering a relationship to someone for the purposes of change. The relationship between counsellor and client is the medium of help.

Effective help rests on the capacity of the counsellor to establish a constructive relationship with client.

To establish a constructive relationship with the client the counsellor must be responsive to the client in conflict.

The counsellor must accept responsibility for giving the interview (the particular form of the experience in relationship that counselling offers) both focus and direction.

The counsellor is responsible for employing effective skills and strategies to enable the client to develop.

It is important that the counsellor keeps their own conflicts and problems under control in the interview so that their own issues do not contaminate the client's work.

Behaviour, regardless of how bizarre, has meaning.

Permanent change in behaviour results from changes in the emotional life of the client.

To understand the behaviour or the conflict of the client, it is necessary to understand the feelings that precipitated the behaviour or which lie behind the conflicts.

Understanding alone does not necessarily produce change.

The counsellor does not impose their own judgements, standards or solutions on the client.

The counsellor's own perspective is kept out of the way for the benefit of the client.

The counsellor respects and accepts the differences between the client and themself including such differences as sex, race, standards of behaviour, goals, social exceptions, values and religion.

The counsellor supports the strengths of the client.

The counsellor will leave the client free to use their own resources in testing solutions or making modifications to changes in the way they live.

The client has the resources within themselves to bring about change, however small.

Points to Remember

If you are genuine about making the client responsible for the content and disclosure in a session, then you must be prepared to take what comes.

Counsellors need to be careful not to project their own feelings on to the client, to interpret their behaviour too strongly, or to burden them with their own value judgements.

The 'here and now' is by and large the territory to get in and stay in.

Many clients may need support outside their session: if so, this needs thinking about.

Silences are important and useful.

Frequently feed back what you think you are hearing to check that you are both moving at the same pace.

Regular sessions help to make counselling part of life and not simply a crisis service.

What goes on in a session is not your property, it is that of your client, and you are not at liberty to use it in any way without their knowledge or consent. You are not on a fact-finding mission for any other agency.

'Presenting problems' are ways of testing out how far the relationship can take stress.

The temptation to give advice is the signal to resist it.

Be willing for problems to have untidy ends.

Don't be over-invested in your own interventions: be willing to let them go and to do something else instead.

Interpretations given too soon may confuse, or make understanding difficult, and make rejection more likely.

The degree of self-responsibility which counselling implies is not always easy for people to assume.

It is essential to remember the circumstances in which individuals have to act out their lives before making any suggestion.

Every problem is important to the person who has it and the solution novel to the person who tries it.

Chapter Eighteen

Problems for Those Seeking Help

To ask for and seek our help requires considerable courage on the part of most people, since our culture places high value on being competent, successful, achieving and so on, and to have to ask for help is often regarded, inaccurately, as the very opposite. Consequently, when a person first begins to notice an issue or problem arising, they push it away or refuse to think further about it in the fond hope that it will go away. When it does not and only grows worse for having been left unattended, it can become even harder to seek help, because the problem has become so big that it would only make the person appear foolish for not having come sooner. The prospective client is caught in their own double-bind. Heads they lose, tails you win.

Many people have the experience of seeking help only to have been met with insensitive handling, abrupt and inappropriate advice or having been patronised at regarding their particular concern as any sort of problem in the first place. This kind of experience deters people from trying again.

Accepting Help

For the reasons given above, it may be difficult for an individual to accept help. Additionally they may have very strong beliefs and convictions which get in the way of accepting help. Those with beliefs about never asking other people for help or always relying upon your own efforts, find it extremely challenging to be open to help.

There are also certain kinds of life crises which have a potentially (and usually temporary) devastating effect upon the individual: examples are divorce, bereavement, and enforced redundancy. These can produce effects of such shock to the individual's self-esteem that having to ask for help, desperately needed though it is, is to place oneself in a position to invite further rejection.

Recognising The Need

It is often the case that those around us are the first to spot the signs that something is 'going on' and that we are not behaving in our usual ways. It is usually over issues that are personally felt that the individual concerned finds it most difficult to recognise or admit that a problem even exists, let alone that help might be required. Alcohol dependence can lead to alcoholism through the denial of the excessive drinker that they have any kind of problem at all. This kind of denial is not unusual.

It needs to be remembered that unless a person takes responsibility for the problem there is little that a helper can do. Sometimes people have to make very painful mistakes before they acknowledge that an issue exists which requires help to sort it out.

Behaviour Patterns

Most people associate change with difficulty, compulsion or even pain. They therefore not unnaturally dislike the idea of change, and will go to considerable lengths to avoid it. Also, well- established patterns of behaviour, or ways of relating to others developed over years of practice, have considerable investment attached to them. Changing such behaviours requires a great deal of commitment over a considerable period of time.

Accepting the Helper

It can sometimes be difficult to accept the helper, not only at the level of individual like or dislike, but because they represent all the competence, skills and ability that is presently absent in the client's own life. Clients sometimes go through a period of challenge in the worth of the helper's efforts, accusing the helper of not understanding their problem because 'You are too well-off, middle-class, young, old, etc.' or of seeking to establish an unrealistic relationship of dependence upon the helper.

Having to Trust

To get help requires trusting in the skill and expertise of another. At a time of vulnerability it means placing oneself in a position of extreme risk, laying the way open to exploitation. Such fears are genuine and should be handled sensitively.

Size of the Problem

The problem may seem too big, too small, too disgraceful, too pathetic, too complicated, or whatever, to seek out help or to accept it when it comes. Helping someone see that whatever the dimensions of the problem, something can be done to give a person greater choice over the options they have in front of them, is an important part of the helper's task.

Chapter Nineteen

The Counselling Process: An Overview

The strategies employed by the counsellor will depend upon the issue under review, the resources of the client, and - just as importantly -the amount of contact they have had. Attempting to define the outcome of counselling too early for instance will only increase anxiety and perhaps lead to the client not fully expressing the complexity of a problem. As in any helping interview, a counselling session will follow a number of stages. The skills used at each stage will vary. There is usually an initial phase in which counsellor and client tentatively open the area of discussion before moving into the final action phase of deciding upon new steps to take as a result of new information, understanding or insight.

COUNSELLING: STAGES OF A SESSION

STAGE	PURPOSE	SKILLS
CONTACT	* Relationship building	* Listening
CONTRACT	* Acceptance of the individual's need to share the nature of the dilemma shows RESPECT.	* Attending * Observing * Asking Open Questions
	* Appreciating the personal significance of the dilemma conveys EMPATHY.	
	* Authenticity in dealing with the individual shows GENUINENESS.	

CLARIFY	* Understanding the implication and effects of the difficulties experienced.	* Reflecting
		* Paraphrasing
		* Focussing
	* To enable the individual to gain a greater understanding of the dilemma.	

CHALLENGE	* To encourage the individual to begin to move toward a consideration of possible options.	* Defining
		* Confronting
		* Immediacy
	* To begin the process of assessing the various options and considering the pressures for and against them.	

CHOICE	* To help move towards change.	* Contracting
CHANGE		* Action Planning
	* To create a climate of choice.	* Goal Setting
	* To enable the individual to take charge.	* Homework

| CLOSURE | * Bringing the work and relationship to a close | |

Chapter Twenty

A Five Stage Model of
A Counselling Session

The model offered here in detail is one of five principal stages. Each stage has a central thrust or purpose for the counsellor and features the use of particular skills. This is not to say that the same skills, such as listening and attending are not important throughout - they are, but some skills will be likely to predominate at different times.

Stage 1: Contact and Relationship Building

Stage	Task	Skills
Contact	Relationship	Matching
		Mirroring
		Pacing
		Leading
		Listening
		Attending
		Questioning

Before any help can succeed helper and client have to form an alliance to work together. It is primarily the helper's job to "model the process"; to indicate how the relationship will work, to indicate the boundaries and manage the efforts of both of them. This in itself can be a major task since some people have never had the experience of really being listened to or being given time and attention by someone else. It may cause embarrassment or anxiety to face the prospect of entering such an unfamiliar space. The helper can do much to put the client at ease by picking up cues from the client early and responding to them appropriately.

There are two principal tasks to accomplish in promoting effective contact:

* The removal of distractions and minimising of the potential for interruptions.

* The promotion of an atmosphere which will enhance the client's safety to disclose those things they need to talk about.

This raises the question of "where to begin".

* If the helper spends too long relating to the client this may be a way of never getting round to the crucial material. Lots of good chat may happen, but nothing much may change.

* If the helper begins with too abrupt a request to get to the heart of things, the client is likely to back off and freeze up.

Much that the helper can do at this stage can be undertaken at the non-verbal level:

* Sitting in an open, expectant but not threatening way.

* Holding an open gaze, rather than a stare.

* Inviting the client to choose where to begin.

* Mirroring the client's overall body posture.

* Matching the client's language and using their preferred channels of communication.

* Pacing the client's world-view in an attempt to understand their **frame of reference** rather than challenging their ideas and beliefs too early.

Once the client begins to feel you are interested enough in understanding how it really is for them and are taking the trouble to learn about their individual **model of the world**, they will be more willing to let you **lead** them into new areas of exploration - the next stage of helping.

Rapport

Rapport is clearly an essential element in the early stages of the formation of a working alliance between counsellor and client. Successful rapport depends upon two major considerations on the part of the helper. These are:

* To begin their conversation at a suitable place that is near to the major purpose of their meeting i.e. somewhere close to the topic at hand.

* To move at a pace that does not upset or put off the client, thereby making it more easy for them to respond well.

Rapport is about establishing an effective relationship, one suitable for the purpose. In that sense those involved do not have to like each other, but they do have to create sufficient confidence and trust that they can accomplish their work together.

The helper's role is crucial in setting the tone and in creating the context for the client to respond in.

Any helping activity has to begin somewhere, but if you do not know the client well there is a danger in starting too close to the subject matter and increasing the client's anxieties. However if you begin too far from the topic, there is every danger of never getting to it at all, or only when the time available is running out.

Rapport can be thought as having five elements:-

* **Willingness** - a genuine interest in accomplishing a result.

* **Freedom from distractions** - the ability to give your full attention to the task in hand.

* **Joining and leading the subject** - the ability to **match** the client's language, **mirror** the client's behaviour and **pace** their belief system, before moving anywhere else.

* **Acuity** - having a sufficient awareness to both detect and understand the signals the client gives and the responses that they make.

The central purpose of establishing rapport is to generate in the client a sense of being understood whilst you are able to gather information central to the task that you are there to accomplish. Rapport can be considered as having four levels:

* There is rapport at the **content level.** You generate for the client a sense of their being understood, by being able to relay back to them what they have said.

* The second is at the level of **feeling.** You can convey to the client a sense of your understanding of what it is that they feel about what they are saying.

The third and fourth levels of rapport are more complex and difficult. However, if you can confidently create rapport in depth, the work that you can do with the client will have consequent benefits.

* The third level of rapport can be called **advanced empathy.** This means being able to take what the client has said and to be able to draw attention to what has not been described but which is also meant. It is akin to filling in the spaces between the words. If done sensitively the client not only feels understood, but also understood in a way that they themselves are groping to discover.

* The fourth level of rapport might be called **projective empathy.** Here the client is not only understood, but the counsellor can so closely identify the **frame of reference the client is using** that they can give other situations which are congruent to the client's world view. The effect is to help the client realise that someone else can understand even that which they are not yet able to express confidently.

Stage 2: Clarifying - Getting the Story

The second stage of a counselling session is to help clarify the concerns the client is attempting to express.

	Task	Skills
	Offering permission	Open Questions
	Identifying Issues	Reflecting
Clarify	Listening for Themes	Restating
	Testing understanding	Paraphrase
		Summary

Someone in difficulty may well seek only an immediate solution to the problem. Nevertheless the issue still presents them with an opportunity to take a further step in their life journey.

It is useful at this stage to remember that clients need their problems, and since they have usually taken a long time to get them, and have spent a while hanging on to them before asking you for help then you can remember that it will do them no great harm to keep the problem until they come up with **their own solution.** This should be sufficient for you to resist all efforts to provide 'solutions'. If the problem or the crisis really were that easy to solve why do you suppose they are so 'stuck'?

Resist helping the client in favour of **gathering a full description** of the problem they experience. It can be tempting to believe that you know the client's problem at this early stage. Yet you cannot possibly know how it is for them even when they tell you. If you are reasonably sure you know what is going on, it will do no harm to keep it for later when the client may well be able to use it. This stage of counselling is focused around helping the client gain **coherence in their account of themselves.** The helpers task is to facilitate that process and gather a sense of how the client comes to have the difficulty they face at this particular time. As the story unfolds the counsellor will be alert to listen for any 'blind spots' the client has overlooked, any **unexamined assumptions** they are making about themself, others, the situation or the world in which they live, which are **limiting their freedom of action.**

It is important to be free to listen to the story as it unfolds and if you are not distracted then you have time to think of how to respond and where to go next.

Stories have both a content, a sequence of events and a meaning or feeling **tone.** The importance of the story lies in the sense of meaning the client has or has not got in what has been happening to them.

Some stories are: complex;
some are only discovered in the telling;
some deepen as they unfold;
and some reveal many possible directions.

Points to remember

* The story may turn out not to be the story.

* What does it mean for this person to carry this issue in their lives?

* How does the person feel about what is happening to themself and about themself from inside their circumstances?

* Some people may show little initial commitment to telling their story.

* The client may believe telling their story won't change anything (and, of course, strictly speaking they are right).

* The story may be deeply moving and the client may need considerable reassurance.

* It is a risk to raise the lid on yourself or to dig your own pit and them jump in.

* Sometimes telling the story is sufficient for the person to gain either insight or understanding about their difficulty.

* Sometimes it is enough just to share the difficulty knowing it is yet no nearer to resolution.

* Most often telling the story seems to remind the client of how far the situation has developed and how much there may be to do before any change is likely.

Stage 3: Challenging Implications

Following clarification of the issue or difficulty, which helps the client reveal to themself something of the understanding they have of their dilemma, the sessions have to move forward. In the clarifying stage the control over what happens next rests very much with the client. They can decide how far to go, just what they disclose and how they tell their story. Once a session moves on from examining the implications of the situations described then the control and influence transfers across to the counsellor who will ask questions that push and challenge the client. This can be done with sensitivity and skill to the point where the client barely notices it, or it can be a very direct, confrontive experience. However it needs to be done with the client's interests paramount and not the need of the counsellor to demonstrate how well they know what the client has overlooked. This is not counselling 'to make sure they have got the right message'.

This is the stage where client and counsellor can begin to look for patterns in the examples given, where deeper feelings may surface requiring sensitive encouragement for their expression. It may be the point at which there is a discovery of the impasse the client faces because of a deeply held and fixed belief.

If the client is to move forward something has to give way, boundaries may have to be challenged, action may be necessary. Part of effective challenge lies in **identifying unused resources, capitalising on unnoticed opportunities** or **hidden potential.**

All this involves risk and uncertainty, the consequences for self image and self esteem one are likely to be high. Can counsellor and client evaluate the issue so as to make the uncertainty manageable?

For a challenge to succeed it is essential that the client 'owns' the issue i.e. takes responsibility for their part in whatever situation they are in. Finding ways to displace the problem away from oneself, to make-up excuses why they can't change or to play games with themself in the hope that the problem will go away all have to be surrendered if the client is to move forward. Energy spent avoiding the issue is energy needed to resolve the dilemma.

In all this the client needs to feel supported by the counsellor. This is the phase of 'tough loving' where attempts to 'rescue' the client from the potential painful realisations they may face will only delay the inevitable; where false reassurance is more likely to be an attempt at protecting the counsellor themself.

In the end we have to exchange blame (upon others) for pain (of realisation) and a counsellor who must keep things 'nice' will help no-one, not even themselves: just as a counsellor interested merely in pushing the client into seeing what they need to do will only be counterproductive. If the client pushes themselves prematurely or does it to please you, where is the real learning? Often such premature efforts backfire and the client is left more demoralised than ever.

The challenge stage requires a **balance between love and power** on the part of the counsellor, a sufficient degree of compassion to be present for the client rather than to see them 'get better', 'make a go of it' or any of the other rationalisations we might put forward and enough power to hold the challenge effectively when the client's frightened, inner child wants to run away to the safety of keeping things the way they have always been. Any anxiety or uncertainty on the part of the counsellor will only get in the way of offering a clear non-defensive challenge. Unsolicited challenge, it is worth remembering, is hardly ever successful and that is why it is worth waiting until this point in a session to offer a challenge, when the relationship can bear the weight of the confrontation of the client with themself.

Sometimes the conflict the client is struggling with lies not in the world, in a relationship or situation they wish to act differently toward, but often the conflict is an internal opposition between competing values, for instance the need for security versus the risk of trying something new.

Many internal conflicts have an **exaggerated** dimension to them: either an exaggerated need for something, approval, recognition, or perfection for instance; or the pursuit of **the one right way** which will make everything alright again; or an exaggerated fear of being rejected, condemned or that some ultimate catastrophe will ensue.

These exaggerated concerns may have led in the past to the client repeatedly using self-defeating behaviour that only reinforces the very pattern they want to change, or may have only seemed to set up evasions and avoidance behaviour.

Working with Challenge

Always allow the client the opportunity to challenge themselves, to discern the discrepancies and incongruences in their account of themselves for themselves. **Self challenge is the most potent form of challenge.** It allows the client the opportunity to assume responsibility for taking themselves through this stage. That way they can take all the credit for themselves.

It is important to challenge the **right** issue. By right we mean the one the client is most ready to respond to effectively, not right as in what you think is most important or what you think the client should tackle. Sometimes the issue you both identify turns out not to be **the** issue and the client has to return to a further stage of clarification. This will only be able to occur if you are steady in holding the first challenge so the client has an opportunity to know where they are in relation to themselves and the issue. It is therefore important not to be side-tracked by following up irrelevant issues or smoke-screens, including exaggerated emotional responses.

Before any challenge can succeed the counsellor and client need to gain **as complete a representation as possible of the internal experience** the client goes through at the time the problem occurs by using **focused questions.** If possible get the client to bring the problem into the room to demonstrate just how they look or what tone of voice they actually use. This will show you how they get stuck and you will not have to rely solely on their description. Counsellors need to be imaginative in finding ways to accomplish this.

Whilst the manner of the challenge the counsellor offers needs to be tentative and tactful and should look to identify examples that identify the client's potential to work with an issue, it is also important for the counsellor to have had experience of being challenged themselves. Openness to challenge oneself offers a valuable role model to the client. The counsellor should remember that **there must be sufficient rapport** for the challenge to hold and that your challenge should be open to being refused: "I'm not ready to deal with that yet," or even rejected: "I think you got it wrong." If you are really there for the client you can always return to the subject at another time. Remember to remain positive in the challenge and not to become over-invested in any result.

Areas of Challenge

There is a whole series of polarities which many issues become reduced to. These are frequently related to self-limiting beliefs about one's own talent or potential or oneself, about moral constraints or fixed ideas about personal identity. Beneath the impasse you will often find one or all of the following issues at work, a sense of **hopelessness** (as in "I couldn't possibly do that") or sense of **helplessness** (as in "People like me shouldn't expect any more or don't have any right to...") or **worthlessness** ("I am just not worth anybody's trouble to put this right. It doesn't really matter anyway.") Helping shift such deep stated beliefs is not easy and a **modest** improvement is the aim.

Other conflicts can often be identified as a struggle between:

What I ought to do	v	What I want to do
What I think	v	What I feel
What I say	v	What I end up doing
What I want for myself	v	What others expect of me
What I think of myself	v	What I'd like to aspire to

The Manner of the Challenge

*	Be tentative	"It's my impression that..."
*	Be tactful	"I've got a sense that..."
*	Build upon success	"When did you last achieve this or anything like it?"
*	Be concrete and specific	"You have said how much you care, but each time, I have noticed your hand hitting your wrist."
		"Are you sure you know how you feel?"
*	Relate it to aspects the client can undertake	"What time could you find to work this out?"
		"How much do you think you will have to give?"
*	Challenge strengths to develop rather than point out failings.	

Challenge Questions

What is the pay-off for things being like this?
What have you already tried?
What happened?
What would happen if you did...?
What is the worst thing that could happen?
What would you really like to do?
What stops you?
Who says you can / cannot?
How do you know?
How do you feel about...?

Challenge is designed to assist the client to move forward, to liberate their own inner resources, skill and potential. The counsellor needs to look for **points of leverage** to alert the client to qualities they already possess but which they could exploit more successfully in their own lives.

Challenge is offered to:

* open a new perspective
* increase awareness
* widen options
* discharge feelings

Challenging Implications

Stage	Tasks	Skills
	Selecting themes	Focusing
	Challenging implications	Defining
	Support through discharge	Specifying
Challenge	Identifying options	Concreteness
		Immediacy
		Challenge

Counter-productive Challenge

There are a series of interventions that can occur any time in a counselling session and which are likely to hinder the client. In themselves they are often experienced as challenging in a threatening rather than productive way. They rarely help. Amongst the most frequent are:

Commanding:	ordering or directing the client to change however benignly expressed.
Warning:	pointing out, however gently, the unpleasant consequences of continuing as they are.
Moralising:	offering, however rationally, your own position as the one to adopt.
Advising:	offering a solution of your own to the client's supposed problem.
Lecturing:	using logically convincing explanations that are supposed to show the client the way.
Ridiculing:	belittling the client's best efforts to help themselves.
Interrogating:	questioning the client to help them face up to what you know they are avoiding.
Humouring:	distracting yourself and the client into letting yourselves off the hook.
Reassuring:	sympathising or consoling the client is not what you are there for.
Approving:	agreeing with the client is irrelevant to the task.

Challenge and Irrational Beliefs

Many of the impasses that we experience in our lives are concerned with the influence of irrationally held beliefs. We become, for example caught in a struggle between two competing choices: we cannot seek the solution to a problem by asking for what we want without feeling guilt in ourselves or thinking we will appear selfish in the eyes of others. Some of the characteristics of such beliefs are set out below:

Demanding: they often include elements of "must", "should" or "ought".

Self-fulfilling: because we have always failed in the past we expect to in the future and we make sure we do - all without realising it.

Self-evaluating: they are highly judgmental of self - the opposite of self-forgiving and self-accepting.

Awfulness: there is usually a sense of heightened emotionality or crisis about events.

Misattribution: there are elements of the situation that claim exaggerated importance, and responsibility is shifted onto self or others or away from self or others in unrealistic ways.

Repetition: we indoctrinate ourselves with other related self-defeating ideas so they assume an often unquestioned consistency.

Five Steps to Challenge the Consequences of Irrational Beliefs

These steps are drawn from the work of Albert Ellis, the founder of Rational Emotive Therapy (RET)

A: There is an activating event.

B: This triggers the irrational belief that determines what the event **must** mean.

C: There are a set of predictable consequences that follow: a pay-off.

D: To change the pattern, there must be a successful challenge or **dispute** of the irrational belief.

E: Leading to a successful effect.

Stage 4: Choice and Change

Change comes about through choice. Two choices is no choice since you have only a dilemma; either this or not this. Choice only begins when there are at least three ways to do something or get somewhere.

Following a successful challenge the client experiences a freeing of energy, an increase in potential, an optimism or at least a sense of possibility that what once could not be influenced is now open to change. The 'being stuck' gives way to the interest to get on with it. Where in the Challenge Stage control passed from client to counsellor it now returns back to the client. The client can begin to take the initiative. With the benefit of a new insight, or change of perspective, ways forward can be envisaged and considered.

This is a time when it might well be the counsellor's task to apply the brakes and to ask the client to consider further, to check again, to rehearse their intended course of action in order to help the client bring their new sense of freedom under **realistic** direction. After all the other people in the client's life will not have benefited from the insight the client has gained. Others in the situation will not have changed their views on what needs to be done. **Consider the system's capacity to bear the amount of change proposed.** Too ambitious an action plan, or one commenced too hastily will only ensure that once it is implemented it generates unanticipated problems.

This is when counselling becomes like work. It is a thought out and considered stage of evaluating options, considering consequences, weighing benefits of courses of action **before planning a strategy** and **devising an action plan** to get there. In one sense the counsellor can be thought of as the **external** monitor that enables the client to rehearse and anticipate the effects of what they intend.

This often involves learning new skills, rehearsing courses of action, practising what "I am going to say when..." or trying out **how what I am going to do feels.** It needs patience and consideration. Sloppy thinking gets sloppy results and much good work gets diluted because the counsellor and client cannot be bothered to work at the level of detail this stage often requires.

Personal problem solving is taken up at a later stage in the manual and much of what could be said here is raised there. For the counsellor however, it is important to remember that nothing changes in the client's life until they begin to act. It is not sufficient to have an insight or come to a decision for change to take place. It has to be implemented. And at this stage the client may well become nervous and anxious all over again at the prospect of what they now know they have committed themselves to. Since practising mistakes and attempting things that fail have no place in counselling, together the client and counsellor have to build a model of action that has **manageable chunks of activity and realistic steps** that the client can with a reasonable degree of confidence expect to accomplish and report back upon.

Reviewing what actually happened in the light of experience is an additional and important source of further learning that the client might overlook but the counsellor should not. Similarly accepting a statement such as "Oh yes it went fine", and not probing what took place actually fails the client. There is everything to learn from a success so that the client can identify those skills and behaviours and then can draw upon them next time. Such exploration begins to generate positive behaviour in the client and help move away from a purely remedial style of working.

Stage	**Tasks**	**Skills**
Choice and Change	Movement towards change	Contracting
	Increase of energy	Problem solving
	Increased freedom to identify alternatives	Goal setting
		Action Planning
	Generate options	Rehearsing
	Client increasingly in charge	Homework
		Revision

Stage 5: Closure

Finally the client has to say goodbye. What they came to learn they now know and the time has come for them to move on even from you. This is not an easy stage to manage or do well. Both parties are likely to have a good deal invested in the work they have done together and the relationship that has grown. A good counselling relationship can become a messy one because the counsellor cannot find a 'good time' to broach the ending or the client 'Isn't sure if they are ready to leave you'. Talking about endings a long time before they are likely can help to prepare both people beforehand.

Closure is about completion, of the work, or the issue. A time to look back and make sure what the client is taking away, of the journey they have made. It is an opportunity for the counsellor to help by pointing out landmarks they too have noticed and offering appropriate disclosures about the meaning the work has had for them too. It is about being real; and partings can be moving. There is no need to pretend you are unaffected in order to make it "easy" for the client.

Stage	Tasks	Skills
	Ending the work	Respect
	Closing the relationship	Empathy
Closure	Evaluating the time spent together	Genuineness
		Authenticity

Chapter Twenty-one

Counselling Skills

A Counselling Skills Framework

John Heron (1986) devised a very useful framework for examining the skills involved in helping situations which can be applied to counselling. The system of **'Six Category Intervention Analysis'** looks at inter-personal interaction as fitting into six broad categories. Each has its own strengths and limitations.

The Six Category System

Different counsellors possess different degrees of skill in different areas. They also have preferred strategies for the various stages of a session. For example, some counsellors are very effective in confronting their clients in a supportive and non-threatening way; others find that they feel they handle such situations less well. Training in the use of counselling skills helps counsellors to identify the areas in which they work well and those which are open to further development. There is no 'ideal' profile of a counsellor. It is much more important to be aware of the strengths and limitations of your own individual style.

Prescriptive: Advice-giving, telling, authoritative intervention offering, large-scale interpretations.

Appropriately used this can help bring about major insight or understanding. If the client is in severe difficulties, giving strong prescriptions can be a caring and responsible form of protecting the client (from suicide, for example), **but** large-scale interpretations can easily be used to demonstrate the skills of the counsellor at the expense of **the client** working things out for **themself.** It is open to the counsellor taking over the client's problem. Clients can become demoralised by all you know about them which they don't understand about themselves.

Informative: Offering new facts and information, interpreting behaviour.

Less authoritative than prescriptive interventions, informative ones offer the client a more immediate interpretation of the current situation. They can usefully serve to move the client forward to new understanding, by helping to fit pieces of the jigsaw together, but informative interventions can remove important learning from the client. The temptation to appear the wise leader has to be recognised.

Confrontive: Challenging restrictive thinking, beliefs, attitudes and behaviour.

Challenging a client in the safety of a session can help to focus on the unanticipated consequences of intended actions. For many of us, there are some areas of conflict between what we would like to do and what we feel we ought to do, and counselling often needs to work in this area. **But** many people, both counsellors and clients, find confrontive interventions potentially threatening and avoid them. Because it is challenging, over-use of confrontive interventions can lead the client to switch-off and not hear.

Facilitative Interventions

Catalytic: eliciting self-direction, assisting the individual to enquire within, and reflecting back the content and feeling of client responses. Enabling full expression of distress can bring about a recovery of attention to problem-solving.

Encouraging openness to feeling positive as well as negative is an important resource for full living. **But** many clients are 'blocked' from expressing certain feelings. Often such feelings are withheld because of personal myths about potential consequences. "If I cry it might never stop," or "Men should always cope," or "Feelings don't change anything [so I'll stay miserable]," are common examples. If clients work with feelings which the counsellor has not looked at and experienced for themself, and the counsellor can not handle them, the client will sense this, with messy results.

Cathartic: working with the feelings of the client.

Enabling discharge of painful feelings or memories. Offering permission to release repressed anxieties to provide 'free attention' to work more productively, but allowing and encouraging feelings can be a great challenge to some clients.

Supportive: being with the client, offering non-judgemental appreciation and positive affirmation of worth.

Bringing clients into a fuller appreciation of themselves is a central part of counselling. Assisting clients to a recognition of what they can do for themselves and have already done can have positive force in dealing with the current dilemma. **But** support that is qualified or partial is damaging, as in "Don't worry about it, we all have to go through..." thus diminishing the individual's difficulties. Support means being there and seeing it out.

Through the use of the six categories, counsellors can identify a profile of their favoured and most troublesome or avoid areas of activity, and to begin the process of practising these skills so as to develop greater flexibility over the whole range. Where individuals are restricted in their freedom of expression, the use of paced exercises can help to broaden the resources available to a client.

Clarifying Skills

Many of the skills used during the **exploratory** stage of a session are those which help the client clarify or enlarge their ideas, thoughts or feelings further. They are designed to elicit **self-direction** in the client. These types of intervention aim to broaden the shared information between counsellor and client:

* To help clarify the issue under review.
* To explore an aspect further.
* To examine the implications of the way things are.
* To consider alternative strategies.
* To increase choice, understanding and self-direction.

Open Questions:

"Tell me more, please."   "Why?"   "How?"
"When, specifically does this happen?"
"What else do you notice that's different?"
"What are you aware of?"

Client-centred Questions:

All questions which seek information about the external or internal world of the client.

Selective Reflections:

Taking a part of a statement from within a longer speech and selectively reflecting the phrase or image back either with similar tone and intonation or with tone and intonation deliberately exaggerated.

Reflecting:

Playing back in full a complete statement to the client in order to enable them to hear it and measure its effect.

Client: "I really hate my father."
Counsellor: "You really hate your father."

Repetition:

Asking the client to repeat a statement, phrase or word exactly in the manner they have just expressed it. (Sometimes asking to repeat it with an opposite intonation).

Client: "I wind myself up before every exam - do I do it myself? I'd never thought of it that way."

Summary:

The counsellor summarises the main points from within a series of statements and provides the client with an opportunity to confirm, deny or change the counsellor's understanding.

Counsellor: "Let me see if I'm sure I've heard what you're saying..."

Testing Understanding:

Deliberate requests to summarise and test out if the counsellor has indeed got the essence of the story or scene. Frequently clients discover what they mean as they talk. Such checks for understanding are therefore useful to both parties.

Empathic Building:

Elaborations of the client's meaning which enable both client and counsellor to investigate the **possible** implications of suggestions. Such elaborations are offered non-possessively and are made to aid the client, not to suggest the counsellor's depth of insight.

Use of Self-disclosure:

The counsellor's use of appropriate self-disclosure, sharing a feeling, an experience or an observation from within their own life, can bring about a helpful release or further work in the same area by the client. To know that someone else has experienced similar events in similar ways can be a great relief and can help the client to accept what is happening in themself.

Challenging Skills

The confrontive dimension moves all the way along the spectrum from mild requests to reconsider the weight of a statement and its appropriateness to the context, (e.g. "Can you describe what you mean when you say you feel angry?") to much more challenging interventions that confront the individual with aspects of thinking, attitude or behaviour which are severely limiting their action. **Confrontive interventions are in**

the realm of feedback, where the counsellor is in the position of an external monitor to the client, able to make helpful comments and suggestions as a result of what they see.

Many people have little clear idea about how their behaviour is seen by other people, and therefore, have little accurate information about its effects on others. The deliberate request for feedback from other people seems an invitation to others to become negative and judgmental. Once we know how our behaviour is being interpreted, we might then decide to change. But before any change is possible, we require **accurate** and **specific** information.

Feedback requires an atmosphere of sensitivity and support because most people find the deliberate request for information about themselves threatening. If I am to learn from what you tell me, if I am to really appreciate your experience of me, then I need **clear** and **direct** remarks that are not wrapped in cotton wool with all the energy drained out of them. If the feedback is coming with the best of intentions, it will be better if it arrives at me 'straight' and uncluttered, not 'packaged' for my protection.

What makes for effective feedback?

Feedback needs to be:

> *Related to specific behaviour.* There is little point in telling someone they "dominate the gathering". They need specific occasions which illustrate what is being meant. For example: "Just now, I felt that you were not really listening to what I was saying, and that you were just wanting to tell me what you think."

> *Identified as a subjective impression.* Feedback is often given as though it is a judgement from on high, delivered with all manner of claims to authority. Feedback can only be a subjective impression. For example, I cannot **know** that you are angry -though I may **believe** you are. To own the impression as a subjective one is both more honest and more productive. To say "I think you look angry: are you?" is to offer a personal impression which does not label the other person, and leaves them free to accept or reject the suggestion.

Directed toward behaviour that can be changed. To offer feedback on aspects of life that the client is powerless to change is both threatening and frustrating. For example, if someone who is self-conscious about their height is told "You look like a dwarf", this is not likely to help them listen next time.

Descriptive not evaluative. For example, it is more effective to say, "When you point your finger like that, it makes me feel as though you are treating me like a child," rather than, "Don't point your finger at me, you creep". The first describes what happened; the second makes a judgement of the client.

Well-timed. Almost always, feedback is better for being given sooner rather than later - providing the receiver is ready to hear it and there is support available.

Requested. It is most useful when the receiver has actually invited the feedback. For example, "Do you find the way I behaved just now threatening?" implies an openness of response to the feedback the individual may receive.

Checked for understanding. Check to see if what has been heard is what has been said and meant, and work at it until it is.

Feedback is a way of giving and getting help. It gives individuals an important new source of information to assist them in learning how well their behaviour matches their intentions. It increases the chances of accuracy, success and confidence in interpersonal behaviour, and helps to promote a healthy and open atmosphere of mutual regard. The free flow of constructive feedback is a powerful tool for the promotion of mutual learning.

Focusing. Focusing means bringing the client's attention to select from amongst a collection of strands those which possess most 'charge' or significance: e.g. "Which of the last few remarks seem most important to the topic we have been talking about?" It is usually experienced as a mildly challenging intervention. By use of such interventions, the counsellor exercises responsibility for maintaining some focus of interest or pursuing some theme.

Pointing out mixed messages. Clients can be alerted to discrepancies between what they say and what they do. Counsellor: "You say you feel happy about it, but you don't seem to be happy - your face is all drawn and tight..." Counsellor: "A few minutes ago you were telling me how good this relationship was, now you seem to be saying that it's too painful." Pointing out a mixed message is not intended to trap clients: if a trap is suggested to them, they will immediately become defensive.

Direct questions. Supportively asking a direct question aimed at the core of the issue - an area the client may be avoiding, concealing or hesitating in sharing - can be a useful confrontive exercise.

Challenges to personal restrictions. When **a client** celebrates **their** inability to do something they like, or has failed at something yet again - in short, when they are recycling familiar stories of failure - interruptions and mimicking their script can be sufficient for them to recognise it for what it is.

Immediacy. Immediacy, or using the 'here and now', occurs when the counsellor encourages the client to draw upon their reactions and responses to the situation they are sharing. Counsellor: "You say you always feel embarrassed when you talk about your appearance, how do you feel talking about it now?"

Being concrete. Asking for a specific or actual example can be useful. Counsellor: "Can you tell me the last time you felt lonely?"

All confrontive interventions ideally come out of a desire to assist the client and not to serve the counsellor's needs. Therefore there should be no great investment in any of them. If the observation does not fit the client, the counsellor does not have to pursue it until it does.

Cathartic Skills

The expression of strong feeling in our culture tends to be reserved for special occasions when few witnesses are present. There are strong social inhibitions about letting go of anger, grief, sadness and so on, and this can strongly restrict the choices individuals make. For example, an individual may ask for time, care and support to "talk about the loss of their parent" without realising that talking about it is only part of the process of grieving: **feeling is also part of that process.** The inhibition about experiencing such feelings fully and openly in the presence of another can give such sessions an unsatisfactory quality. There are times when clients dip in and out of feelings, unwilling or unable to choose either to express them or ignore them. Ultimately it must be the client who decides, but the counsellor's own willingness and experience in working with feelings of anger and distress will come to play a very great part in the client's decision. It seems unlikely you can ever take anyone to places you haven't at least visited yourself in emotional terms.

Physical support. Physical contact is another area of social taboos. Who can touch who where and in what circumstances is a matter full of variables. However, in counselling what is being acknowledged is the human need for contact at times of acute crisis. The holding of a hand, or an arm or a shoulder can simply tell the client that they are not alone.

Validation. To share strong feeling is a considerable risk, appreciation and respect for having taken the risk, gentle encouragement and support as it happens are ways to validate the client.

Critical scene descriptions. The client can be invited to relive some traumatic scene by retelling the events from within the present tense to evoke the unfinished and incomplete elements of the original experience.

Psychodrama. The client can be invited to return to an earlier occasion and say all the things not said at the time as though the person or group were present now.

Associations. When people begin to speak of emotionally laden events, their attention may switch, signs of feeling may become apparent on their face, breathing may become more rapid and shallower, and so on. Inviting the client to share the thought image or words they might be hearing internally can enable them to more fully experience the emotion.

Contradictions. Simply asking the client to repeat the opposite of a negative statement can have a powerful effect and can bring to the surface material to work with. For example, if a client says 'Life is just a waste of time', the contradiction 'Life is wonderful' is much more likely to bring to their awareness what the original statement actually hides.

Facilitating Change

It seems from the evidence provided by research studies that to facilitate helping it is important to:

Communicate in such a way that the client feels able to trust.

Communicate clearly and unambiguously so as to be aware that behaviour matches intentions and to know how to handle feelings.

Have a genuinely positive attitude toward the client.

Be able to be mature enough to allow the client their separateness and to respect your own, so that you do not become engulfed by their fear or overwhelmed by their grief.

Enter fully and sensitively into the world of feelings and meanings and accept the client as they express it.

Behave in a way which provides the safety for growth. The more free from threat the client feels, the more attention there is available to deal with the feelings of conflict in the client.

Respect the client's ability to make choices even and especially when they differ from those you might like to suggest.

"The degree to which I can create relationships which facilitate the growth of others is a measure of the growth I have achieved for myself", says Carl Rogers (1961).

Chapter Twenty-two

Personal Problem-Solving

People in the helping professions often refer to the difficulties of those seeking help as 'personal problems' in a loose kind of way, well aware that not all the difficulties people experience are either 'personal' in the sense that they have their origin in decisions the clients have made for themselves or 'problems' in the sense that they have a clear solution. In what sense is the loss of a parent a problem? It is rather a naturally occurring life-crisis which the majority of people will one day have to face. Some people will meet this and other crises with little or no need of outside support; others will not. This is not a judgement upon those who at times of crisis seek out a listening ear to help them shape their experience into understanding. Some people are fortunate to live in a network of support that is freely available, but many people have no such network. In times of difficulty they are without close contacts to share their difficulties and must look outside for support. It is often the case that people who are seeking help find it difficult to request it openly and may offer a more tangible and practical need as the reason for seeking help in the beginning. In such cases, helpers need to be alert to clues which might suggest that other issues or concerns are present and to provide opportunities for the client to broach them.

Even when an individual experiences a dilemma, issue or concern in their life as a problem - for example, the desire to lose weight, give up smoking, and so on - such problems may not be capable of solution in a straightforward fashion, as the suggestion to 'eat less' to someone with a weight problem immediately demonstrates.

When people say they "do not know what to do" they are really saying they have no reference system for making a decision.

A reference system for making decisions about whether to stay in a relationship or whether to buy a house or to change jobs will not necessarily be the same. However, most people use the same strategy to do everything which means they will be good at some things and not others but not know why. They will then set about doing the same thing over and over until it works - a sure way to fail. **If at first you do not succeed - then do something else.**

If, for example, you use pictures from your past to determine what you do in the future, then you may condemn yourself to living out the same relationship with a lot of different people. It may be a good strategy for certain kinds of thinking problems - building roads say, but not people problems.

So when people confess to not knowing what to do in a particular situation, it is usually not that they lack the kind of information everyone else has, or that they lack important information. It is that they have more information that they can use. What they lack is knowing what to make of it - what the information might mean.

Problems occur in some context. The context is determined by what you pay attention to and what you pay attention to is related to what you value. And people often do not know what they value.

Meaning lies in people and people **code their experience differently.** They may all experience the same event but each one will represent it in a highly individual way.

There is a difference between an experience and how it is represented - the meal and the menu, and for much of the time people are not responding to what is actually 'out there' in the world, but to what they think it might mean or what they think they should be doing about it.

Decision making is about choice. To have only one option is to be a machine; two alternatives equals a dilemma, three possibilities represents choice. Choice is a multiple response to the same set of stimuli. It is about having a range of ways to obtain what you are after.

But you have to know what it is that you are after, the outcome you want, and this means specifying it accurately because sloppy language gets sloppy results. You then have to be able to alter your behaviour to get the outcome you want - this is termed **behavioural flexibility.**

Most personal problems have some function or purpose in the total life circumstances of that individual. Somehow and at some time it made sense to acquire whatever habit or behaviour pattern they now seek to change. If change were such a simple and straight forward matter, helpers would quickly be out of business. The fact is that problems give people certain kinds of **secondary rewards:** ways of getting certain kinds of attention that are extremely important to them and which they believe they can not get in other ways. If, for example, I am repeatedly complaining of my ill-health and it gets me noticed, although I may complain of it a great deal of the time, I nevertheless remain heavily invested in staying the way I am, since it gets me something that I want - time, sympathy and attention.

Making technical suggestions to solve a personal problem is the least difficult aspect of helping. More important is establishing what the pay-off of the problem is and finding better ways for the client to get the same reward more safely and more effectively.

Assumptions

There are a variety of approaches that have been designed to help individuals solve personal problems. Many are recent in origin and derive from techniques developed in the 'new therapies'. The approach outlined here is based upon a learning and information model.

The underlying assumptions are:

People can learn to solve their own problems, and when they do, they acquire skills transferable to other situations.

Many people lack sufficient information in their awareness to solve their problems. The role of the helper is to help the person with the difficulty to raise the information into their awareness so they can act for themselves.

Many problems are capable of improvement through the help of another.

Such an approach would not be suitable for dealing with long-standing emotional difficulties or critically serious disruptions to an individual's life, unless it were accompanied by skilled specialist help. It is important, therefore, for anyone undertaking the role of helper to ask themselves if they possess the necessary skills to help and if this approach is suitable for the problem.

Force-field analysis is an additional resource for personal problem-solving and draws on the work of Kurt Lewin (1946) and Gerard Egan (1975).

Identifying the Problem

It may be unfortunate, but it is true that the only behaviour you can do something about is your own. You cannot change other people: you can only help them to change if they want to. The problem may appear to be centred in someone else, but the only parts you can act upon immediately are the parts that influence and affect yourself. Once you have taken the first step and begun to concentrate upon your own behaviour, you can begin to apply the steps below.

Problem Solving and Decision Making Strategy

What is the problem?

Express the essence of the problem in one sentence that a seven year old could understand.

What have you done so far?

Briefly outline your responses from the time you first became aware of the issue.

What have you not done but might try?

Note any efforts you have considered but discussed or discounted and consider why: generate other suggestions, however extreme.

What gets in the way?

What factors restrain your efforts?
What are you telling yourself that you can't do?
What other self imposed limitations might you be victim to?

What do you want?

What is the outcome you are aiming to get? Make it specific and relevant to the bit of the world you can influence - yourself.

Is it realistic?

How does your outcome stand up to the cold light of day - be rigorous.
A modified plan and more thinking is better than pain and frustration.

Chunk-it:

Reduce the overall aim to manageable proportions.
Have a realistic time-scale.

Implement the strategy:

Put the first steps into effect.
Ensure there is sufficient support if needed.

Evaluate

Review the actual events against your expectations. Invite feedback.

P:	Pose the problem accurately.
R:	Refine the problem areas into manageable chunks.
O:	Outline the 'right' kind of questions to ask.
B:	Bring back the data.
L:	Look for solutions.
E:	Evaluate options.
M:	Make a decision.
S:	So what next?

The Three Components

To solve any problem successfully, you require as much reliable information as you can get.

There are three aspects to the solution of any problem. There is a **knowing** component (what you think) a **feeling** component (how you feel about the way things are), and an **action** component (doing something about it). Most of the time it is very much easier to gather the information than it is to act upon it, and the way a person feels about things will have great influence upon what they decide to do.

Knowing

To gain information quickly, it is often better to seek someone who already knows the information you require than to try to do it all by yourself. But make sure the source of the information you seek is reliable. It is your responsibility to ensure that the information is accurate and relevant to your needs.

Ask yourself:

What do you already know about the problem?

What do you need to know?

How could you find out?

Who might be able to help?

Feeling

Having information relating to a problem does not always lead to an individual taking positive action. The evidence connecting cigarette smoking and lung cancer is in itself not sufficient to actually stop many people from smoking, though it probably makes most people think harder about giving it up or guilty if they continue. For some people, to admit that they have a particular problem would be to lose self-respect or self-esteem. Denying the problem is a way of avoiding having to confront the implications and the challenge to an individual's self-image. Alcoholics often refuse to admit they have a 'drink' problem until it is acute and therefore harder to change. Sometimes solving a problem is resisted or avoided because the person concerned would then have to consider what to do instead of complaining or feeling sorry for themselves.

Ask yourself:

How do you feel about the problem?

Do you feel that way at other times?

How important is it to you to solve the problem?

What effect would it have upon your life if you were without it?

Acting

Knowing all that is required to solve a problem and then becoming motivated only gets one to the starting-point. A problem is only solved by **doing** something about it. It is important to identify the sequence of activities and skills required to achieve a solution, and to isolate those which are most difficult or require most support or practice before trying them out.

Once those behaviours which are most difficult or most risky have been identified, they can be practised away from the situation until confidence has been developed and until the person feels easier in trying them out in the real situation. Talking is a form of practice, and so is role-play. The advantage of this kind of practice is that it provides an opportunity to evaluate the results in a risk-free environment which allows you to modify anything with which you are not satisfied.

Reviewing

Stay involved. Once you have put a plan into action, it is important to check how you went about it so that you can remember it next time or go over the areas of difficulty. Reviewing enables people to build upon their success and to identify skills they already have and use.

Force-field Analysis as a Problem-solving Method

Force-field analysis can be used when working with someone on a problem they wish to change. It provides a step-by-step approach that covers all the factors in the situation, including those which promote change and are therefore helpful, and those which oppose change and are therefore restraining.

(i)   *Identify the Problem*

* Is the problem owned by the client? (Are they willing to take responsibility for the problem?)

* Is the problem soluble? (Is the problem expressed in concrete terms understood by both parties?)

(ii)   *Clarify the Problem*

* Break down the problem into sub-parts and explore their interaction.

(iii)   **Establish Priorities**

* Choose a 'chunk' of the problem to begin with which can be handled easily. Ensure that it is under the control of the person being helped.

(iv)   **Establish a Workable Goal**

* State the object in a behaviourally descriptive way that ensures that you will have indicators of its achievement.

* Ensure that the client owns the goal and is committed to attaining it, and is not merely saying so to keep you quiet.

* Break the goals down into workable units.

(v)   *Means to Achieve the Goals*

* Look at all those forces, however incidental, that may well facilitate and encourage the client to achieve change. Include internal approval, for success, external praise, environmental support, etc. Do the same for all those factors which will undermine, inhibit or restrain the client from moving ahead easily. Put this into two columns as below:

Facilitating	**Restraining**
1.	1.
2.	2.
3.	3.

Developing a Behavioural Strategy

In identifying a strategy of change, it is important to remember the principles of behaviour change - shaping (approximation to the desired performance), avoidance, reinforcement - and the lack of usefulness of punitive or negative support for failure.

Implementation

Gain a clear contract of commitment to achieve specific goals in an agreed time.

Evaluation

Revise the information and include unintended as well as expected outcomes.

Agree success

Or check where things went wrong.

References

Avila, D.L., Combs, A.W., and Purkey, W.L.: **The Helping Relationship Source Book.** Vols. I & II. Boston, Mass.: Allyn & Bacon, 1977.

Bandler, J., and Grinder: **Frogs into Princes.** Real People Press., 1976.

Carkhuff, R.R.: **The Development of Human Resources.** New York: Holt Rinehart, 1971.

Coombs, A.W.: **Studies in the Helping Professions.** Florida: 1969.

Egan, G.: **The Skilled Helper: a Model for Systematic Helping and Interpersonal Relating.** Wandsworth, 1975.

Fielder, F.E.: 'The Concept of the Ideal Therapeutic Relationship'. **Journal of Consulting Psychology,** Volume 14., 195), pp. 239-245.

Heron, J.: **Six Category Intervention Analysis.** Guildford: Department of Adult Education, University of Surrey, 1976.

Jourard, S.: **The Transparent Self.** Princeton, New Jersey: Van Nostrand, 1964 (revised edition 1971).

Pietrofesa, J.J., Hoffman, A., Spekte, H.J., and Pinto, D.V.: **Counselling, Theory, Research and Practice.** Chicago: Rand McNally, 1978.

Rogers, C.R.: **On Becoming a Person.** Boston: Houghton Mifflin, 1961.

Truax, C.B., and Carkhuff, R.R.: **Toward Effective Counselling and Psychotherapy.** Chicago: Aldine, 1967.

Select Bibliography

Halmos, P.: **The Faith of the Counsellors.** London: Constable, 1978.

Heron, J.: **Helping the Client.** London. Sage, 1991.

Kopp, S.: **If you Meet the Buddah on the Road, Kill Him!** London. Sheldon Press, 1974.

Miller, J.C.: **Tutoring**. London: Further Education Curriculum Review and Development Unit, 1982.

Peck, M. Scott.: **The Road Less Travelled.** London: Arrow, 1990.

Rowan, J.: **The Reality Game.** London: Routledge Kegan Paul, 1983.

Rowan, J.: **Feeling and Personhood.** London. Sage, 1992.

Vaughan, F.: **The Inward Arc.** London. Shambhala, 1985.

FULFILLING THE CONTRACT

KD GRACE

Published by Xcite Books Ltd – 2014

ISBN 9781908766359

Printed and bound in the UK

Fulfilling the Contract *is dedicated to the many intriguing facets of sexuality and the pleasure and connection they bring.*

Thank you, with all of my heart to:

Renee and Jo and all of the lovely Ladiez at Sh! Thanks for all of your inspiration, wisdom and encouragement. You are truly my heroes! Hugs and kisses and my deepest gratitude.

Hazel Cushion, Elizabeth Coldwell, Gwennan Thomas and all the fabulous people at Xcite Books.

Lucy Felthouse, for boundless PR expertise and even more boundless patience when it comes to staving off more than a few panic attacks and encouraging this neurotic writer to soldier on. Thanks for all that you do. I couldn't have done it without you, EP!

Kay Jaybee, for being my partner in crime, my "terrible twin", and for just being your fabulous, beautiful self. The journey has been so much more fun because we've shared it. You're amazing!

Chapter One

Letting his cock do the thinking was never advised, Nick Chase thought as he pulled Tanya – what was her last name? Something Slavic – through the back door of the bar and into the desert swelter in the alley, kissing and groping as he went.

'Fuck me here,' she gasped, managing for a split second to take her delicious tongue out of his mouth. 'Is sexy here, outside. You have the condom, no?'

'No, I mean yes, I have a condom, but I'm not having sex with you in the alley.' He grabbed her hand and pulled her around the end of the building. 'My car's over here.' He nodded to the black Lincoln Town Car parked in the shadow of the building.

'You drive limo?' she asked. Did he imagine the disappointment in her voice?

'I own a limo – several, in fact,' he corrected. What the hell, was he bragging to get laid? How adolescent was that? Was he really that desperate? Forget desperate. It was compensation he was after. The night had gone straight down the crapper early on, and he deserved something nice to make up for it.

His last fare had had a heart attack in the back of his limo while banging a woman half his age. OK, people using his limo for sex was something he didn't get his boxers in a knot over. This was Vegas. But heart attacks, even minor ones, those were boxer-knotting experiences,

experiences that didn't do *his* heart a lot of good either! The woman who caused the man's meltdown had bailed at the first stoplight like they were in some shoot-'em-up film. It might have been funny if she hadn't left Nick to rush Casanova to the emergency room. There he'd waited until the angry wife arrived several hours – and what would have been several good fares – later. He figured a minor heart attack was nothing compared to what the man would get from his wife when she got him home. Nick didn't mind being a good Samaritan, but when a man twice his age and three times his weight got a good hard riding in the back of his limo, while he was reduced to slapping the sausage when he actually had time to be horny, it was hard to be sympathetic.

If that wasn't bad enough, he left the hospital to find that his limo had been towed. By the time he'd found out where it was, paid a taxi to get him there, and paid the fine to release it, he was pissed off, tired, and $300 poorer for his night's efforts. Feeling pretty damned sorry for himself, he'd stopped at the Mango for a much-needed drink. He couldn't actually drink anything stronger than a Coke and drive on home, but home was a fair ways yet and, at least, some caffeine was in order. That's where he met Tanya. She was a busty blonde with eyes the colour of toffee and a sexy Slavic accent that stirred him right in the crotch area. She sat down on the stool next to him, offering him a kick-ass smile as she ordered a Cosmopolitan. At first, he wondered if she were a hooker. But when she ignored the attentions of the guy on the other side of her and politely hinted that she wasn't interested, Nick figured she was just a tourist who either got lost or adventurous. And when the man wouldn't take the hint, it was Mr Good Samaritan to the rescue again.

'Hey buddy, she's with me.' Nick offered a don't-want-any-trouble sort of smile, to which the guy lifted his hands in response, mumbled an apology and took his beer over to the slot machines.

Three Cokes, a couple of strong coffees, and several Cosmos later, and Nick had forgotten all about his ambulance run. In fact, he'd forgotten all about everything except Tanya. He'd like to say it was her accent, or the fact that she was a good conversationalist, and both were true. But honestly, it was Tanya's well-displayed cleavage that had his full attention.

'If you want a real drink,' she said, 'is no problem. 'You order it. I will take it in my mouth, swish it all around. And then I will kiss it into your mouth. Like this.' She demonstrated with a mouthful of Cosmo and a cranberry-flavoured lip-lock that had his cock hard-pressed in his jeans. She came up smacking her lips. 'And that way you will get the flavour and I will get the alcohol.'

'Tanya, I could do that all night, but I think your science is flawed. I'd be both drunk and horny and I'd have to call a taxi to get both of us home.'

'Is true. I swear,' she said. Then she offered him a wicked smile. 'As for the horny part – well, is a side-effect of the procedure, I'm afraid.'

That was when he dive-bombed her mouth with his, coming up breathless as her hand snaked up the inside of his thigh, and he returned the favour by toying with the hem of her curve-hugging minidress, all bright with the sort of tropical print Vegas tourists often wore.

The flirting became foreplay as she opened her legs to give him a glimpse of a skimpy red thong before sliding to the edge of the barstool and pulling his hand up against the triangle of fabric moistening next to her goodies. Her cherry red nails made less than gentle scratching motions against his fly as his mouth found hers once more. After another serious wrestling match with her tongue, he pulled her from the stool and

3

practically dragged her toward the back door, groping as they went.

The parking lot was full of expensive cars, and two things quickly became clear. Tanya had had a few more Cosmos than necessary for an alcoholic buzz. And Tanya had a car fetish. 'Oooh! A Humvee!' she squealed. And before he could stop her, she raced over to the vehicle. That was no small feat in her outrageously high heels, and even more astonishingly, she actually stepped out of her red thong as she did so. Then she hoiked her skirt and hopped onto the hood of the black Humvee that was waxed to an eye-dazzling sheen even in the glow of the streetlights. Once she was up, her heels clunk-clunking on the waxed surface, she spread her legs wide and squatted, giving him a tantalizing view of her pussy before she arched her back and thrust her hips forward in just such a way that said pussy was up close and personal with said wax job giving it ... well, a wax job. '*Bože!* Oh *bože!* Is good,' she moaned. 'Is so good! Come! Join me'

'Jesus, Tanya! Get off there! Come down from there,' he hissed, anxiously stooping to pick up the shed panties and stuffing them into his pocket. Three men came out of the bar and got an eyeful when Tanya chose that moment to flash her very excellent tits from her position high atop the hood of the Humvee.

The men made no attempt to look away, and Tanya made no attempt to hide what she had. And Nick had to admit that in the competition between his very impressed cock and the fear of getting arrested as an accessory to Tanya's indecent exposure, his cock was winning, hands down. 'Come on, come down here. Now!' He gave another look around the parking lot and offered her his hand. Giggling loudly, she took it and slid, open-legged, off the Humvee, leaving a very wet path right down the centre of the hood that left no doubt as to what'd caused it. From there she launched herself at him mouth first, with her magnificent and still uncovered tits not far behind.

'Ooooh! There's a Porsche. I love Porsches.'

Nick figured if the Humvee made her wet the Porsche would probably give her multiples, but he wasn't risking another scene. He kept his arm around her waist and half escorted, half carried her to the limo. Before he could get the door unlocked, she spat on her hands and slathered her nipples with a good dose of saliva. Then she gave the driver's side window the full-frontal rub-up. Tit prints. Nick had tit prints on the window of his limo. Looking rather pleased with her artwork, Tanya leant on the back door, fingering herself while he unlocked.

'Do the people ever have sex in your limo when you are driving them?'

'Yup.' He decided not to tell her about his last unpleasant experience.

'Oooh, is sexy!' She managed a grope at his fly and rubbed up against him before he opened the back door and pushed her in, with her pulling him in on top. 'Do you watch them in your mirror?' she asked, tugging loose his belt and going to work on his fly. 'Do they sometimes make you come?'

'Not so far, no.'

She made a tut-tut sound with her tongue before she slipped it back in his mouth. 'Do they ever ask you to join them?' She slurred the words across his lips.

'I've had offers,' he managed, pulling away far enough to tug at a delicious mouthful of nipple. 'Wouldn't be very professional me joining the orgy, though, would it?'

'Spoilsport.' She offered him a pout before she squirmed out from under him, and slid down his body to take his very agreeable cock into her mouth. And wow, could the woman suck cock! Her throat was seriously deep and her grip was tight enough to suck the paint off a mop handle. And her tongue – holy Christ on a pogo stick, her tongue was warm and wet and all over the place. He curled his fingers in the masses of blonde hair while she sucked and licked his cock like it was the best lollipop ever. Her skirt was still hiked up over her hips, exposing the shift and grind, shift and grind of her pert little arse as she rode her hand like a rocking horse. And the door was still open!

The smell of her pussy filled the dry desert air with a humid sea scent of female heat, and he could almost make out the wet sounds of her fingers dancing over her snatch above the slurping and licking of her tight mouth. But as delicious as her mouth was, it was her pussy he wanted. And she must have read his mind because, just as he reached for the condom in his pocket, she came up gasping and wiping her mouth.

'Fuck me. Please fuck me, Nick. I need you to fuck me now.'

It was all he could do to hold her off until he got suited up for business, then she shoved onto him so hard that she left him gasping for breath and grabbing her hips in self-preservation, at least until he caught her rhythm. And then he let her ride him hard.

'Your cock is so good. It fits so tight up in my pussy,' she half whispered. 'I need to come, Nick, I need to come so bad, so bad.'

As much as he wanted to knead and caress her luscious breasts, he couldn't bring himself to shove her hands away from the filthy mauling she was giving them. Her nipples were engorged like fat cherry gumdrops that made his mouth water. Surely it must hurt, the way she pinched and tugged and squeezed.

He raked the nib of her clit until it pearled and jutted from under its hood and raked back against his finger, wet from the flood of her juices lubricating his sheathed cock.

'Is hard. My clit is so hard,' she sighed. 'And my pussy is eating your cock like hungry mouth.'

Yup, it was doing that all right, and very well getting the job done. One last stroke of her clit and her orgasm broke in a vice-grip clench on his cock. 'I'm coming! I'm coming!' she keened, just as two more men stepped out – probably to take a piss in the alley. But they only registered as a minor distraction because Tanya's tight grip and bounce and her fierce orgasmic tremors along his cock had Nick coming too. Tanya's spasms milked every last drop from him, and it was a lot. He was amazed there weren't broken bones or pulled muscles for their efforts.

He had just disposed of the condom and she was wiping herself clean with the box of tissues he kept in the back of the Town Car when another limo pulled up, way too close for politeness considering there was plenty of room in the parking lot.

At the sight of it, Tanya cried out, and it wasn't with the delight she'd had over the Humvee. She tossed the wad of tissue she'd been using and turned to run just as a man the size of a small freight train stepped out and grabbed her by the arm. 'You need to come with us, Tanya.'

'No! No! Don't let them take me, Nick. Please don't let them take me.' She hammered her little fists ineffectually on the man's chest. 'Leave me alone. I haven't done anything wrong. I haven't.'

'Did you fuck him?' The man asked, in a voice that seemed way too soft for anyone that size. When she began to sob, the man simply shook his head and helped her into the open limo. 'You can explain everything to Elsa when you get home.'

At that, Nick attacked. Well, it wasn't much of an attack. The man just shrugged him off and pressed him up against the hood of his own limo with one beefy hand. 'This is not your concern, Mr Chase.'

'It is if she doesn't want to go, besides … How do you know my name?' Nick didn't strain against the man's stiff arm hold. He knew it wouldn't help. 'She doesn't want to go,' he said, as if repeating it louder would send the big man packing in fear. Jesus! Where was his sense of self-preservation? Was he out of his mind? This could be Mafia; maybe this man was her pimp. Hell, he knew thinking with his cock was a bad idea. 'I'll call the cops,' he threatened.

The man raised an unimpressed eyebrow. 'And tell them what? Tanya's drunk. And when she's drunk she becomes a drama queen. She shouldn't be here and she knows it. I'm just taking her home. That's all. And I'd advise you to stay out of it.'

He gave Nick a half-hearted warning shove before he got back in the car and drove away with Tanya yelling, 'Please, Nick! Don't let them take me! I don't want to go. I want to stay with you!'

And Nick, stupid man that he was, hopped in his limo and followed.

Chapter Two

Nick followed the limo into a deserted part of the parking garage at the Cosmopolitan. There it stopped and Freight Train Man, who seemed neither surprised nor upset that Nick had followed, got out and held the door for Tanya. She ran to Nick and threw her arms around his neck. 'Don't tell her anything,' she sobbed onto the front of his shirt.

'Tell who? What?'

'Elsa Crane. Is best we don't tell her anything.'

Still holding onto him for dear life, she addressed the big man. 'You don't have to tell her this. Please, Pagan, it will be our little secret. I made mistake, that's all. It won't happen again. I can pay you.'

'You can't pay me enough to incur Elsa's wrath, Tanya. Sorry.' And the big man truly did look sad about his decision.'

They entered the Cosmopolitan through the casino like they were tourists, like whatever was happening was nothing out of the ordinary. The constant jangle of slots and bells and buzzers of electronic gaming surrounded them as they made their way through to the hotel elevator bank, Tanya clinging possessively to Nick. The guy she'd called Pagan flanked her on the other side and practically filled the elevator he escorted them into. To Nick's surprise, they got off on the 20th floor and made their way to one of the suites. Granted, the suites in the

9

Cosmopolitan were nice, but Nick had been expecting mahogany and leather in a private apartment that reeked of money and intrigue. Pagan knocked softly on the door. Tanya held Nick's arm in a fingernail-gouging grip and whimpered softly.

A man who was as tall as Pagan but built much more like a dancer opened the door and nodded them in. He was dressed like Tarzan in a leopard-print loincloth that left little of a well-worked-out physique to the imagination. His only other fashion accessory was a pair of unlaced black Converse high-tops. That it didn't seem strange to Nick was a testament to how long he'd been working in Vegas.

The man gave Nick a curious onceover then, with a jerk of his head, nodded them toward one of the bedrooms.

Sitting in the middle of the big bed was Tarzan's Jane. Her loincloth and halter top barely covered the goodies, and it was obvious that the goodies were exceptionally fine. Her heavy auburn hair was in the process of escaping a large tortoiseshell clip, and a good bit of it hung in wild ringlets down her back and over her shoulders. Her do was all topped off by a bright blue headset that got lost in the crown of her hair and reappeared from the silky dark mass just in time to cup her ears. She wriggled bare toes at the end of well-muscled legs that went on for ever before disappearing under the small laptop upon which she typed madly.

At last the woman looked up, and Nick was astounded that someone with such dark hair had such blue eyes. The smile she offered was very bright and very brief as she took in the way Tanya still held onto Nick like she was about to walk the plank.

'Did you two have sex?' she asked without so much as a how-do-you-do.

'That's none of your business,' Nick said.

10

'It is my business.' She pulled off the earphones and shoved them and the computer to Tarzan before crawling off the bed with all the grace the leopard print would imply. It was only as Tarzan settled into her place that Nick noticed the bedroom was buried in an array of monitors, keyboards, and other electronics he couldn't identify. There were also two telescopes pointed out the window.

The woman came to stand in front of Tanya. 'Did you have sex with him?' she asked.

'It was just once, Elsa, and we used the condom.' Tanya's voice was a breathless tremble. All trace of her alcohol buzz was gone.

'Of course we used a condom. I'm not stu –'

Elsa raised her hand to stop him. 'Mr Chase, though your use of a condom is commendable, it fails to absolve Tanya of what she's done.'

'What she's done? She had sex. People do that, you know?'

She ignored him and focused her attention on Tanya. 'You've got a month paid on your flat, and your two months' severance pay'll be deposited first thing in the morning. Pagan'll go with you to clear out your locker, then he'll drive you home, since you've been drinking.'

'What?' Nick exploded. 'You fired her for having sex with me?'

'No, Mr Chase. I fired her for having sex with anybody other than her approved partners.'

Before he could protest, Tanya spoke up. 'What about my bonus? I still get my bonus, no? Is so close to the end of my contract.'

Elsa held her gaze. 'You're in breach of contract, Tanya, so no. You don't get your bonus, and you knew that when you went off and broke the rules yet again.'

Tanya burst into tears. 'But I need the bonus. I have to have, or how will I pay for my mother's surgery and

11

her convalescence afterward? That is whole reason why I need the bonus.'

'You can't be serious,' Nick said. 'OK, fine. Fire her if you have to, though I think it's pretty stupid to fire someone because they had sex on their own time. In fact, I'm pretty sure if Tanya wanted to hire a lawyer, we'd find that what you're doing's illegal.'

For a second, Nick thought Elsa would laugh at him, the way her lips curled in a smile, the way her lungs filled with air, and then she spoke once again to Tanya. 'Want to hire a lawyer, Tanya?'

'Well of course she'll say no if you intimidate her enough.'

Elsa rubbed the bridge of her nose and shook her head. 'I'm not intimidating her, Mr Chase. No one is intimidating anyone, but she won't hire a lawyer.'

Then Nick twigged. 'Wait a minute; is she a prostitute, then?'

This time Elsa did laugh and Tanya wailed. 'No, she's not a prostitute, but she knows she's in breach of contract, as she's known the past four times she's had sex outside the boundaries of that contract, and I've let her get away with it. But not this time. Not this time.'

'You can't do this to me, please, Elsa.' Tanya wept openly, grabbing the woman by the hand. 'Please, just give me one more chance.'

Elsa pulled away, somewhat more gently than Nick would have expected. 'I've given you way more chances than I would have given anyone else, Tanya. Now I'm sorry, but what's done is done.'

'But it's only two more months. Just two more. Please! What about my mother?'

'You should have thought of that before breaching your contract. There are charities, places you can go for what you need, Tanya, but I can't help you.'

'Wait a minute.' Once again, Nick butted in where it

12

was none of his damn business instead of saying thank you very much and scramming fast. 'So you're getting two months' severance pay?'

'And it's a lot,' Elsa said. 'MV pays its employees well.'

'Is not enough, though.' Tanya bit her lip and wiped at her nose with the back of her hand. 'It will never be enough.'

'And she only gets the bonus if she finishes the contracted period?' Nick said.

Elsa nodded. 'It's a three-year contract with a very large completion bonus.'

He took a step forward. 'How large?'

'Two hundred and fifty thousand dollars,' Tanya sobbed.

'Jesus! A quarter of a million? That's one helluva bonus,' Nick said.

'And it would have been mine in two months, just two more months.' Tanya wept against his chest.

'How can you be so heartless? And just because the woman wants to have sex? Who doesn't?'

'It's a contract, Mr Chase, and one that Tanya's broken repeatedly. As for sex, it's readily available to her. Even you she could have had if she'd only followed the rules.'

'It's just two months, damn it! And there are extenuating circumstances.'

'Extenuating circumstances which Ms Povic chose to ignore each time she spread her legs for a stranger.' Elsa raised a hand. 'I don't blame you. It's not your fault. As you say, everyone wants sex. But since you don't fully understand the circumstances, then it's best you stay out of it.'

'Sorry to interrupt,' Tarzan said from his cross-legged position on the bed, which did little to hide his junk. 'But someone's complaining about the noise

13

coming from room 2031.'

'Who?' Elsa's attention shifted instantly to the hodgepodge of electronics set up on the dressing table. 'I need a room number, Pike, I need a room number!'

'Uh, 2039.'

Elsa slid another headset over her mass of hair while her fingers flew over the keyboard of another computer. 'Damn it, they must be really loud. I was sure we'd cleared enough rooms so no one would be disturbed. Pike, when I connect, tell Beetle to moan and shout she's coming.' Raising a hand, she pointed at him as she spoke into the headset. 'Hello, Mr Hegel, this is the front desk.' She batted her eyelashes and smiled. 'Yes, I'm calling about the disturbance. Oh my! Yes, even I can hear that. Mm hmm, uh huh, I see.' The smile on her face never wavered. 'Mr Hegel, I'm so sorry for the inconvenience. Really, it's a mistake that you're even in that room. The whole floor's being used for a film. No, not a porn film. It's a romantic comedy.' Once again she nodded and smiled. 'Yes, I know, the industry's certainly pushing the boundaries these days. Nothing decent to watch any more.'

She listened politely and nodded, then cut in. 'Mr Hegel, obviously the hotel can't stop the filming, but what we can do is give you $500 worth of credit in the casino. Yes, that's right. We'll also give you an upgrade for your room as well. One of our terrace suites is available. We can have the bellboy come up now and move you if you'd like.' She gave the cue to Pike again. Even Nick could hear someone shouting, "I'm coming, I'm coming!" over the headset. Elsa nodded and kept smiling. 'Oh, you want to wait till morning. Well, if you're sure you can endure it, Mr Hegel. We'll have you moved first thing tomorrow. You're welcome. Sorry for the inconvenience.' She punched a few more keys on the computer, pulled off the headset, then turned her attention back to Nick and Tanya.

'Surely you can give her one more chance. I mean it's her mother,' Nick said. 'And really, it was my fault. I'd had a bad day and I wasn't on my best behaviour.'

Elsa tossed the headset back onto the dressing table and rubbed the back of her neck. 'Mr Chase, unless you want to fulfil Tanya's contract for her, this conversation is over. It's been a very long day, and I've had enough. Pagan will escort the two of you back downstairs, and since Tanya no longer works for me, I don't care if you fuck her brains out. Now if you'd –'

'All right,' Nick interrupted. 'I will.'

Suddenly, all eyes were on him. 'Tell me what to do and I'll fulfil the contract for her. After all, it's my fault she's in breach.'

Tanya gave a little yelp that sounded like a kitten in distress and Elsa laughed out loud. 'Mr Chase, you don't even know what Tanya's contract involves.'

'I assume it has something to do with what's going on in room 2031. It's not prostitution is it?'

'No! No, is not prostitution.' Excitement vibrated through Tanya's voice. 'Is nothing like that.'

'Actually, it's something like that,' Elsa corrected. 'My people get paid for sex.'

'I don't understand,' Nick said.'

She nodded him over to one of the telescopes set up at the bedroom window. When he balked, she nodded again. 'Go ahead; check out what's going on in room 2031.'

Nick nearly knocked the scope out of focus at his first view of the naked arse of a man pistoning his cock into a woman bent over a big bed. Her head was buried between the legs of another woman, who was pinching her own nipples for all she was worth and writhing beneath the serious tongue action.

'Then they are prostitutes.' Nick's voice dropped to a

whisper, as though he feared he might disturb the people he viewed through the scope.

'No.' Elsa leant close to him as though she could see over his shoulder. 'They all work for me, and they get paid a lot of money to have sex with each other while someone else watches.'

With difficulty, Nick took his eyes off what was going on in the scope. He suddenly felt dizzy. 'Let me get this straight, these people –' He nodded around the room. 'All of these people and those –' he pointed to the scope '– have sex with each other and people pay money to watch.'

Elsa nodded 'A lot of money.'

'And that's what Tanya was doing? That's what the contract's about: having sex and letting people watch?'

'That's what the contract's about,' Elsa said. With a smirk, she pulled Tanya's red panties out of Nick's pocket where he'd forgotten he'd stuffed them after he'd picked them up from the parking lot at the Mango. She handed the tiny scrap of fabric back to Tanya and replaced it with a black business card, briskly patting his pocket as she did so. 'I know how much you loathe your job, Mr Chase, and I can almost guarantee you'd find what Tanya does a lot more satisfying. But –' she ran a hand down and gave his crotch a quick grope '– it takes some serious balls.'

He elbowed her away and shoved past Tanya and Pagan. 'You people are all crazy if you think I'd … if you think I might …'

Elsa offered him a smile that he felt, much to his discomfort, right down between his legs. Then she lifted an eyebrow and gave a shrug that made the dark gloss of her hair shimmer in the subdued lighting. 'You asked.'

That was it. With his heart hammering and his cock shoving at his fly, he fled the suite with Tanya wailing behind him, 'Please, Nick! Please don't let her do this to me. Please, Nick!'

He could still hear the echo of her words as he fled the Strip, fled the lights, fled the city limits. He found himself driving out toward Red Rocks before he pulled off on a dark side road. He opened the door to the cool desert air and undid his jeans. He wondered how he could possibly be horny after what had happened to poor Tanya because of him. But, Jesus Christ, he was! In fact, he was so turned on he'd feared he might have to pull into an alley and get some relief before he even left the city.

He wrestled the heft of his cock from his boxers with a grunt, as though the weight of it was almost too much for him to lift, and damned if it didn't feel that way. He gave his balls a cupping, biting his lip and sucking in a heavy breath as he did so. Then he spat on his hand and ran it down his length in a tight fist, feeling a shiver pass up his spine at the anxious stretch of himself. He jerked and tugged to thoughts of Tanya exposing her pussy and wiping her juices over the waxed hood of the Humvee. By the time his thoughts shifted to the view through the telescope, the tight clench and release of the man's arse as he jackhammered the woman bent over the bed, feasting on pussy, Nick had dragged himself from behind the wheel to lean against the limo. His efforts with his cock had turned into a tense thrust and squeeze of a battle. Yes, what they were doing was outrageously hot, and if he'd been alone in the room, gazing at the action through the scope, he'd have undone his fly and had a good hard wank, maybe even more than one. Precome sheened the end of his cock as he recalled he hadn't been the only one watching the trio. Someone had paid a lot of money to watch them do the nasty.

His grunts and groans filled the silent desert night as he worked himself, kneading his tight balls and thrusting into his fist like it was a pussy, like it was Tanya's pussy. The limo rocked from the press and shove of his body as he put Tanya and himself in the hotel room instead of the threesome, as he bent her over the bed in his imagination, her snatch spread slick and begging. The pressure built as he thought of the audience viewing him from an anonymous place, tugging at hard cocks, maybe fingering wet pussies, as they watched him slide into Tanya, as she quivered and grasped and begged him to fuck her harder. And the anonymous audience, suddenly and surprisingly, had Elsa Crane's face. Elsa in her leopard print, Elsa with her hand up under her loincloth, Elsa shoving aside her halter to fondle breasts that were surely magnificent. Then Elsa joined Tanya in his fantasy. In fact, Elsa replaced Tanya on the bed, face up. She lifted her loincloth until he could see every wet fold of her silken slit, until he could see the hard press of her clit, until there was no longer any denying himself the woman lying there on the bed, legs spread, arms open, pussy pouting.

As he imagined thrusting deep into Elsa's hot tightness, the world behind his closed eyelids burst in a kaleidoscope of colour and light, and when he came, the explosion rocked him to the core as he shot streamers of semen onto the desert floor, glistening pearlescent in the lazy moonlight.

Chapter Three

After a very long, very strange night, Elsa was up early to Skype Rita Holly. In the three and a half years since Rita had become the head of the High Council of The Mount in London, the two had become fast friends. Rita was making a trip to Vegas in a few weeks, and Elsa could hardly wait to meet her in person. She sipped at her third cup of coffee and listened as Rita updated her with the latest news from the London coven. Rita was so much easier to work with than her predecessor, Vivienne, had been. Vivienne had always treated Elsa like she was some bastard relative and kept contact between the two covens to a minimum. OK, Mount Vegas was only a very small outpost of The Mount. It didn't have coven status yet, but Elsa knew that it was already making a good impression with the rest of The Mount; in no small part due to her hard work and the work of her brilliant team.

Rita Holly Martelli had breathed new life into the London Coven. That wasn't much of a surprise, since her mother was the head of the High Council in Rome, which was the oldest, most respected coven of The Mount. Like mother like daughter, Elsa thought. It must have taken a Martelli feat of genius to wrest the reins of power from Vivienne. Elsa didn't know the details, but she hoped to wheedle them out of Rita over dinner and a nice bottle of Malbec while she was in Vegas.

'Elsa, the scenario you're planning sounds totally yummy.' Rita squirmed in her chair and offered a thousand-watt smile. 'I discussed it with Edward, and he's in. We haven't done any roleplaying in a while, and it'll be fun to do it for an appreciative audience.' She squinted at her computer screen. 'Sweetie, you look tired. I know I got you up early, but what's going on?'

'I had to let Tanya go last night,' Elsa said.

'Oh no. Just what you didn't need right now. And with her so close to completing her contract. Same problem?'

Elsa nodded. 'It's more than that, though. She's run up some serious gambling debts as well, and I have a feeling she was ... trying to make a few bucks on the side. She swears she didn't take money for it, and the guy she was with tonight – well, I'm sure no money was involved there. He definitely wasn't the type. But I just can't turn a blind eye any more, Rita. The rules are in place for a reason. I hate it that she won't get her bonus, but what else could I do?'

'You did the right thing.' Rita said. 'Every time she goes off on her own like that she puts everything and everyone in jeopardy. And maybe this will be her wake-up call to get help with her gambling problem. What about the man she was with?'

Elsa smiled to herself. 'A really nice guy, actually. Really sexy. I felt sorry for him. I'm pretty sure it was the first time he'd ever picked up someone at a bar. He blamed himself for Tanya's bad behaviour – and oh, the man's guilt was so sexy.' She sighed at the memory. 'He nearly tore me a new one for being so heartless to Tanya. And he even offered to fulfil the last two months of her contract so she could get her bonus.'

Rita nearly choked on her tea. 'Are you serious? Wow! That's a first. So what do you think? Could he do it?'

'I doubt it,' Elsa said. 'When I explained to him what we do here at Mount Vegas, he couldn't get out the door fast enough. But I did stick a card in his pocket.' She giggled. 'Believe me, I've already had a few wicked fantasies about how much fun I'd have teaching him the ropes, but that's probably as far as it'll go.'

Rita gave a sympathetic nod. 'Well even at The Mount, a girl still has to have her fantasies. Anyway, send me over the specs for Mrs Keyser's fantasy, and Edward and I'll have a little fun with it. Gotta run. I'm meeting Leo over at the Zoo to see one of his new pets. Apparently she's quite something.'

The two women said their goodbyes. For a long moment, Elsa sat looking at the Mount Vegas logo, thinking of how much fun it would be to have Rita and Edward playing the lead roles in Mrs Keyser's fantasy. Mrs Keyser was a regular client with a fuck-ton of money, which she loved spending on pervy scenarios. Sadly, the woman didn't have a lot of imagination. She paid top dollar for generic cleaned-up kink. But she did pay top dollar, so no matter how pedestrian the fantasy was, Mount Vegas provided it.

Elsa looked down at the specs she had discussed with Mrs Keyser. It was another "virgin loses her cherry to a surly billionaire" scenario, which would be nicely spiced up by having the head of The Mount in London and the owner of its club playing the billionaire and his virgin. Their involvement would raise Mount Vegas' profile considerably within the organisation, and it would be a voyeuristic treat for the whole team.

Originally she'd had Tanya in mind for the role of the virgin with Deke playing the brusque billionaire dom – he looked the part. Thankfully, the idea had totally intrigued Rita and Edward or Elsa would have ended up playing the virgin. Though she never thought of herself as anything but worldly, she had the look that would

21

have worked. She loathed the role of sub almost as much as she loathed the role of a virgin. With Tanya gone, though, she supposed she should get used to it. They had been asked to supply at least one billionaire and virgin fantasy a month since *Fifty Shades of Grey*.

She forced her attention back to Mrs K's specs, which she had entitled *The Billionaire Buys a Virgin Bride.* The plot was simple. The billionaire buys the virgin as his bride to pay off her family's gambling debt. Of course, that bit was all in Mrs K's head. The actual fantasy would begin in The Wedding Chapel. Mrs K wanted that part included, with a kinky little scene beforehand in which the billionaire checks out his merchandise just to make sure he gets what he paid for. Well, that was a nice touch, Elsa thought. She wrote down a few notes about a discreet but filthy feel-up and probe of the little innocent to make sure she really was a virgin under all that white taffeta. Elsa added some very naughty ideas about the groom guiding his little bride's virgin hand to the fly of his tux for her first fondle of his very expensive junk. It was shaping up nicely for a billionaire/virgin fantasy.

After the happy couple said "I do" there would be hot, sexy foreplay in the limo on the way to the hotel. Elsa could imagine lots of dirty talk on the part of the billionaire about his new bride's lovely tits and her tight little slit that he was all bulging and hard to fuck. All the while the coy virgin would be blushing and squirming and moistening the crotch of her wedding panties, or lack thereof – oooh, that was better yet. Make the little dear walk down the aisle without any undies!

'Oooh Mr Chase, please be gentle with me. I've never been with a man before and you're *sooo biiig*,' Elsa said out loud in a mock-girlish voice. Foreplay in a limo. Of course it would be Nick Chase she'd think of. After he had stormed off last night, she'd given herself a serious finger-fucking when she was alone in her bed trying to unwind after a day that had gone on for ever. It wasn't just the thought of him coming into Mount Vegas to finish out Tanya's contract, all knight-in-shining-armour-like, it was that he'd even consider such a thing to begin with – blaming himself for Tanya's bad behaviour. OK, so he'd left in a huff when he found out what fulfilling her contract would involve, but he'd left with a hard-on, and one it didn't take 20/20 vision to see. Five would get you twenty he'd had to stop and jerk off before he got back home. She wondered if he'd even made it out of the building before he'd had to answer the call.

God, how she'd love the chance to handle that cock! Wouldn't it have been something if Nick Chase had agreed to see out Tanya's contract? Elsa's panties got moister at the thought. Wouldn't she just love the chance to train that boy up? With those drowning-deep cinnamon eyes and that slightly mussed bedroom hair that had the bronze shimmer of desert heat about it, training him would be no hardship. He'd be a huge hit with the clients. She wished she'd have found a way to get that shirt off him. It was quite obvious the man was built for filth, and he was not the kind of man she figured spent hours in the gym to get that way. He spent time in the sun, she'd bet. The bit of research she'd managed before he stormed the castle to rescue Tanya said that he owned a place with a couple acres outside town and that he'd inherited the limo business from his father. Not his first choice, the Vegas limo business, especially not for someone with Nick's background. She wondered if his hands were calloused. She loved the feel of callouses against her more sensitive bits. She crossed her legs to get a good squeeze where she needed it and thought about guiding Nick Chase's fingers to those sensitive bits to check for callouses.

It was hard to get comfy in her chair as she read through Mrs K's specs. Seriously, she would almost be willing to play the submissive virgin if Nick Chase was her billionaire, and certainly he had that surly billionaire look about him. And oh, the way he did guilt! Mrs K would burn out her vibrator in a fit of lust at the sight of him "devirginising" Elsa.

Elsa was just reaching in the drawer for her own vibrator to see where fantasies of Nick Chase devirginising her might lead when there was a knock on the door, and Pike, her second in command, stepped in without waiting for her invitation.

He smiled as she stuck the vibe back in its place. 'You thinking about last night? I had a good wank afterwards. Chase is hot. I don't mind saying I was disappointed to see him leave so quickly.' He nodded down to the drawer where she kept her toys. 'You want me to give you a few minutes? Or I can take care of you if you'd like.'

'Thanks, Pike.' She offered him a wave of her hand. 'I'd love to take you up on it, but today I really don't have time, so it's a good thing you got here when you did. Now that we're short-handed, I've got to reshuffle everyone for tonight's little adventure. Deke's set to play our big-name magician – turns out he even knows a few magic tricks – but Tanya was supposed to be his buxom assistant who gets it up the ass in the disappearing cabinet.'

Pike nodded. 'That was a nightmare to get cameras set up in. Leave it to Darnell Peters to complicate things.'

'Yes, but he pays well and he's kinky as hell. And he adores watching Tanya.'

Pike sat one tightly jeaned arse cheek on her desk and smiled down at her. 'But he likes watching you even better.'

'She was prepared for the role. I'm not.'

'That never stopped you before, Elsa. You're great at pulling an act out of your ass. You're upset about letting Tanya go, that's all.'

She stared past him at the wall behind. 'It was the right thing to do, Pike.'

He rolled his eyes. 'If it had been me, I'd have done it ages ago. Nobody's that good. Personally –' he leant over the desk and brushed a quick kiss across her lips '– I'm still hoping our lovely Mr Chase will have spent a sleepless, guilt-ridden night and rush back to us all ready to take on Tanya's contract. I saw you slip the card into his pocket.'

She forced a little laugh. 'Always an optimist, aren't you, Pike?'

'Always a pessimist, aren't you, Elsa?' He stood and rubbed his hands together in anticipation. 'I think we haven't seen the last of Mr Chase. If I were to venture a guess, Tanya'll harass him until the poor guy'll take on her contract just to get her to leave him alone.'

'Or he'll take out a restraining order,' Elsa said. Then she added. 'Even if he did come back and he did agree to finish out Tanya's contract, he'd never last two months. Hell, I doubt he'd make it through one week.'

'It's Vegas,' Pike said. 'I'll bet you he'll call back in less than 48 hours, probably unable to shut out the guilt or Tanya's badgering, or all the nasty thoughts he's had about what he saw last night.'

Elsa was reminded again why she loved Pike so much. Her second in command had a way of always convincing the pessimist in her that the glass was half full. 'All right,' she said. 'I'll bet you we won't see him again. If I win, I get one of your fabulous back rubs.'

He offered her his filthiest look. 'With all the trimmings?'

'All the trimmings,' she said.

'And if I win, like it or not, you'll be my sub in the next dungeon fantasy. Though I suppose before we shake on it, I should warn you I've stacked the deck.'

'Oh?' She folded her arms across her chest and glared at him.

'I accidentally sent Tanya Mr Chase's cell phone number last night before I went off to beddy-bye.' He stopped her response with a quick kiss. 'And no need to play shocked. I got it from you, my lady. You're not the only one who has access to Mount Vegas research.' He made quotation marks in the air with his fingers to emphasise the word "research."' He looked at her from under a dramatically drawn brow. 'You weren't thinking of calling him yourself, were you?'

'I certainly wasn't,' she replied. 'Frankly, I don't think it'll matter even if you did give his number to Tanya. He fucked her once and got more than he bargained for. End of story. And he doesn't have to answer his calls, so yes, Mr Smart Ass, I'll take your bet.' She stretched in her chair and twisted her neck from side to side. 'I really could use a good back rub.' She offered him her hand.'

'It's a bet, then,' he replied, shaking on it. Then he dusted a kiss across the back of her knuckles. 'I'll have the dungeon made ready.'

She reached up and gave his cheek a playful slap. 'You do that. I always like my people to have a well-prepared workplace. Now can we take a look at this week's agenda and see how we can minimise the loss-of-Tanya damage.'

Chapter Four

The damned alarm went off in the middle of the hottest fuck Nick had ever had. He came up out of the dream roaring like an angry bear and practically slapped the clock off the nightstand in his efforts to shut it off. There was no going back to sleep, not with his heart hammering and his dick stretching out between his legs like it owned the place. Cursing between his teeth, he stumbled to the bathroom with only one eye half open. Not bothering with the stop at the commode for the piss he knew he couldn't manage as hard as he was, he shoved his way into the shower and cranked the hot water. No cold showers this morning. He had every intention of giving this dream a good send-off. For a minute he leant against the wall, letting the jets from the shower massage work their magic. Then, when he was nice and wet, he soaped up, still not bothering to open his eyes, still doing his best to capture the vivid images from his dream. Once his chest and armpits, lower back and arse were well lathered, he went to work where he needed it most. And when his pubes felt like they were mounded in thick whipped cream, he closed his fist around his sudsy hard-on and began to stroke, letting the dream flood full-on back into his head.

It had all started on the top of the Humvee in the parking lot at the Mango. It was right there in broad daylight. He had Tanya Povic's tropical print skirt shoved up over her arse, ploughing into her fast and

27

furious while he kneaded her gorgeous tits like they were bread dough ready to bake. They were grunting and thrusting and shoving, and she kept on saying in that sexy Slavic accent, 'Is good! Is so good! Fuck me harrderr, Nick Chase, I vant to come!' And he was happy to oblige.

The parking lot was full of people with scopes and cameras, of all things, and they were all watching Nick mount Tanya on top of the Humvee. Some of the men had cocks out, tugging and jerking like they'd lose control. The women either had hands in their panties or on their tits, which they were happy to expose to the desert sun. Some of the watchers were even humping each other while Tanya kept begging him to fuck her harder.

Elsa Crane had her keyboards and monitors and electronic surveillance equipment set up on the hood of his limo. She was bent over with her leopard-print loincloth barely covering her magnificent arse. Then, all of a sudden, she turned to Nick and Tanya and said in a loud voice, 'Tanya, you're fired. Get off Nick and let me fuck him.' Nick watched with his cock in his hand while Elsa gave Tanya's tits a fondle and made her bend for a good pussy-probing, as though she might be trying to stash something in that tight little hole – like office supplies, maybe. It was a dream, after all.

As Elsa stroked and spread and examined Tanya's cunt, Tanya turned her attention back to Nick's hard-on, giving him a sucking that would have made his eyes cross if he hadn't been so keenly focused on what Elsa was doing.

Finally, Elsa gave the woman a hard smack on her pert little backside, and Tanya went in and out among the crowd, offering to suck cock or lick pussy for anyone who would fulfil the remains of her contract so she could get her bonus. Then, the next thing he knew, Elsa had her top off and her loincloth hoiked, as she crawled up onto the Humvee and mounted him in a seductive squat, her tight pussy sheathing him like a surgical glove. Then she grabbed him by the hair and pulled him up to nurse on her luscious tits, a task he was totally up for. People with their cameras and scopes moved up close and personal, to where he could even hear their heavy breathing, which was no small feat above his own. With Elsa Crane gripping and squeezing and rocking and riding, he was about to go off like a nuclear warhead. And then ... Then the damned alarm clock went off instead of him.

The tug, tug, tug on his cock against the bounce of his lead-heavy balls was just about to get him there under the pulsing of the shower, though why it should be Elsa Crane who got his cock iron-stiff, he didn't know. She was a hard-ass, if ever there was one, and she'd all but laughed at him when he'd offered to fulfil Tanya's contract. Tug, tug, tug. She probably did laugh when he turned and left. Jesus, it was insane what they were doing. Filthy insane. He thought about the ménage he'd viewed through the telescope. Tug, tug, tug. He thought about him standing in the desert jerking off from the experience, and it was Elsa Crane he'd been fucking in his fantasy. Jesus, what was it about that woman? Was it that avalanche of thick, shiny hair? Those deep blue eyes? The fact that the leopard print did little to disguise the fittest body he'd ever seen? The slight gravel to her voice that he just wanted to rub up against? Tug, tug, tug.

But as the dream gave way to his fantasy, Elsa wasn't begging him to fuck her harder. She was hardly the begging type, was she? In his fantasy, she rode him like she was a jockey and he was her stud. She didn't need to ask him anything. She took what she wanted, and he was happy that she took it from him. Suddenly, the cameras and the scopes and the watchers were almost on top of them and it was enough. All of them watching Elsa Crane fuck him until his balls exploded – it was enough. He came in a convulsing, backbreaking ejaculation that belied how hard he'd come in the desert just a few hours ago. The cascade of steamy water from the shower washed the evidence of his lust down the drain.

Out of the shower, still thinking about why both jerk-off sessions had involved being watched, he dressed in his uniform of choice – black jeans and a black cotton shirt. He had a couple of drivers who actually dressed in livery, but he was only driving because he was a man short. The last time he'd worn a proper suit with a tie had been his father's funeral. His aunt Reba had teased him about it, had said that she hoped the next time she saw him all spiffed up – that's how she put it – would be for his wedding. He'd told her not to hold her breath.

He called Lou-Ann down at dispatch before he headed out. 'Any good news for me?' he asked when she answered.

'Yup,' came the reply. 'Good news is that my divorce is final and now we can elope.'

He smiled through the windshield as he checked the mirror and started the engine. ''Bout damn time, woman. You know I've been lusting for that hot cougar bod of yours.' He'd known Lou-Ann since he was fresh out of university; when his father hired her on to replace Aunt Reba, who'd moved away to Taos to open a gallery. He was sure that without her the Vegas Chase Limo Service would have fallen apart ages ago. Certainly he couldn't have continued the business after his father's death without Lou-Ann's knowledge and her sense of humour.

The woman offered a chirp of a laugh. 'I'm yours on a silver platter, stud, but as for finding another limo driver, no dice. Sorry, sugar.' Then she gave him the address of the first pick-up at the Elara.

He was there in 30 minutes, his thoughts still on how he could find another driver so he could back off and leave the business in someone else's hands. In fact, he was so preoccupied that he hadn't noticed until he got out to open the door that his client was Tanya Povic. She was dressed in hot pink shorts that could have been painted on her excellent arse and a white chemise top that did everything but advertise her gorgeous breasts on a billboard.

'Where to, ma'am?' He spoke around the sudden spike of guilt that made him feel like all of the people milling around at the entrance of the hotel knew that he'd fucked this woman last night and cost her a job and possibly her mother's health. He glanced over at the valet behind the podium, who was making covert glances at Tanya's bottom.

'I don't care where.' She spoke softly, holding his gaze. 'Just drive, and I will talk to you.'

He wanted to tell her there was nothing she could say. He wanted to tell her to get out of his limo and leave him alone, but he couldn't, could he? Not when he was the one responsible for her situation. So he waited until she was in, then closed the door behind her and pulled out onto the road.

When they were back in traffic, he glanced at her through the rear-view mirror. 'You all right?'

'Of course I am not.' Her reply was nearly a sob. 'I don't know what I will do.'

'Tanya, I'm sorry, but surely you can see that I'm not able to fulfil your contract. Christ, I'm working double shifts in my own business at the moment. There's not enough of me to go around. And really, I'm just not the kind of person who could … do what you people do.'

'Do what you people do? *You people*? You mean like the prostitutes and the drug dealers and the organised crime. Those people?' Her voice rose with each example. 'Is that what you mean?'

'No! Damn it, that's not what I mean. I mean that I just don't think I could have sex while people are watching me. That's all.'

She leant forward in the seat. 'You didn't seem to mind last night in the parking lot at the Mango; in fact, your cock seemed to like it just fine.'

And damn it, in spite of himself, his cock jerked in his jeans at the mention of last night. 'Do you have any idea what you're asking me to do? Like I said, even if I could get away from the business to do it?'

'I'm asking for you to be my hero and save my mother's life. That's what I am asking you to do, Nick.'

Jesus, the woman didn't have a subtle bone in her exquisite body.

'I would give you sex in exchange. You could have me whenever you wanted.' Christ almighty, did she just offer him a modest blush? 'Is all I have left to give you, Nick, and I am desperate.' Her shoulders shook with a sob, then she added, 'Turn left here.'

He did as she asked. The limo was awash in a soundtrack of soft snuffles. A glance in the rear-view mirror and he could see her dabbing at those huge, bright eyes. If he hadn't felt like a cad already, he did now.

She swallowed back a sob that made her shoulders shake and said, 'Now make a right at the light.'

'Look, Tanya, I'll talk to Elsa again. Maybe I can make her see reason. She gave me her card. I mean, I'm sure there must be some kind of arrangement that can be made under the extenuating circumstances, will that help?'

She offered him a watery-eyed smile and leant forward until her cleavage was well and truly on display in the mirror. 'That is good, Nick. Thank you! You're good man.'

'Where are we going?'

'You can drop me here,' came the reply. 'My apartment is very close and perhaps is best we don't be seen together until after you talk to Elsa.'

He pulled over to the side of a well-manicured street lined in palm trees, got out and opened the door for her, refusing her offered payment. She slid her arms around his neck and her tongue into his mouth for a goodbye kiss that had him both hard and breathless by the time she pulled away.

'Thank you, Nick. Thank you so much.'

'I can't promise anything, Tanya. I said I'd talk to Elsa. That's all I can promise.'

She kissed him again and smiled up into his eyes. 'I trust you, Nick Chase. You will do the right thing.'

Then she turned and hurried away, leaving him standing hard, breathless, and wondering what the hell he'd gotten himself into.

Back in the limo, he resisted the urge to jerk off for the outrageous third time in less than 12 hours. Instead, he pulled out his wallet and dug for the card Elsa Crane had given him. It was a black card with a pearlescent purple sheen. In the middle, printed in stylised white letters, were the words *Mount Vegas*. In the upper right-hand corner was a phone number and an email address.

He took a deep breath and punched the number into his BlackBerry.

Chapter Five

'Hello?' Nick called out softly, just in case there was some orgy going on he didn't want to disturb. The suite seemed deserted. There was an array of dirty cups and glasses and plastic soft drink bottles on the kitchen counter and several take-out boxes on the table. The lounge was empty and quiet. In one bedroom, the bed was piled high with clothes and the floor littered with sandals and flip-flops. The other bedroom was set up with the same equipment Elsa had been in command of at the Cosmopolitan two nights ago. There were two telescopes, a couple of keyboards, and three monitors. One was blank. One focused on people scrambling around a pool. They appeared to be getting ready for a shoot. The sound was off. But it was the third that got his full attention.

'Let me feel your pussy.' The male voice breaking the silence made Nick jump in his tracks. As he moved closer to squint at the screen, he recognised Pike. Only this time he wasn't dressed as Tarzan. This time he wore a pair of low-slung, faded jeans and nothing else.

'Please,' the woman, whose bottom was now front and centre, cried out. She was bent nearly double over a wicked-looking wooden bench, bound with leather cuffs so that her legs and her arms were spread wide. The dimly lit room was filled with ominous wooden racks, and one wall was hung with what looked like an array of whips and chains. Nick shivered.

The woman wore only stockings and a garter belt under a miniscule skirt that was pushed up to expose her whole arse. 'Please, sir,' she begged. The voice sounded familiar. Nick took a step closer and listened hard.

'Please, sir, what?' Pike demanded. He slapped her bottom hard with a riding crop and she squirmed and moaned.

'Please, sir, fuck me,' she whimpered.

'Let's just see how bad you need to be fucked, slut.' He shoved two fingers up between her legs, and by the time Pike brought her juices to his lips to taste, Nick's cock was paying full attention.

'I need it bad, sir, so bad,' the woman half sobbed.

Just as Pike thrust his juicy fingers into the mouth of his captive, the camera angle changed, and Nick's stomach went into freefall. There, beaded with sweat, lips swollen, eyes smudged and cheeks blackened in running mascara, was Elsa Crane, licking her own juices off Pike's hand.

'I don't think so, not just yet, you little whore.' Pike gave her clearly abused butt cheeks a squeeze that made her eyes water. 'I don't think you're quite there yet, and I think you need to do something for me first, don't you?' With one hand, he unzipped his fly; with the other, he grabbed her by the hair and yanked her mouth onto his heavy cock until she sputtered and gagged then began to suck furiously, a stream of saliva trailing down her chin.

Pike grunted and thrust, grunted and thrust, as though she was nothing more than a hole for his cock, and she kept sucking. He grabbed up the crop and brought it down against her arse, causing a muffled cry around his penis. Nick cried out along with her, sucking air between his teeth at the pain he was sure she must feel.

'You look at me when you suck my cock, slut. Don't close your eyes. Do you understand?'

She nodded and sucked furiously, her eyes locked on his.

No matter how much Nick wanted to run away, no matter how much he didn't want to see Elsa like this, he stood riveted to the floor, his gaze locked on the scene unfolding in the monitor.

Pike ran the soft tip of the crop up between Elsa's legs, and the camera angle switched to take in her wet slit, gripping and releasing at the crop's teasing. Nick felt heat crawl up his face, and he jerked involuntarily when the man began to tap the flexible end of the crop against Elsa's exposed pussy, Elsa squirming furiously against her bonds. With a sharp thwack, Pike brought the crop down, first on one buttock then the other, laying a criss-cross of bright pink welts over her arse in rhythm to his thrusts. 'You're almost ready for me, I think, slut,' he said.

Nick's insides squirmed with anger toward Pike and empathetic humiliation for Elsa, almost as if by watching he shared in her degradation. His head spun with a cocktail of emotions he couldn't sort and, in spite of it all, his cock felt like it would explode in its fullness. He refused to open his fly and get some relief. Perhaps they were watching him, and even if they weren't it felt like he deserved to suffer with his arousal unsatisfied for watching Elsa's humiliation. In some strange way, it felt almost like watching made him responsible.

'I'll spank your ass and fuck your mouth until I think you're ready, slut.' Pike spoke in rhythm to his strikes.

Nick could see the mascara-darkened tears on Elsa's cheeks, he could see the way she cringed and squirmed each time Pike struck her, and he wanted to look away. He wanted to tell someone to make Pike stop hurting her. Surely she didn't like it. Surely she hadn't asked for it. How could anyone possibly ask for it?

More than anything, he couldn't stand the thought of Elsa Crane begging, of Elsa Crane so subdued, so why couldn't he look away? Why couldn't he just leave? He didn't really owe Tanya anything, did he? Surely she was better off out of this perverted place?

'Are you Nick Chase?' a male voice called from behind, and Nick whirled around like he'd been caught in the act. Before he could answer, the man said, 'You're supposed to wait in the lounge.' The newcomer looked like he might be Native American. Beneath the heavy headset, his black hair was caught back in a ponytail. He wore faded jeans and a Gold's Gym muscle shirt and, from the size of his arms, he looked like he'd earned it. 'This area's off limits,' he said in a voice that was a deep rumble. 'There's beer in the fridge, soft drinks, wine. I think there may be some pizza left. Help yourself. Elsa will be with you shortly.'

One last glance at the monitor showed Pike was now buried cock-deep in Elsa's pussy, humping her in quick, staccato thrusts. 'Come, you little slut –' Nick heard him say '– come for me.'

In his fevered imagination, Nick could see himself shoving Pike aside and taking over. And Elsa was pleased by the switch-out.

What the hell was he thinking? This was not sex. This was crazy. This was out of control. And yet his cock ached against his fly.

Back in the lounge, he paced in front of the big window, looking across the Strip at New York New York Casino. He wasn't interested in food or drink. He couldn't get trussed-up Elsa Crane out of his head, or out of his groin. What the hell was the matter with him? How could what he'd just seen both repel him and make him hard? He wanted to grab Elsa and shake her and ask her why the hell she would allow Pike to do it. Shit!

Worst of all, there was a part of him that wanted to take the crop from Pike and lay a few stripes across her pink, upturned bottom himself. After what Elsa had done to Tanya, she deserved a good spanking.

Jesus! What was he thinking? She didn't deserve a spanking. He didn't know what the fuck she deserved. He found the bathroom and splashed cold water over his burning face. What he needed was a cold shower. He absolutely would not rub one off in the john. He was ashamed he'd even consider it. He walked out into the lounge just as the door burst open and Elsa shoved through. She wore a loose-fitting sundress, her face had been wiped clean of mascara, and she walked carefully. 'I hate you!' she called over her shoulder to Pike, who followed her in.

'You're just mad because you lost the bet,' came the reply. He was in the same jeans and now wearing an untucked denim shirt.

'No, this time I really hate you,' she said, rubbing her arse. 'It was a stupid bet in the first place and –'

Both she and Pike froze when they saw Nick.

'Ah, Mr Chase. I hope I haven't kept you waiting too long.' Suddenly Elsa was all business. She walked to the fridge and grabbed a bottle of water. 'You want something?'

He shook his head, and she turned her attention to her abuser. 'Pike, help Horse with the pool scene.' Then she offered Nick a smile. 'Sorry, we're running a few minutes late. Pike had a flat tyre on the way over.'

'It didn't take you long. To get here, I mean.' Nick said. 'Not after he finished … beating you and then had … sex with you.' God, he sounded stupid. Why didn't he keep his mouth shut and not say anything until it was time to talk about Tanya.

Elsa stood for a moment studying him, holding her forgotten water in her hand. Then she yelled into the bedroom, 'Horse, did you let him watch?'

'I was in the crapper,' came the reply. 'Sorry about that.'

'Horse? Seriously?' Nick said.

'Yep, seriously, and yep, exactly for the reasons you're thinking.' She offered him a filthy smile. 'He's very popular with the ladies. Give me five for a quick shower and then we can talk.' She nodded to the bedroom containing the technical equipment. 'You can go watch the fun in the pool if you want.'

'But I thought I wasn't allowed?'

She smiled again. 'Oh, you're allowed to watch. I just didn't want you watching me get my ass beat.' She gave said arse another rub and disappeared into the bathroom.

Elsa really was out in five, her wet hair hanging around her shoulders in a tumble of curls. She wore a loose cotton sundress that was nearly transparent with the backlighting from the bathroom, transparent enough for him to tell she wore nothing beneath it, but no doubt her bottom would not have appreciated anything tight. She motioned him away from the lesbian scene going on in the pool at the Flamingo, closing the door on Horse and Pike.

'We get a lot of requests for girl-on-girl action,' she said. Then she nodded down to his cock. 'I see you agree.' Before he could decide whether to be offended or tell her it was none of her damn business, she went on, 'We all agree, actually. Me, I'm always up for a little girl-on-girl fun, but from a voyeuristic point of view, I'd just as happily watch a little guy-on-guy action.'

He followed her into the lounge area and sat down on the sofa to which she nodded. She disappeared for a second and returned with a pillow from one of the beds, upon which she sat very carefully, uttering a soft curse.

'You like getting … spankings?'

She sucked a breath between her teeth and pulled a

39

wicked smile as she squirmed to get comfortable. 'Not nearly as much as I like giving spankings. Why? Are you in need?'

When he failed to see the humour in her words, the smile disappeared and she eyed him for a second. 'It was an act, Nick. We all do what we have to around here.'

'Does Tanya do what you just did?' he asked.

'Yes, in fact when we have a client who wants to watch a submissive being well dominated, Tanya was our go-to girl.'

'She likes … that sort of thing?' he asked.

'You sound shocked, Mr Chase. Tanya would have loved tonight's little session in the dungeon.'

It took a second for the thought of Tanya bottom up with someone wailing on her gorgeous arse to sink in, and when his imagination sharpened the picture to include Elsa wielding the crop, Nick wished he had Elsa's pillow to cover his bulging junk.

'Then why did you let her go?' The words were out before he could stop them, and his reason for being there settled his cock at least a little bit.

She shifted gently toward the control room and called out, 'Pike, bring me my iPad.' In almost the same breath she addressed Nick. 'Tell me something, Mr Chase. Suppose you were to hire a driver for that position you're trying to fill, and he was a brilliant driver, best driver ever. All of the clients loved him, he was on time, always got repeat customers – you know the kind I mean.' She waved a hand and sipped her water. 'But suppose this brilliant driver takes one of your limos out for a joy ride from time to time, with whoever he picks up at a bar or a casino. And in these wild forays he puts both your property and the people he's driving at risk.' She leant toward him and winced slightly. 'How many times would you let him get away with it before you sent him on his way?'

'I might view it a little differently,' Nick said, 'if there were a bonus in play and it was to pay for his mother's surgery.'

Pike chose that moment to deliver Elsa's iPad. She grabbed it from him with no thank you. He offered a bow and left, but not before Nick caught a twitch of a smile at the corner of his mouth. With a few flicks of her fingers, Elsa pulled up a document and handed it to him. 'This is the standard contract, the one Tanya signed, the one everyone who works for Mount Vegas signs. Read it.'

When he tried to push it back to her, she glared at him. 'I said read it. Then we can talk.'

She sipped slowly on her water and watched him while he read. He let out a low whistle. 'This is the contract she had?'

'Yup. Housing paid for, living and clothing allowance, and a wage that I'm sure you'll agree, Mr Chase, is way more than generous, even without the added incentive of the bonus. Yet she chose to ignore the terms of the contract – repeatedly, even though she supposedly had earmarked the bonus for her mother's surgery.' She nodded to the iPad. 'Surely you can understand why the contract demands that Mount Vegas be made aware of and approve the sex partners of all those who work here?' She gave a sweeping gesture with her hand. 'To lessen the hardship, any person who works here is always willing to offer sex to fellow employees in need. Tanya wasn't living like a nun, Mr Chase. You were the only one who wasn't getting any, which is why you fell in with Tanya in the first place.'

'It was a bad night,' he said. 'I hate driving at the best of times, but … It was a bad night.'

'Well?' They both jumped at the sound of Pike's voice. He was standing next to the dining table with his hands on his hips. 'Ask him.'

'Go away, Pike,' Elsa practically growled. 'I'm not talking to you right now.'

'Then I'll do the talking.' He came to sit in the chair across from them. 'Tanya deserved what she got, Mr Chase, whether you believe it or not. But the deal is still on the table. If you want to finish out her contract for her, then she'll still get her bonus, or rather you'll get it and what the hell you do with it is your business.'

Nick looked from Elsa to Pike and back again. Elsa only shrugged.

'I can't fulfil her contract,' he replied, not even attempting to hide the tremor in his voice. 'I'm a driver short and it's a busy time.'

'Mr Chase –' Elsa shifted, sucked a painful breath, and shot Pike a withering look. 'Mr Chase, if you'll check your BlackBerry, you'll find an email from your dispatcher, who has received the perfect résumé from the perfect driver to fill your needs. He's willing and ready to start work tomorrow if you need him.'

Nick fumbled his device from his pocket and, sure enough, there was a message from Lou-Ann and a résumé attached that looked like a match made in heaven. It took Nick a second to realise both Elsa and Pike were watching him. He slid the BlackBerry back into his pocket with a sweaty palm. 'I – don't think I could do … what you did.' He nodded to Pike.

'You won't have to do what he did,' Elsa said. 'Fortunately, Pike's very good in the dungeon. But –' she held his gaze '– you will have to be comfortable with people watching you have sex, and with having sex with multiple partners in kinky situations.'

'I – I don't know if I can,' Nick managed, but even in a situation that was electric with nervous tension, his cock strained toward Elsa.

Just then the door burst open and the two women who

had been having sex in the pool came into the room, laughing about how cold the water was. They wore only thin tank tops and sarongs.

'Beetle, Deb –' Elsa spoke without taking her eyes off Nick 'Mr Chase here has been watching your performance, and he's very uncomfortable. Perhaps you could help him relax?'

The willowy redhead giggled and stepped forward. 'Mr Chase, are you going to fulfil Tanya's contract?' Before he could answer, she slipped out of her top and dropped the sarong to the floor. 'That's worth at least a blowjob, I'd say, wouldn't you, Beetle?'

The other woman, who was a Goth right down to her black, spiky hair and matching nails, nodded her agreement and dropped her clothes. They both stood looking expectantly at Elsa, who nodded to Nick's crotch.

Deb, the redhead, dropped to her knees between Nick's legs, and whatever protests he was about to utter died in his throat as she gave him a hot, wet lick through his jeans that nearly sent him into orbit.

'Oh Jesus,' he gasped. 'Elsa, please. This really isn't necessaree.' His last word ended in a tight hiss as Deb, holding his gaze, unzipped his jeans and freed his cock into the strong squeeze and stroke of her hand.

'Oh, I think it is, Nick Chase,' came Elsa's reply. 'I think it's very necessary. Beetle –' she addressed the Goth '– introduce Mr Chase to your nipples.'

Beetle came to Nick's side, leant over the end of the sofa, and undid his shirt with a practised hand. Just as she straddled him, offering access to small breasts with enormous, ripe-berry nipples, Deb took his erection into her mouth – all of his erection, all the way back. There was no other way to describe the sound that escaped his throat but a whimper, and not a very dignified one at that. Beetle pulled his head to her right breast to nurse, and guided his other hand down to her smoothly shaven pussy. 'Oh Mr Chase,' she said in a little-girl voice, 'I'm still so wet from all the naughty things Deb did to me in the swimming pool, I hope you can help me feel better. Oooh, and your hands are so strong, and your cock … Mmm, Deb, you have to let me have a taste.'

'I don't think so,' Elsa said. 'I think you're going to let Mr Chase push that big cock way up in your tight little snatch, Beetle. Would you like that?'

'Ooh yes! Ooh yes, Elsa, I'd like that so much.'

Deb disengaged from her exquisite deep-throating. 'Hey, that's not fair, Elsa, what about me? My pussy needs fucking too.'

'I'll take care of you, sweetie,' Pike said. But as he started to undo his fly, Elsa raised a hand.

'No. You don't get to come this time, Pike.' She shot him a vicious half-smile. 'I need you to man the controls. Horse!' she called to the Native American. 'Deb needs a good fuck.' She turned her attention back to the crestfallen Pike. 'Put it away, and keep it put away. You've had yours for tonight.'

With some difficulty, the man zipped his cock back into his jeans and stood to go, but before he did, he offered Elsa a wicked smile. 'I still won the bet, and it was still worth spanking your ass.'

She flipped him off as he left the room, and Horse came in with his fly already open, revealing the reason for his equine nickname.

'What do you think, Deb?' Elsa said. 'Will our clients like watching us play with Mr Chase's cock?'

'Oh yes, Elsa. He has a fabulous cock and nice, tight balls. Look how they nestle up close in all those lovely, silky boy curls.' She gave his pubes a tickle that made him squirm against the couch.

Beetle slipped the shirt off his shoulders and ran long, black nails over his back and biceps then down his chest where she raked his nipples to torturous points. 'And he has such a delicious body,' she said, gripping his fingers with her tight pussy lips. 'Please, Elsa, can we keep him?'

'That's entirely up to Mr Chase,' Elsa replied.

'I know what you're doing, Elsa,' Nick managed around a nibble and lick of Beetle's engorged areola, unable to muster enough self-control to disengage from his very enjoyable task.

Elsa batted innocent eyes at him. 'I can tell them to stop if you'd like.'

'Please, Mr Chase.' Beetle sighed. 'Don't make us stop. I so want to ride that big cock of yours, and I promise, I'll hold on tight.' As if to demonstrate, she gripped his fingers with powerful girlie muscles and his cock surged in Deb's mouth, causing her to moan and lift her arse for Horse, who had slipped out of his jeans and released his enormous cock.

'Oh pleeeze, Elsa! I can't stand it,' Beetle keened. 'Please let me fuck him now.'

Elsa nodded permission. As Deb pulled away, Horse handed her a condom, which she unwrapped, and rolled onto Nick's cock with her mouth. Jesus, he thought that only happened in porn films. She stepped back, holding her pussy lips open for Horse, who took up the position behind her. Her face alone was nearly enough to make Nick come with its mix of grimaces and smiles and concentrated biting and sucking of lips and teeth as she grunted and pushed until she was fully impaled. All the while, Horse held very still and did nothing more than guide himself home.

'That's a girl,' Elsa said. 'Horse'll keep your tight little cunt good and busy while you watch Beetle make our Mr Chase come.'

'Why don't you make me come, Elsa?' Jesus, where did he get the balls to ask that?

Beetle offered a little pout and Elsa simply smiled. 'I'm not on the menu tonight. I've already had my bottom royally thrashed and my ass fucked hard. However –' her smile turned positively evil '– I can have Horse do you, if you'd prefer.'

Nick held her gaze and returned her evil smile, feeling way more playful than he should under the circumstances. 'I doubt my little asshole's up for that tonight. And besides, Beetle here's good and ready.' With that, he grabbed the Goth by her hips and pulled her down onto his anxious dick.

Her grip was fist tight. He cried out and held her still, for a horrible moment fearing he'd end the show before it even began. It was only then, as he grabbed Beetle by her short, raven hair and pulled her into a hard tongue kiss that he realised he *was* putting on a show, and he was doing it for Elsa Crane, just like she'd planned, just like she knew he would. God, the woman was devious.

He fingered the Goth's little beaded clit and she quivered and clenched. Once again, her tight grip demanded his full concentration to hold his wad. Out of the corner of his eye, he could see he had Elsa's full attention. Her cheeks were flushed, her breath accelerated. Good! If she wanted a show, he'd see she got one.

He pulled away just enough to speak. 'Your little clit's like a rock, Beetle. Shall I stroke it for you? Oh yes, you like that, don't you? I bet you can come as often as you'd like, can't you?'

She bit her lip and nodded. 'Shall I come for you, Mr Chase?'

It was Elsa who responded. 'Oh yes do, Beetle. Your sweet pussy gets so tight and yummy when you come.' She offered Nick an innocent smile. 'She'll make you feel so good, Mr Chase.' She batted long, dark lashes at him, and he braced himself. Christ! How was he going to hold out for … For what? Just so he could impress Elsa Crane?'

'I'm coming! I'm coming,' Beetle gasped, raking her clit against his pubic bone and gripping his cock in a sweet, wet stranglehold that had him seeing stars and holding his breath to keep from exploding.

The wave had barely passed and he was just about to pat himself on the back for surviving round one, when Deb shouted, 'I'm coming, oh I'm coming too. Put it in my ass, Horse. I want to feel that piece of meat up my asshole!'

Elsa leant forward and patted Nick on the bare thigh. 'Oh, you're gonna love this. Deb didn't get the nickname Stretch for nothing.'

Fuck! If Nick had even had a tiny bit of his brain that wasn't focused on his crotch, he would have closed his eyes to give himself some breathing room, but how could he possibly look away?

Deb eased herself up off Horse's cock, and he sat back in one of the dining room chairs. Her sopping slit still convulsing in aftershocks, Deb squatted on his muscular thighs so the whole of her was splayed for Nick's viewing pleasure. Then she shifted her hips and spat heavily on her hand. Horse did the same.

While she slathered his enormous cock, he rubbed and probed and lubed up her anus, which sucked first two, then three wriggling and scissoring fingers. Then he gripped her arse cheeks as though he would pull her apart, spreading her until Nick could see her dark, round hole dilated and ready.

Nick felt the buzz of arousal from the tips of his toes all the way to the crown of his head. His balls were approaching critical mass. And how the hell could Beetle's grip just keep getting tighter?

'You want to watch, don't you, Mr Chase?' Elsa's voice was little more than a whisper. 'And no matter how manly you are, and how much you like pussy, a part of you would like to know what it feels like to have your tight little asshole so used, so abused.'

Nick couldn't manage a reply. He was pretty sure he'd totally forgotten how to speak. And anyway, Elsa already knew the answer.

Deb huffed and groaned and bit her lip in fraught concentration as she bore down, her gaping back hole swallowing Horse's enormity centimetre by grudging centimetre, and Nick couldn't have looked away if his life depended on it. He'd gone to shallow breathing mode. He tried desperately to think about something boring, something unsexy, anything unsexy, but his brain wasn't having it.

'Oh God, oh God, oh God,' Deb chanted in tight little gasps. And Horse, still holding her arse cheeks in kneading, fisting palms, thrust up into her until the slap, slap of flesh against flesh metered the heavy breathing in the room and Deb's chants. Horse's balls bulged and rocked, bulged and rocked as Deb rode him. Then her chant changed to, 'I need more, I need more, I need more!'

Fuck! How the hell could anyone possibly need more than Horse?

She slapped at the table like a wrestler tapping out when he'd been defeated, until her fingers caught on the edge of the fruit bowl, catapulting fruit in all directions. Plums and apples rolled onto the floor. Grapes smashed beneath the slap of her hand. Then her fist closed around a ripening banana. Nick's heart lurched and his balls tensed. Dear God, surely she wouldn't? Surely she couldn't …?

Just then Beetle began to wail, 'I'm coming, I'm coming, I'm coming!'

'Fuck! Oh fuck!' Nick gasped. The Goth's grip clenched like iron bands around his erection, just as Deb shoved the banana deep in her gaping pussy.

One thrust, two and three, and she joined Beetle in a trembling chorus of, 'I'm coming, I'm coming, I'm coming.' She would have bounced off Horse's lap but for the anchorage offered by his monster cock up her arse. Her tits bounced, her body convulsed, and Horse roared like a lion, gripping her buttocks hard enough to bruise.

Before Nick could congratulate himself for being the last man standing, he caught a glimpse of Elsa out of the corner of his eye, shifting on her cushion. The light fell against the hammering of her pulse in her throat, and he was certain she was trembling out a stealth orgasm. Why else would she shift so on her sore bottom? Why else would she suck her bottom lip so intently? Why else would her eyelids flutter and her gaze become suddenly unfocused? And it was certainly nowhere near cool enough in the room to make her shiver so hard.

He'd made Elsa Crane come. Jesus Christ, he'd made Elsa Crane come!

And that was it, he could hold his wad no longer, and he came like there was no tomorrow while Beetle crooned against his ear, 'That's it, Mr Chase. Come for me. Come hard. Oh, that's so good, isn't it, your yummy cock pumping out all that hot jizz you've been holding back. My oh my, we're all gonna have so much fun together.'

Then, for a long moment, there was nothing but the sound of heavy breathing. Before anyone could do more than moan and gasp, Pike burst from the control room and handed a memory stick to Elsa, then stood back, making no attempt to hide his hard-on.

'You got it, then?' Elsa asked.

'I did.'

'Good.' She stood carefully and handed it to Nick. 'This is for you. A memento of tonight's adventure. Hal

Easter will show up tomorrow morning to fill your position as limo driver, and you are to report to the address on the memory stick if you want to fulfil Tanya's contract. Because that's the only way she'll get her bonus.'

She bent down and brushed a fleeting kiss across his lips, grabbed up her bag, and disappeared out the door, leaving him naked and still buried to the hilt in Beetle's wet pussy.

Chapter Six

This time, Nick barely made it past the entrance hall in the suite at the Bellagio before Elsa joined him. She was wearing a backless red sundress with her dark hair piled carelessly on top of her head. The matching heels made her calf muscles swell and flex exquisitely. The dress was not curve-hugging, but quirky and lightweight enough that he could again make out the length of her legs beneath the fabric as she stood backlit by the late afternoon sunlight streaming in the window.

His cock threatened a takeover as he recalled the way he'd seen Elsa last night, all trussed up and exposed. Even more so as he recalled her on the sofa next to him watching him fuck Beetle, watching him and acting as though she were above it all. But she wasn't. She had come! He had watched the little sex romp featuring him and the Mount Vegas people over and over after he got home, always fast-forwarding to the shots of Elsa. Pike had made sure there were more than a few, but then he'd made sure there were plenty of shots of everyone. This wasn't a porn film. There were no close-up crotch shots, no come shots. This was the kind of camerawork that an amateur might shoot of a voyeuristic experience. Somehow that made it all the hotter.

Perhaps Pike had chosen to integrate so many shots of Elsa because Elsa was the only voyeur in the room. Everyone else was a participant. But Nick was certain, as he played back through the shots of Elsa, that she had most definitely come. That he had been the reason for her orgasm left him feeling way more satisfied that it probably should have.

'You're late.' The slight gravel in Elsa's voice, as though she'd just got out of bed after hot sex, had his full attention and, fuck, if her head to toe inspection of him didn't have him blushing like a schoolboy.

He stood shifting uncomfortably from foot to foot, doing his damnedest to hold her gaze. Jesus, the last thing he wanted was to come across nervous in front of the woman, but he just couldn't help himself, not when he knew why he was here. He finally found his voice. 'I … wasn't sure I would come at all right up until I found myself being escorted upstairs by that big guy.'

'Pagan.'

He nodded. 'Does he ever … you know.' Jesus, could he sound any stupider?

'He does, yes. In fact he much prefers showing off for the clients over being our resident badass, but he's good at both.'

'Have you and he ever …?'

'Yes, Pagan and I have fucked. In fact –' she motioned him into the kitchen and poured them both coffee '– I'll just clue you in right now, everyone here has fucked everyone else. We've fucked each other in just about every combination you can easily imagine, and you'll do the same for the next two months, *if* you can handle it. Oh, you've got fabulous equipment and the makings of seriously good control, but last night was just for you, Mr Chase, not for an audience.'

'You were watching.' He couldn't quite block the video of her out of his head.'

She offered him a soft chuckle and nodded him to the table, where she sat across from him. 'Yup. That I was, but I'm a very forgiving audience.'

'I doubt that,' he said.

She only shrugged, then held him in her exquisite blue gaze while she sipped her coffee. 'So you think you're up for it, then.'

'I … don't want to spank you.' Jesus! Why had he suddenly taken to speaking every word that came into his mind?

'Good, because I don't want you to spank me,' she replied.

'Then I won't have to …'

'Not if I can help it,' she said. 'Now, if you really want to do this, if you really think you're up for it, I'll try to bring you up to speed and answer any questions you have. But first, I have to ask, why are you doing this for Tanya? She doesn't deserve it, you know.'

'You're pretty quick to judge,' he shot back at her, feeling more wounded than he should.

'No, Mr Chase –' her gaze cooled '– I'm not quick to judge. Have you told her?'

'Not yet. No.'

She raised a perfectly shaped eyebrow. 'I'd have thought you'd call her with the good news before the limo left the building last night.'

'I told you, I was still deciding this morning.' That wasn't entirely true. He had decided before he went to bed in the wee hours, but even if he hadn't, he just couldn't bring himself to share what had happened last night. He was sure Tanya would have questions, questions he just didn't want to answer. Besides, he figured he'd have to deal with her soon enough. It disturbed him he'd nearly forgotten why he was doing this until Elsa reminded him.

'I'm sure she'll be thrilled that you're trying.'

'You don't think I can do it?' He felt the tension in his shoulders like tight fists.

'I'm reserving judgment.' Her response felt like a

slap in the face after last night, and he wondered if he'd made a mistake in coming back. It had never been his intention to even consider fulfilling Tanya's contract until – until what he'd seen, what he'd done, what Elsa Crane manipulated him into.

'You don't want me here.' God, he sounded like a pouty little kid.

'If I didn't want you here, you wouldn't be here, Mr Chase. But being here and succeeding here are two very different things.'

She turned her attention to her iPad on the table in front of her before he could argue further. And really, what was there to argue? He wouldn't even be here if he had half a brain. But he now had a driver so he'd no longer have to face the loathsome task of driving horny tourists around Vegas in the wee hours, and he owed Elsa for that. Christ, even in his own brain that sounded lame.

'Do you … does Mount Vegas have offices or do you always meet in hotel suites?' he asked, mostly to fill the stretching silence.

'We have offices, yes. But we meet in hotel suites because they're practical for what we get up to. In the course of the night we run anything from one to three fantasies for different clients. Sometimes we do daytime acts, but not often.' She shrugged. 'This is Vegas. We find the most centrally located hotel, set up the equipment and run everything from one site. The office is a much more private affair. We take care of other business there.'

'Other business?'

'You know – accounting, planning, organising, that sort of thing.'

He felt a nervous twitch developing just below his left cheekbone. He took a long drag at his coffee for courage and set the cup down. 'Will you … will you train me?'

'As much as we can in such a short time, yes. I've had Pike download some books and info you'll need to help familiarise yourself with terminology and help you understand situations such as you witnessed last night with Pike and me, as well as those you'll soon be participating in. There are several good glossaries and notes on all sorts of kink and fetish, and there's a basic set of rules for life under contract with Mount Vegas. Most of those you've already seen from the outside in.'

There were so many questions he wanted to ask her about what he'd seen, but it seemed an invasion of privacy, even though he knew someone somewhere was actually watching. Someone had actually paid to watch Pike abuse her! He still couldn't quite get his head around that. Of course he wasn't totally ignorant of the kink that underpinned the foundations of Mount Vegas, but being aware of and actually seeing first-hand were two very different things. Beyond the privacy issue, he just couldn't bring himself to ask the kind of questions the whole incident had evoked. He felt like a teenager, afraid to ask about sex. He'd have to get over that right quick, he figured.

'I suppose you could say that we're exhibitionists showing off sexually for our voyeuristic clients,' Elsa said, 'but we're more just acting out for them what they want to see and setting up a way for them to watch that makes them feel like thcy'rc sneaking a peek. The majority of what we do is pretty pedestrian. We have lots of generic watching sex in one hotel room through a scope in another. Now, thanks to *Fifty Shades of Grey*, we have lots of billionaire and virgin scenarios.

'Most of what we do is without condoms. We're all checked regularly and we're all clean. Tanya was the only one of us who ever had sex with a partner outside the Mount Vegas team. And that's OK as long as you let us know in advance and use protection. You understand; it's to keep everyone safe. And with the provisions in the contract no one suffers from lack of sex.'

'I can't even remember the last time I had sex before Tanya.'

'I know,' she said. 'I know most things about you by now, because if I didn't I wouldn't be considering doing this insane thing that you've asked me.'

The nervous twitch along Nick's cheek went into overdrive. He tried to force it out by smiling harder. 'That's not really fair, is it? You knowing everything and me knowing nothing.'

She held him in a drowning-deep gaze that made his pulse jump against his throat as he struggled to meet it. 'Oh, you know way more than nothing, Mr Chase. Way more. And you'll know a whole lot more before the day's over.'

'Nick,' he said, his voice sounding breathless and thin on the ground. 'If we're going to work so closely together you should call me Nick, unless I get a nickname like everyone else.'

She smiled, and he felt like the sun had just come out. 'You have to earn your nickname, Nick.' The play on words made them both chuckle. 'Anyway, I like Nick. Nick is nice.'

He liked Elsa too. He liked the way it slid over his tongue like something almost too hot to taste and yet way too delicious not to.

'Now, grab yourself some more coffee and I'll show you how we set up and what's going on, then Pagan'll drive you over to one of the sites so you can see how things happen from that end.'

Nick had just got his coffee doctored when the bedroom door burst open and Pike poked his head out. 'We've got problems, Elsa. You'd better come.'

Nick followed her into the designated control room.

Pike gave him a nod for a greeting and turned his attention to his boss.

'Deke's completely lost his voice and he's running one hell of a temperature. Pagan's driving him to the doctor. Whatever it is he can't pull off tonight's act for Mrs Bromley and even if he could manage to do his part, Deb sure as hell isn't gonna want to share the love. Horse is still in Arizona for the next two days.' Already Pike's eyes were locked on Nick.

'No.' Nick shook his head like he was trying to shake it off his shoulders and his insides plummeted into freefall. 'No, I've not had any training. I'm not prepared.'

Elsa looked him up and down. 'You'll be involved in a fairly pedestrian fantasy. It doesn't take any special skills. No spanking or getting spanked.'

'There's nobody else,' Pike said. 'Mrs Bromley's one of our best paying customers. We can't postpone her big night.'

'You're already comfortable with Deb,' Elsa said, 'so it wouldn't be like being with a total stranger, though that's what you need to make Mrs Bromley believe.'

'I'd be more comfortable with you,' Nick blurted before he could stop himself.

She offered him a smile that went straight to his crotch. How the hell could she do that? And why the hell was it her he wanted to be with when she was the cause of him being in this mess in the first place? 'I'm involved in another act, Nick. I wouldn't be able to get back in time to perform with you, but Pagan will be in charge of the control room, so you'll be in good hands.'

'Why can't Pagan star in Mrs Bromley's fantasy then, instead of me?'

'Can you run the controls on three fantasies?' Her gaze suddenly went from sexy to stern.

'No, but –'

'Then you either do Mrs Bromley's fantasy or you take up Pike's role in the dungeon, and we've already discussed that, haven't we?'

'Yes, but –'

'Look, Nick –' she thrust her hands onto her hips '– do you want to do this or not? It won't get any easier, and putting it off until tomorrow, which is the biggest grace period I can give you, isn't going to make it better. Now, are you in or are you out?'

Nick looked from Elsa to Pike, who stood looking at him expectantly, and back to Elsa again, whose expression was now unreadable. The room felt too hot. He hadn't even had a chance to peruse the basic rules and regulations for Mount Vegas let alone study terminology and kinks and fetishes he might have to deal with. He should walk away. Hell, he should run, fast and far. Instead, he took a deep breath from under tight shoulders. 'All right. What do I have to do?'

Pike smiled broadly. Elsa only offered a neutral nod. It was Pike who replied. 'You'll be playing a wealthy businessman who's been gambling into the wee hours. You always stay in the same suite because it has a scope, and you like to watch the action in the other rooms. You know exactly which rooms have all the kink and when the fun begins.

'Deb is the hotel maid, Beth. Since you're out late gambling, she cleans your room late so she can look through your scope and have a diddle. You return early and catch her mid-diddle.'

'And?' Nick asked.

'Well, that's it,' Pike replied. 'Imagine you're the rich businessman returning to your room from a night of winning at blackjack. You come back expecting to indulge your voyeuristic desires and find your scope already occupied by a very voluptuous, very horny hotel maid who, if you report her, will get her ass fired. What would you do?'

'As the rich businessman, not Nick Chase,' Elsa added.

'I got that,' Nick said.

'Rely on Deb to help you if you get stuck. Keep in mind, she's a horny little maid, and she'll do anything to keep from getting fired.' Elsa batted her eyes. 'Anything to show her gratitude for you keeping her secret. Get him over to wardrobe,' she said to Pike. 'He's broader in the shoulders than Deke is, and the tux has to make him look like James Bond, not Farmer Frank in his Sunday best. I'll take over here.' She looked at her watch. 'Now hurry up. Time's wasting.'

As Nick stood in front of the three-way mirror being measured and fitted for a tux that even he had to admit looked fucking good on him, he wondered how the hell he was going to pull this off. He had a sudden, vivid flash of Elsa rocking on her wounded arse against the pillow, quietly trembling out her orgasm as she watched him do Beetle. He had made her come, and without even touching her. That was at least a little boost to his ego. Then it hit him; that was the way he'd get through this nightmare. He'd go about the whole experience as though Elsa Crane were watching him, as though she were on the other end of the telescope with her fingers in her panties, strumming her clit and darting in and out of her pussy. And suddenly his trousers were tented and he was in danger of staining them properly before he even got to Mrs Bromley's fantasy.

Chapter Seven

'Mr Garland has agreed to an earlier start for his fantasy,' Elsa said. 'That way I can be back here and –'

'And what?' Pike interrupted. 'You can't suddenly take over for Deb.'

'No, but I've sent Pagan to wardrobe and got him suited up for the businessman role. That way if I get back in time I can take over the control boards and he can do Mrs Bromley's fantasy instead of Nick.'

'She won't like it,' Pike said. 'You know she's not keen on body-builder types.'

'Maybe I can give her a discount. Surely she would be amenable to that.'

'Why don't you just have a little faith in Nick and let him get on with it? He's with Deb right now, and they're walking through the act. Besides, you know Deb; she's pulled more than a few disastrous acts back from the brink.'

'How can I have faith in him when I know his motives?' Elsa paced in front of the monitors, already dressed in the corset and feather boa that she was supposed to masturbate her way out of. Mr Garland had paid top dollar for the fantasy, and the space they'd rented looked identical to the dressing rooms of a burlesque show. Thankfully, the man was as anxious to get on with the performance as she was.

Pike was dressed in his jeans and the flip-flops he'd

remove when he got to the dungeon, where Beetle would be waiting for him. He was lucky Elsa was talking to him at all. When she was forced to do a dungeon scene with him, as long as her arse stung from his spanking, or any other part of her body was any worse for the wear, she usually snubbed him. But this was too important. 'You saw the way he was last night. I think the guy's a natural exhibitionist. He just doesn't know it yet.'

'What?' she said. 'Are you that attracted to him?'

'Of course I'm attracted to him. So are you. So's everyone else, and the way he came to bat for Tanya sure hasn't lost him any brownie points. I mean, we all like Tanya. We all wanted her to stop fucking up and complete her contract. Nick Chase basically did what the rest of us wish we could do. Even you, Elsa.'

'Don't tell me what I wish, Pike. You don't know what I wish.'

'Elsa, you gave the woman four chances. I know what you wish. And Nick Chase is the solution to our Tanya problem.'

She nodded down to the monitor that now showed the empty hotel room where very shortly Nick Chase would discover Deb, the hotel maid, rubbing one off behind his scope. 'You really think he can handle this?'

'I do.'

'For two months?'

Pike's lips curled into the mischievous smile that Elsa could never stay truly mad at. 'I think he'll not only stick it out for the two months, but I think he'll want in as a permanent member of the team after.'

'Whatever he does after two months is not my concern right now, Pike.' She looked up as Pagan came into the room dressed in shorts and a muscle shirt with a garment bag slung over his shoulder. 'I've given this a lot of thought and I think he's probably right. We probably are pushing him a little too hard. Now I gotta go, but I'll be back as soon as I can to take over for Pagan.' She turned and left the room.

When he was sure Elsa was gone, Pike laid a hand on Pagan's shoulder. 'I have an idea, but I need your help. I need to give Mrs Bromley a quick call. Then I'll fill you in on the details.

When it was all sorted, Pagan heaved a sigh that made him look like his chest was a giant muscle-shaped balloon inflating. 'Elsa won't like it.'

'I know,' Pike answered. 'But the blame'll be on me, and after last night in the dungeon, she'll feel a whole lot better if she can lay into me. Anyway, Nick can do the job, and if he's going to fulfil Tanya's contract, let him get on with it, I say.'

Nick got the heads-up from Minnie in wardrobe, who was leaning over him fussing with his hair when her BlackBerry rang. She did nothing but listen for a couple of seconds, grunted affirmation, then hung up. 'Mrs Bromley's wanting to start 15 minutes early. Seems she's anxious to gaze upon your studliness.' She made another pass of shimmying fingers through his hair. 'Well, you're as ready as you're ever gonna get, but I'm recommending to Elsie that you get a haircut. There's only so much I can do.'

Nick didn't mind 15 minutes early. It was better than standing around stewing in his nerves while he waited.

Minnie was giving him the final inspection in front of the three-way mirror when the BlackBerry rang again. She picked it up, listened and then said, 'He's on his way.' She looked up at him and offered a motherly smile. 'You'll do great, Nick. Now go make Mrs Bromley squirm.'

By now, Deb would be looking through the scope with the front of her black maid's blouse unbuttoned enough to get to her nice rack. One hand would be assaulting an exposed nipple while the other would have shoved aside the crotch of her panties under her hiked skirt, and Mrs Bromley would be getting an eyeful. It wasn't quite as well choreographed as all that. Mrs Bromley was a voyeur, which gave some leeway to improvise. Deb confided that Mrs Bromley liked her men a little shy and bumbling. Well, that part he wouldn't have to pretend at, would he?

As the elevator opened, for a split second Nick had the urge to push the down button and run. But then he thought of Elsa watching him, and he took a deep breath and moved forward.

The card key clicked in the lock and, with a sweaty palm, he pushed the door open. He knew where Deb was in the room, he knew what she was doing. But he took his time, shed his jacket and tie, and unbuttoned and untucked his shirt. Humming softly to himself, he slipped off his shoes and socks. He was, after all, planning a good wank in front of his scope, and he wanted to be comfortable. He wanted Elsa – and Mrs Bromley, anticipating what would happen when he discovered the naughty maid in his hotel suite. At the bar, still standing with his back to where he knew Deb was, he poured two fingers of Glenfiddich into a cut crystal tumbler and, after a sip that really wasn't more than touching it to his lips, he turned for the encounter. Deb let out a little squeal of surprise, and with way more ease than he would have thought possible, Nick found his voice.

'What the hell are you doing here?'

'What the hell is he doing there?' Elsa growled.

Pagan offered her a guilty look and stepped back from the monitor. 'Mrs Bromley decided to start her fantasy 15 minutes early.'

'Jesus!' She pushed him aside and shoved forward,

ignoring the image of Pike inserting ever larger dildos into Beetle's pussy while the woman squirmed and moaned helplessly from where she was tied spread-eagled to the bondage bed. Elsa's focus was totally on Nick. He looked positively edible with his white shirt undone and untucked to expose the open button of his tux trousers, which rode low, just above his bronze pubic curls. Elsa's pussy clenched at the sight, and when he spoke, she nearly gushed in her panties.

'You're supposed to clean my suite, not play with your pussy while you watch my neighbours fucking. That is what you were doing, isn't it?' Before Deb could do more than whimper, Nick moved closer and slid a hand between her legs. Deb's eyelids fluttered and she gasped. 'Whatever they're doing across the way must be pretty damned good to make your little snatch so slippery.'

Elsa and Pagan gasped in unison as Nick gave her pussy a hard finger-thrusting. Deb bit her lip and quivered all over.

'You know, I could have you fired for this,' Nick said. There was a slight growl in his voice, as though he suddenly spoke from a place deeper inside his chest. The sound of it went straight to Elsa's pussy.

'Oh please don't, Mr Smith. I need this job.' Deb laid on a thick Southern drawl. 'Honestly, I've never done anything like this before. I don't know what came over me. Please. I'm putting my baby sister through school back in Dallas. I can't let her down. Please Mr Smith –' she batted her eyelashes and shifted on his fingers '– I'll do anything. Anything you ask.'

'What were they doing over there –' he paused long enough to look down at her nametag '– Beth? What were they doing?'

'The guy was licking the woman … down there, and his thing! My oh my, it's a whopper.'

'Do you think he's about to fuck her?'

'Oh yes, Mr Smith. I'm pretty sure.'

'Then come on, you don't want to miss anything, do you?' Nick pulled his fingers from Deb's pussy and licked them, then gave her a little push until she stood once again in front of the scope. When she was bent over, looking through the eyepiece, he moved in close behind her and lifted her skirt. He yanked the crotch of her panties over one buttock and cupped her arse, his thumb sliding along her crack and stroking until she shivered and moaned. 'Here's what's going to happen, Beth. You're going to watch our horny neighbours and you're going to give me all the juicy details.' He thrust a hard finger into her pussy and she yelped. 'If you don't want me to tell your superiors what I found you doing in my room, you're going to talk dirty enough to make my cock so hard –' he twisted her arm around behind until her palm rested on the bulge in his trousers '– that all I have to do is shoot my wad up your sopping wet cunt.' He nibbled her ear. 'Or maybe I'll fuck your tight little asshole, Hmmm? Would you like that?' With his thumb, he stroked her anus. She quivered all over and wriggled back tighter against his probing. 'Mmm, I can tell you would, you naughty thing, you. Now what are they doing?'

'Oh Mr Smith, this is so embarrassing. Please don't make me say it.'

'Say it –' he reached around and squeezed her tits hard '– or you'll be needing another way to pay for your sister's education.'

Deb whimpered and pressed closer to the eyepiece. 'He's … he's licking her … down there and, oh dear lord, he's got two fingers up her … you know.'

'Up her what, Beth? Use the word. Tell me where he has his filthy fingers.'

Back in the control room, Pagan stroked himself through his trousers. 'Jesus, boss, you were worried about *him* not being able to do the job?' he gasped.

Elsa shushed him and pulled up a chair in front of the monitor just as Nick, with incredible grace, kicked Deb's legs apart and stepped in closer, rubbing his still clothed hard-on up against her exposed pussy. Deb shoved her arse back against him and he thrust so hard that the scope nearly went over. 'You want that, Beth? You want my cock in your tight little cunt? Where are the man's fingers?'

'Up her ... up her bottom.'

'Say it, Beth.' He gave her a shake. 'You're not in Dallas any more.'

'Up her asshole!' she said with a sob.

'That's it, Beth, say the words. I want your mouth to be as filthy as your little pussy, because I like to fuck a filthy mouth as much as I do a filthy snatch. Now tell me what else they're doing, and don't say it like some tight-ass Sunday School teacher.'

'Oh my, for mercy's sake! He's licking at her ... asshole and she's wiggling and bouncing on the bed back against his tongue, and his thing ... Oh, for heaven's sake! Mr Smith, he's going to put his thing, I mean his ... cock up her ... asshole, but I don't know how he's going to do it. He's so big. Oh dear lord in heaven, Mr Smith, he's doing it up her ass.'

'Doing what, Beth? Tell me what he's doing.'

'He ... he's f-fucking her back there. He's fucking her up her ass!'

Elsa held her breath as Nick dry-humped Deb through his tux trousers, his other hand working on her blouse, opening it far enough to slip his palm inside and fondle.

'I want to see your tits, sugar. Take off your shirt.'

Deb quickly dispatched with the rest of the buttons and shimmied out of her blouse. Before she had it completely off, Nick unhooked her bra and ran his hands around to cup her breasts. 'Very nice,' he moaned. 'Beautiful tits. Turn around, hon, I want to see your tits.'

'But what about the neighbours?' Deb said.

'I think we've seen enough of the neighbours for a while, and now, my naughty little maid, I think it's time you let them see you.'

'What?'

'Come.' Nick took her hand and pulled her to stand in front of the huge window. At first, they both stood in profile with Nick cupping and stroking Deb's breasts. 'I bet my scope isn't the only one in these hotels here. What do you bet, Beth?'

'No, Mr Smith. Please, I don't want them to see me.'

'I don't care what you want, sweetheart. You owe me, remember?'

He bent and, starting with her nipples, gave each of her breasts a lapping tongue bath that had Deb gasping and shifting her hips and had Elsa doing her own little lap dance against the chair. As for Pagan, Elsa wasn't sure he was even coherent, he was so aroused.

Then, in a move that had everyone gasping, Nick turned Deb and shoved her up against the window. She squealed and then moaned at the feel of the cold glass. Then he moved in close behind her. 'Now, my darling, let's us give those neighbours something to watch, shall we?'

With Deb's upper body pressed tight against the window, Nick unzipped her skirt and let it fall to the floor. Then he tugged the crotch of her panties up between her labia, making her shift onto her tiptoes with a gasp, before he pulled them completely off.

'And now that you've shown off those gorgeous tits, I think it's time you showed everyone just what a filthy little pussy you have, don't you?'

Nick turned her around again and rearranged and adjusted until she was bent over, open-legged, with her

67

pout splayed right up tight against the glass. 'You have such a filthy little cunt, don't you, hon?'

She offered only a sob and a nod.

'Say it!' He pinched a nipple hard and she yelped.

'I have a filthy little c-cunt,' she whimpered.

Back in the control room, Pagan unzipped his fly, and Elsa didn't try to stop him. She was using all the self-control she had to keep her fingers out of her panties.

'There now,' Nick said. 'That wasn't so hard, was it? And while everyone is enjoying the view of your naughty little snatch, I think I'll take full advantage of that dirty mouth of yours.' He pulled out his cock and shoved it, without preamble, into her mouth. She cried out, gagged slightly, then began to suck like it was her life's ambition. Nick curled his fingers in the back of her hair and pulled her on and off as though she were nothing more than a fuck toy.

'God, I hope he knows what he's doing,' Elsa said. 'They're only halfway through. He's gotta hold his wad for at least a little longer.'

Just then, Pike and Beetle rushed into the room. 'Holy shit,' Beetle managed.

'Sonovabitch,' Pike added. 'That's sizzling.'

On the monitor, Nick pulled away and turned Deb back so that her tits were once again splayed against the window. 'Is your cunt wet?' he said, fingering in between her pussy lips. 'Because I want to fuck you now, so I need you to tell me.'

'Yes,' she gasped, her breath fogging the window. 'Yes, my cunt is wet.'

'And what do you want me to do about that?'

'I want you to fuck me. I want you to fuck my pussy,' she cried. 'Please.' She opened her legs wider and pushed her hips back, and Nick shoved into her and began to thrust.

Deb was close, Elsa could tell from the way she held

her breath, from the way she bore down on Nick's cock. Then Nick grabbed her by the hair and pulled her head sideways and back so he could kiss her hard on the mouth. 'You don't get to come until I say you can come, Beth. You were a very naughty maid and naughty maids come last and then –' he gave a hard thrust that made her gasp '– then only if they're good.'

Her breasts thud, thud, thudded against the safety glass as he fucked her. She practically went through the roof when his arm snaked around her waist and between her legs. His laugh was positively wicked. 'I found your stiff little clit, hon, and believe me, it wasn't hard to find.' He tweaked it, and she groaned. 'Does it make you want to come when I rub it like this and pinch it?'

Deb was too far gone to do more than nod and gasp for breath.

'Well, maybe I'll let you come after I've shot my wad, and it's one helluva wad, sweetheart. I've been saving it up, looking forward to my time with the scope, but you invaded my privacy, didn't you?' He withdrew his hand and fondled her breasts, thumbing her nipples until she sobbed in frustration. 'I'm not in any real hurry, sugar. I could hold my wad and tease you all night. What do you think?'

'Oh please, Mr Smith. Pleeaase! I need to come sooo bad!'

Deb could be over the top sometimes, but Elsa was pretty sure the need at this moment was genuine. Hers certainly was.

Nick nibbled Deb's neck, then began again with her clit. 'All right, darlin'. I'm not a cruel man. And I've always believed in ladies first. But then you're not a lady, are you, Beth?' She shook her head wildly and Nick laughed. 'Never mind. It's all right. I don't think that little puss of yours can take much more, so it's OK if you come. In fact, I want you to come with me.'

In the control room, the only sound was heavy breathing. Elsa didn't have to look to know all of her colleagues were masturbating. But she held herself. This wasn't her fantasy. This wasn't what she wanted to do with Nick, and even as she watched, knowing that she would come too before his little performance was done, her own Nick Chase fantasy was unfolding in her head.

The silence was broken by Deb keening at the top of her lungs, 'I'm coming, I'm coming!' It was easy to tell Nick was about to follow suit, but just as he reached the point of no return, he roared like a lion, pulled his cock from Deb's still convulsing snatch, and shot his wad up her back and across the picture window in huge, arching spurts.

'Jesus,' Pike managed just before he jizzed into a handful of tissue.

Beetle was trembling out her orgasm in spastic jerks and gasps, and Pagan grunted his load into the trashcan at the end of the dressing table.

Elsa sat very still, feeling the tremors pass through her pussy and climb up her spine again and again. She sat with her eyes locked on Nick Chase, who had now dropped to his knees, his shoulders heaving for breath, his cock still gripped in his hand as Deb slid down the window like she was made of Jell-O.

Then Pagan stumbled back to the keyboard. 'All right, Nick, Deb, you're clear.' He spoke into the mic, gulping air like he'd just run a marathon. While the sounds of zipping and tucking filled the room, he turned his attention back to the control centre and busied himself checking the recordings that were a part of each paying client's package.

'Wow,' Beetle said, 'I think all of us are gonna want a copy of that little number, Pagan.'

'I'm already on it,' the big man called over his shoulder.

Just then, Elsa's BlackBerry rang. She answered, and her pulse went into overdrive.

'Hi Elsa, it's Rita here. Edward and I are still recovering from your Mr Chase's fantastic debut. My God, he's a hot one!'

'You saw it?' Elsa managed.

'We more than saw it; we had a hot little session of our own while we watched. He's definitely a keeper.'

'You were watching?' Elsa repeated.

There was a pause on the other end of the phone. 'Sorry about that. It was a very last minute request, but Pike said he was sure you wouldn't mind.'

Elsa glared at Pike. 'Pike is just so helpful, isn't he?' She ground her teeth. 'I'm glad you enjoyed it, Rita.'

There was another pause. 'Elsa, whatever you do, don't let Nick Chase get away. He's exactly the kind of man you need … the kind of person Mount Vegas needs to strengthen its ranks.'

Elsa nodded dumbly.

'Look, sweetie, I have to go,' Rita said. 'Totally starving after that little performance. I'll Skype you tomorrow.'

Before Elsa had time to question Pike, the door burst open and Nick and Deb blew in. Deb was practically bouncing off the wall with excitement. As Elsa stood to greet them, Deb threw her arms around her boss and hugged her tight. 'Did you see? It was amazing. Nick was amazing, wasn't he?' Before Elsa could answer, Deb was hugging everybody else in turn, leaping onto Pike and wrapping her shorts-clad legs around his waist to get a more effective bear-hug.

When Deb finally settled with both feet on the ground, Elsa turned her gaze to Nick. 'Yes, he truly was.'

Deb barely heard her. She kissed Nick hard on the mouth, then gave him a giggly bear-hug. 'You were amazing, Nick. We were both amazing, Mr Smith,' she said in her thick Southern drawl. Then she smacked her lips. 'I feel like I swallowed the desert. I need hydration.'

She waltzed off to the kitchen for a bottle of water, leaving Nick and Elsa standing practically nose to nose. In a move that was fast and hard, Nick pulled Elsa into his arms, forcing a little grunt of air from her throat before he took her mouth, and it wasn't a thanks-boss-glad-you-liked-my-work sort of kiss. He pulled her whole body against him, running his large palm up under her loose shirt to stroke her back, and fuck if his hands weren't calloused, just like in her fantasies. Any semblance of professionalism she tried to maintain between herself and Nick Chase went out the window as she threw her arms around his neck and returned his kiss. His inquisitive tongue explored her mouth, and she returned the favour, pressing herself up tight and close to the rumpled trousers he still wore, trousers that couldn't disguise his very interested hard-on.

'Mmnm,' he moaned into her mouth, his hands finding their way down inside the waistband of her shorts to cup her bottom, resulting in a harsh intake of breath and a flinch. 'Sorry. Forgot you're tender down there,' he said, and his groping became stroking with his fingertips just grazing her cleft.

She was on her toes, the very tips of them, in an effort to get up high enough for him to make contact with her ache. The undulation of his body was proof that it was exactly that contact Nick was aiming for, and at the moment, he didn't seem to care that they were very much the centre of attention.

Deb returned to the room and offered a little sigh of surprise at their antics. They'd had group sex before; there was nothing they hadn't done to each other and seen each other do. It was the nature of the job they did, and yet, being held by, being kissed and fondled by Nick Chase felt way more intimate than anything Elsa could ever remember feeling.

Somehow he had shoved and groped up her shirt until her breasts pressed hard-nipple tight against the muscular rise and fall of his chest. With a hand that had a mind of its own, she battled several unruly shirt buttons to expose him enough that flesh touched flesh – hot, needy, oxygen-starved flesh and, Christ, she'd never felt anything like it! She'd forgotten the two of them weren't alone. Even if she remembered, it didn't matter. Her hand slid low to caress the path of soft down under his navel. She wriggled her fingers into the gaping waistband of his trousers until they brushed his tight pubic curls, until the thick base of his cock tightened still further against her touch. He grunted as though she had punched him, shoving and thrusting to get closer to her hand.

'Elsa.' He whispered her name into her mouth. 'Oh God, Elsa. I want … I want …'

And she wanted too. She wanted what she'd never had before, what she didn't even have words for. But for a hot, tense moment of clarity, she was sure whatever it was, Nick Chase could give it to her.

And then Pike broke the spell.

'Get a room, you two. You're making the rest of us jealous,' he said.

Elsa couldn't help herself. She pulled away from Nick in an effort that would have been wrenching but for the knot of anger spurring her on. She turned on Pike and grabbed the front of his T-shirt in a tight fist, pulling him close to her. 'If you ever, ever go over my head like that again, Pike, when I'm finished with you, I'll make what you do in the dungeon seem like a waltz in the park.'

'Oh come on, Elsa, it was the right thing, and you know it. Besides, you were already starting your act

when Rita Holly called, so you can't blame me for that.'
Pike's mistake was not quite being able to wipe the smile off his face.

'I didn't ask for your opinion, and we'll discuss this in my office in the morning.' Then she turned and walked out of the room, walked out of the suite, walked out of the hotel.

Nick turned to follow her, but Beetle grabbed his arm. 'Trust me, you don't want to catch up with her right now. Give her a little chance to cool down.'

Chapter Eight

The slap, slap, slap of Victor's balls against Tanya's bottom, his tense grunts and the way that he grabbed at her hips told her that he was near to his climax. She wished that he would hurry up and just get it over with. She was bent over the end of the dressing table with the red silk négligée up over her butt. He'd got bored with tugging at her clit, which was just as well because she was pretty bored with it too. She glanced down at her watch. She was always proud that she had the ability to come any time she wanted, but she wasn't so good at it when she was under a threat. Threats were not at all arousing, so she found herself doing something that she seldom had to do. She found herself faking her orgasm.

'Oh, I'm coming, Victor! I'm coming! Is so good, so good,' she cried out with all of the enthusiasm she could muster. At the moment she was pretty sure Victor wouldn't care one way or the other if she was coming, but a little stroking of the man's ego was good idea under the circumstances. She knew the man didn't mind slapping women around when he was in a bad mood.

'Of course you're coming, you little bitch,' he said. Then he grunted his load into her pussy as though his balls were busting. He had barely finished his coming before he pulled out and went into the bathroom. She tidied herself and poured two glasses of red wine. At the moment she would have rather had vodka – lots of it –

but it was best to keep her wits. She could hear him pissing. He was a pig really, and he was a lazy fuck. He didn't bother with finesse. Perhaps she wouldn't have even known the difference if she hadn't fucked so many men who were really good in bed, and who treated her with respect.

She heard the toilet flush, then the water in the sink was running. Around the edge of the bedroom door, she could see one of his colleagues watching porn on her television. Victor wouldn't like that. A man wasn't at his best with the hard cock, Victor would say. But she didn't care. The man was nothing to her. All she wanted was to get Victor off her back and out of her flat. She glanced back at the bathroom door and then found her iPhone and pulled up the text that Nick Chase had sent.

Have agreed to finish out your contract. My first act is tonight. Will be in touch.'

It was very impersonal from the man who had agreed to take on such a big responsibility, but then they had only ever fucked once, and she was amazed that he would even consider fulfilling her contract under the circumstances. She had never expected him to, and she had never expected Elsa to agree that he could do this thing. There was no doubt Nick Chase was her hero, but heroes often got themselves killed, and Nick was a nice man, too nice for the situation. She would make sure to reward him the next time that she saw him.

She checked her watch again. She was worried about how everything was going with Nick. There was still no message about how the act had gone. Nick was a very good lover, but she thought he was very conservative. She couldn't imagine him to be involved in any of the Mount Vegas acts. Such things would not be easy for him to do, but do them he must if he would fulfil her contract. And those things worried her very much considering that Victor knew about Nick already, even before they knew if he could do this thing or if he would try.

It was a text from Pagan that put her mind at ease, at least a little bit. It said *Nick's a natural, T! Don't worry about your bonus. If anyone can get it for you, he can.*

The flood of relief she felt was tempered by the disappointment that Nick hadn't told her himself. But then he was probably worried that he wouldn't be able to do it and he didn't want to tell her until after, just in case.

'Well? Any news about our boy?'

Tanya jumped, startled at the sound of Victor so close to her. She was so caught up in her thoughts that she had not heard his return. He took up one of the glasses of wine and drained it, then nodded to the iPhone in her hand.

'He has done very well. The bonus will be secured, just as you asked.'

Victor sat down on the bed next to her and gave her a hard kiss that tasted of wine and the cigars that he always smoked. He reached inside the front of her robe to play with her breasts, squeezing them like they were sponges full of water that he needed to wring out.

'Well, that's a start, sweetheart; that should take care of the interest you owe me. And now we can talk about the principle.'

'Interest?' She slapped his hand away. 'You didn't say anything about any interest, Victor. You didn't say that there would be interest.'

He shoved his hand back into her robe and pinched her nipple hard enough to make her yelp. 'This is Vegas, Tanya. What did you think, just because you entertained me with your slippery little cunt I'd make an exception for you after I put myself out so to pay off your gambling debts?' He gave a nasty giggle. 'Come to think of it, I did make an exception.' He curled his fingers in her hair and yanked her close. 'You're still alive, aren't you?'

Tanya held very still so Victor's grip wouldn't hurt so bad, but really, the pain was nothing compared to the fear. 'How do you expect me to get more than the money from my bonus?' she managed without crying.

He kissed her ear. 'Well, I'd say for starters you'd better get that pretty little head of yours thinking and make sure Nicky-boy can't keep his cock away from your hungry snatch. Once you have him between your legs, I'm sure he'll tell you everything we need to know in order to bring Elsa Crane and her empire down. Then all we have to do is set our little plan in motion.'

'I don't know how much he will know,' she said, trying to keep from trembling. 'That all depends on how close he can get to Elsa.'

He took her face in his hands and kissed her hard, so hard that she felt like she couldn't breathe. And then he bit her lip, and his eyes were hard and cold when he looked at her. 'It's simple, really. You'll just have to make sure he'll do anything for you; even get close to Elsa Crane. And once you've helped me bring down the woman, then I'll consider your debt paid in full.' He squeezed her chin hard between his thumb and forefinger. Then he kissed her again and left her sitting there on the bed, trembling.

She listened for the door to her flat to close. And then she drank the other glass of wine to help her to calm her nerves. And when she had pulled herself together, she called Nick Chase.

'Hello?' When he answered she could hear that his voice was breathless and full of expectation.

'Nick, this is Tanya calling. I wanted to call and say to you how thankful I am for all that you have done for me. Pagan said that it was good?'

'Oh hi, Tanya.' Was it disappointment she heard in

his voice? This was not what she wanted to hear.

'Was good? No?'

'Oh yes. It was good. It went really well. I wasn't sure I could do it, but it was OK. It was all right.'

'Am I interrupting something? I know sometimes the party goes on after the act is finished, to help everyone to relax.'

'Oh … no. No party. I'm just tired.'

'Then … you are at home?'

'Yes. At home.'

'Nick, you are my hero for doing this thing. You know this, yes?'

'Yes, I mean no. I mean I'm not a hero, Tanya. I'm just doing the right thing.'

'You are special man, Nick Chase,' she said. 'I would like very much if you would come to my place and let me show you how much I appreciate.'

There was silence that lasted long enough she was afraid their connection had been lost. 'Nick? Are you there?'

At last he spoke. 'That's very tempting, Tanya, but not tonight. I have a lot to think about, and I'm afraid I wouldn't be good company. Plus I'm really tired.'

'Of course. I understand. Is often exhausting doing the work for Mount Vegas. It will be good if you get some rest, my darling, and then we will speak later.'

She hung up, feeling not so certain and much more desperate. If the man was willing to fulfil her contract so that she could get the bonus, then it would only be reasonable that he liked her very much, and right now, after Victor's little revelation, she needed him to like her very much. But he acted like he didn't care for her. She stood and paced the floor of her bedroom. She would have to do something and do it very soon. Victor was not a patient man. But what to do was not so clear.

Nick laid his BlackBerry down on the nightstand. He sat on the edge of his bed with a towel still wrapped around his hips from the shower. He felt more disappointed than he cared to admit that it was Tanya who had called him instead of Elsa – Elsa who had been in his arms, so responsive, so ready he could almost taste her need; Elsa who had nearly climbed him and rode him right there in front of the whole Mount Vegas team. And he would have welcomed her. Elsa who had then turned just like that and left.

Damn the woman! He just didn't understand her. Sometimes he wasn't even sure he liked her, and yet even as sexy as Tanya and Beetle and Deb all were, as soon as he met Elsa Crane, she was all he could think about. It made no sense. After she'd left without so much as a see you later, he had declined the offers of the rest of the team to go out for a late dinner and then back to Pike's place to enjoy the hot tub. He was sure the offer included plenty of sex with whomever he wanted, but it was Elsa he wanted. The possibility of being with her after the act had helped him get through the evening. It wasn't that he pretended Deb was Elsa. He couldn't begin to imagine Elsa as a hotel maid. What he wanted from his leading role in Mrs Bromley's fantasy was to be solely responsible for her orgasm. He wanted to make Elsa Crane come.

He pushed up from the bed and made his way to the kitchen. For the course of the time he'd spent in front of Mrs Bromley's scope, he felt as though he had expanded beyond himself, as though he might have truly experienced himself for the first time. In all of his wildest fantasies he could have never imagined doing what he'd done tonight. And now, after what had happened with Elsa, he felt as though someone had given him a harsh shove back into his own skin, which no longer seemed to fit quite right.

He pulled a beer from the refrigerator along with a slice of cold pizza from yesterday. Still wrapped in his towel, he walked out onto his deck and peered into the brightness of the night sky. He was always stunned at the view of the stars, at just how many were visible in the clear desert darkness. He ate the pizza without tasting it, then slipped back into the house and back into his bedroom. He'd never be able to sleep, he was sure. So he grabbed his iPad and plopped down in the middle of his bed, taking a long pull on his beer, then he opened the first of the documents Pike had sent.

He was just browsing a glossary of terms for kink and BDSM when his BlackBerry rang. He bit back a curse and picked up, all ready to lie to Tanya and tell her that, really, he just wanted to go to bed and get some rest.

'Nick? It's Elsa.'

Both his pulse and his cock responded before his voice could.

'… Are you all right?'

'I'm fine,' he managed around his sudden struggle to breathe. 'You? You seemed … upset.' He shifted on the bed, ignoring the towel as it fell loose.

'It had nothing to do with you, and I apologise for being so badly behaved when your success was so deserving of celebration.'

'There for a while I was actually thinking you might celebrate with me.'

The silence on the other end of the phone made him wonder if he should have kept his mouth shut.

Her delicious bedroom chuckle made his dick stretch tight against his belly almost as though it were reaching to get closer to the sound of her voice. 'If I hadn't lost my temper, I might have taken you up on it, though I'm not sure it would have been a good idea.'

'Why? And don't tell me it's because you don't have sex with the people who work for you.'

This time her voice sounded almost shy. 'That's true enough, but you're not exactly a regular member of the crew, are you?'

'I'm doing the work of a regular member,' he said, his hand straying down to his cock. 'And if I'm doing the work, I want the benefits.'

'You've got Beetle and Debs. You'll have Kandi, when she gets back from holiday, and any of the guys if you feel like experimenting a bit. Then there's Tanya. In fact, if she hasn't called you to offer her services already, then I'll be surprised.'

'But it's you I want, and I'm not stupid. There in the hotel suite, you wanted me too, didn't you?'

'I was overly tired and stressed about … the way the night had gone.'

'That's it? You were so delirious from exhaustion and stress that I could have been just anybody off the streets, and you would have fallen into my arms and kissed my face off?'

Her laughter was like warm fur moving over his skin and the half-hearted touching and caressing of his junk became fisted stroking. 'I didn't fall into your arms, Mr Chase. You … enveloped me, and I'd say it was a pretty stiff competition as to who would kiss whose face off.'

He shifted his arse against the bed and put the BlackBerry on speakerphone so he could use his hands for more urgent tasks. 'Oh, it was stiff all right, but then you'd know that, wouldn't you, being … enveloped as you were.'

'It was definitely stiff. In fact, I was amazed it could get that stiff that fast after the way you'd just decorated Deb's backside and the hotel room window for Mrs Bromley.'

His efforts were no longer mindless. His efforts were totally focused on the woman whose voice made his body tingle with the want of her, the woman who had

82

been in his thoughts the whole time he'd been performing with Deb. His hips rocked and ground against the bed and, fuck, it was like every single conscious thought had somehow migrated to his groin. He ached with a fullness he hadn't even felt when he was playing with Deb.

'Elsa –' he spoke her name around gasping efforts to breathe '– I wasn't performing for Mrs Bromley. I'm sure she's a lovely woman and all, but I was performing to make you come.'

Her own breathing seemed heavier and her voice somehow more humid. 'Nick, I –'

Before she could say anything he didn't want to hear, and he was pretty sure the words were right on the tip of her tongue, he interrupted. 'You can't tell me that you don't fantasise about other things, other people, sometimes when you're performing – other people you'd rather be with, other people you'd rather be making love to.'

And suddenly she was all business-like. 'Of course that happens, Nick. I mean, as you've seen, all the people on the team are very skilled in the sexual arts, and everyone has a very high libido. They have to in order to do what they do. Still, what happens in someone's head sometimes is a lot more arousing than what's happening to someone's body. But –'

'And did it work?' Jesus, she had to know what he was doing, he wasn't even trying to be subtle about the pull and tug, the rock and shift and the battle to breathe around his arousal.

Her laugh was husky, way too breathless for the business-like tone she had just pretended.

'Did it work? Did I make you come?'

'Nick, I –'

'Elsa, tell me, because just talking to you, just hearing your voice on the other end of the phone, just

83

thinking about the way you feel, the way you taste, makes me hard and full and uncomfortable, and I can't help thinking that just maybe –'

'Yes.' Her answer came out long and heavy on the "s", like steak sizzling on the grill, like the heat and humidity of her outrageously tasty mouth was enough to set her BlackBerry on fire, right where she held it close to her face, close to the feather-softness of her cheek. 'Yes, Nick. You made me come. You made me come last night and you made me come tonight.'

Before Nick could let that delicious fact sink in and mix with his already raging lust, the damned doorbell rang.

Unfortunately, Elsa heard it too. 'Aren't you going to answer that?'

'Whoever it is can fuck off,' he growled. 'Now where were we?'

'Seriously, Nick, you should probably answer. It might be something important. I mean, you do own a business, and things happen.'

'And when things happen, normal people call,' he said.

'Just check, OK?'

Silently calling down curses on whoever had dared to disturb the most intimate time he'd had with Elsa so far, he slid into the pair of sweat bottoms, which were nicely tented with his hard cock. Then he pressed himself against the wall to peek out of the bedroom window. From that angle, he could just see down to the porch where the motion detecting lights bathed the untimely visitor in golden hues.

'It's Tanya,' he said, trying not to grind his teeth.

He wasn't sure if he detected a chuckle or a curse in a little burst of air over the speakerphone. 'I don't know how she found me, but I'll send her away,' he said.

'No, don't do that. She's no doubt come to thank you,

and a bird in the hand, you know ...' Elsa's voice sounded way more neutral than he'd have liked. Damn it, he wanted to finish what they'd started. Phone sex with Elsa Crane had to be way hotter than physical sex with anyone else on the planet. 'Besides,' she added, 'I've been on the receiving end of Tanya's gratitude and it's an enjoyable place to be. You should take advantage. You've earned it, and she owes it.'

'Elsa, I don't want –'

'Goodnight, Nick. Enjoy Tanya.'

And with that, she hung up.

He was hard and uncomfortable and none too happy at the way things had ended with Elsa. He had every intention of sending Tanya away. But the minute he opened the door, she launched herself at him, pinning him to the wall in a lip-lock and a full-frontal rub-up that, even if his brain could have ignored it, his cock certainly could not. She wore a burgundy spandex miniskirt and a black corset that barely covered the stippling of her areolas, offering up her tits like ripe, round peaches ready for the plucking.

Before he could say anything, she squatted in front of him, perched on impossibly high heels. He flinched at her long, painted fingernails raking over his hips and sliding his sweats down to release his cock, which shot, as though it were spring-loaded, right into her waiting mouth. As the tight depth of her throat sheathed the length of him, the sound that escaped his lips was nothing intelligible. Her hands cupped his buttocks in kneading, separating motions that exposed his butthole to the air conditioning and stretched it with each grope just enough to remind him that it was there, that it was exposed, and that it was sensitive. She tugged and pulled at his cock in the humid velvet of her mouth until he surrendered all thoughts of banishing her and curled his fingers into her hair, pulling her still closer, thrusting hard into her tight, wet grip.

He felt mean-spirited enough by his disappointing disconnect with Elsa that he would have happily come in Tanya's mouth and sent her home. But the woman had worked for Mount Vegas. She wouldn't make it that simple. Just when he was ready to give himself over to the pleasure, she pulled away and began to unhook the front of the corset. 'I know you are tired, Nick, but I had to come over and thank you for all that you are doing.' She freed her ripe, heavy breasts into her hands and thumbed her nipples to urgent pink points, giving him almost enough time to gather his thoughts and tell her to go away. Almost. Then she scooped herself into her hands and leant forward, first running her wet tongue over the head of his cock, then angling her body so that, almost by instinct, he knew what had to be done. He bent forward, took both her breasts in his hands, kneaded and sculpted and scooped until the dark tunnel of cleavage became the perfect place in which to bury his aching dick.

Tanya ran her tongue over her full top lip and whimpered a sigh just before she bent her head close to her chest and licked the tip of him with each thrust, making little sounds like a kitten lapping cream. Once again, she brought him to the point at which he was ready to let her take what of his jizz into her mouth she could manage while he unloaded the rest across her tits and chest. Then she pulled away.

'Nick, I want you to fuck me. Fuck me any way you would like, only please fuck me. I am all yours to have. I am your fuck toy for the night. I only want to please you.' She looked up at him from beneath well-mascaraed lashes. 'I have condom.'

Once again he was all ready to tell her to leave; he just needed to catch his breath a little bit. But she didn't give him time for that. Instead, she inched up her skirt until he could see the swollen pink pearl of her clit peeking from beneath its heavy hood and the slickened sheen of her splayed pussy. She offered a little sigh that caught in the back of her throat, and she began to tweak her tight nib between her thumb and forefinger, each tug and pinch making her slit even wetter and shinier with her readiness. Then she bit her lip and gave him a little-girl pout. Even then he might have been able to resist, but she leant back and shifted her hips until he could see the grip and surge, grip and surge of her anus, dewy from the abundance of her girlie juices, as though it too were begging for his cock. Her tongue flicked over lips red and swollen, her fingers danced over her clit. The spread of her legs offered exquisite views of pussy and arsehole, all begging for Nick's attention, all begging for Nick's cock in hypnotic undulations and quivers of exquisite feminine muscles drenched and dilated, ready to accommodate.

When he only stood there staring down at her, Tanya pulled a condom from a tight pocket in the scrunched-up skirt and rolled it onto his cock. Then she rose, lifted her arms around his neck, and shifted forward. The rest was instinct. The rest he managed from some state of sexual hypnosis ruled by his penis and his heavy balls. He cupped her bottom in his hands and lifted her, with her half climbing his body until she squirmed and wriggled her way deep and tight onto his cock.

'I want to make you come, Nick Chase. I want to make your big cock feel so good.'

She accentuated her words with a hard grip of her pussy lips, and Nick began to hump, carrying her to the kitchen table, where he settled her, ploughing into her hard as she wrapped her legs around his hips and thrust up to meet him. And even then she wouldn't let him just mindlessly fill her. Once again, she pulled and wriggled off him.'

'What the …?' was all he could manage before she

turned onto her hands and knees, her arse practically in his face.

'You want this, don't you, Nick?' She ploughed her cupped fingers between her sopping pussy lips and spread the accumulated juices over her anus just before she thrust three wet fingers into her tight back hole with a grunt and a nibble of her bottom lip. 'All men want this but many are afraid to ask. You don't have to ask, Nick. I will always give you what you want, what you need.'

Nick had to battle hard for control at the sight of her pussy, empty and gripping in muscle memory of his cock that had filled it only seconds before. Tanya rammed and probed and stretched her dark sphincter until it grudgingly opened and spread and gaped for him. 'Is all right, Nick,' she gasped breathlessly. 'You can fuck me there in my asshole. I would like that, and see, I have it all ready for you. So ready.'

Nick didn't argue. He shoved his cock hard into her pussy for one last coating of her juices and then, with her grunting and straining, let her guide him into her delicious tightness. 'Is good, no?' she managed in a tight little breath. 'So good, and so good for me too Nick.' With his first hard thrust, she nearly lost her balance, but then she stabilised herself on hands and knees and shifted her hips back so that, for Nick's cock, it was a straight shot in, deep and hard, with Tanya chanting, 'Is so good, Nick. Feels so good, so good.'

She whimpered. 'But now my pussy is empty, and she needs to be filled too.' She took his hand, guiding it down around her waist to slip two then three fingers into her drenched slit.

By that time, Nick wasn't entirely sure of his own name. He was buried to the hilt up the arse of a beautiful woman who wanted him badly and, just as Tanya began to jerk and convulse in orgasm, he found himself wishing like hell that Elsa were watching, wishing she secretly had a scope set up to view his house and she had planned the whole meeting with Tanya so she could watch and play with her pussy, so that Nick could make her come again. He imagined that she was addicted to the orgasms he gave her when she watched him. He imagined it was him she wanted, him she needed. That was enough to send Nick over the edge, filling the condom with his load; a load made heavier, once again, by thoughts of making Elsa Crane come.

Chapter Nine

'I expected you to look a whole lot better slept with this morning,' Rita Holly said, squinting at Elsa through the monitor.

Elsa offered half a growl in response and gulped enough coffee to burn her tongue.

'You mean you didn't invite our lovely Mr Chase over for a personal party? Oh Elsa, what on earth's the matter with you?'

'There were ... complications,' Elsa said, feeling an unwelcome ache below her breastbone when she thought of what almost happened. 'Besides, he works for me and I –'

'For fuck's sake, everyone at Mount Vegas works for you and you fuck all of them, and he's the most fuckable hunk of manliness I've seen in a long time. Well, not counting Edward, of course, because I'm sort of partial where Edward's concerned.' She waved her hand as though she were erasing a chalkboard. 'Never mind that. Look, I know you were really upset with Pike. He told me that you probably would be, and you should be, I agree. He went over your head, but sweetie, this time he was right.'

Elsa closed her eyes and rubbed the bridge of her nose. 'I know he was right. That's what's driving me crazy. I don't have any trouble admitting when I'm wrong. I have a pretty healthy ego, but that I made such a mistake, that I backed down when I was the first to push for Nick to be in Mrs Bromley's fantasy, that's what bothers me. Why would I do that, Rita? Why would I second guess myself?'

Rita sipped from a bottle of water and puffed out a heavy breath. 'Well, sweetie, at the risk of sounding obvious, maybe you didn't want to share him?'

'That's ridiculous. Everyone shares everyone here at Mount Vegas, and if he wants to take up Tanya's contract then that's a part of the package.'

'And a lovely package it is.' Rita offered Elsa a mischievous smile, which turned sympathetic. 'Hon, you haven't fucked him yet, have you?'

Elsa felt Rita's words like a hard gut-punch, which made her even angrier. Why should she feel anything one way or another where fucking Nick Chase was concerned? 'Well, there really hasn't been a chance, has there? I mean, he's only just started and I really am trying to break him in as gently as I can and –'

Rita nearly sprayed her mouthful of water on the monitor. 'Come on, Elsa! Break him in gently? I know about the little game you played with him the night before, letting Beetle ride him while Horse shoved his monster cock up Deb's arse. Jesus, if that's breaking him in gently than you're one helluva sadistic bitch. Why didn't you join the party?'

'My ass was sore.'

'Big deal. So you'd been in the dungeon with Pike. Don't you think the man who's conscientious enough to offer to fulfil Tanya's contract would know how to fuck you gently and protect your little wounded arse?'

'Rita, please. Do we have to talk about this?'

'Of course we have to talk about this. Why the hell do you think I so gladly got you up in the wee hours? Nick Chase is hotter than hot. He's the best thing that's happened to Mount Vegas in a long time, and clearly you like him, Elsa Crane.'

'Well of course I like him,' Elsa blustered. 'I like all of my team, and I wouldn't have hired him if I didn't like him.'

'Then why didn't you invite him back to yours and fuck his brains out last night, sweetie? After all, you're the boss.'

'I was … he was … and then I called him but … Tanya came and I figured he would … they would … Well, you know.'

'Right. Thanks for that concise recap of events.' Rita said. Behind her, Elsa could see Edward fresh from the shower with only a towel around his waist. He bent and kissed Rita on the neck, than blew a kiss to Elsa, who blew one back. 'So you were probably the only one in Mount Vegas who didn't get laid last night. Oh Elsa, that's just so wrong. What kind of an example are you setting for your team?'

Elsa glared at her. 'Now you're toying with me.'

Rita's smile turned sympathetic again. 'No, I'm just telling you how it is. You like Nick Chase and it's clear he likes you.' Rita rubbed her hands together as though scheming something very naughty. 'You want him. He wants you. So all you have to do is fuck him and get on with it. You see, sweetie. Problem solved. Oh, and then you have to tell me all about it, of course.'

In spite of herself, Elsa smiled back at her. 'Next time we Skype I'll try to be ready to titillate.'

'Good. You'd better,' Rita said. 'Oh, and one more thing, Elsa, don't be too hard on Pike. His instincts were spot on and, even though he might have gone about it all wrong, he loves you, and he'd never do anything to hurt you.'

'I know,' Elsa said. 'Pike's a good friend, but he's never gone over my head before, and it … well, it hurt as much as it made me angry.'

'Then you need to tell him that when you talk to him.'
She leant forward. 'Are you going to punish him?'

Elsa shook her head. 'That's not really my thing any more.'

Rita studied her through the monitor. 'Whether or not it's your thing, Pike understands the relationship he shares with you way better than you do, Elsa. He understands what he deserves, and he deserves to be punished by the Mistress of Mount Vegas. Trust me on this one, Elsa, you'll both feel better if you do it properly.'

Pike settled in the reception room of Elsa's office. He usually walked right on in unannounced. The two of them had been friends with benefits from the start and they had never stood on ceremony. It was neither a surprise, nor a thing of resentment that Elsa became the head of Mount Vegas. Elsa had created Mount Vegas as something unique within all The Mount, created it even before she knew The Mount existed. It was because of her creative mind and her business acumen that Mount Vegas was quickly heading in the direction of full coven status. So even though they were best friends, it was Elsa who held the reins of power, and she held them well. Pike knew better to push his luck when she was angry. And she was really angry. In fact, he wasn't sure he'd ever seen her so angry.

Knowing that, he waited for her to invite him in. She'd been behaving strangely ever since Nick Chase came into their lives. On the one hand she didn't want Nick here; on the other she'd given the whole gang permission to play with him. On the one hand she practically forced him into yesterday's act for Mrs Bromley; on the other, she tried to pull him out at the last minute. And then there was the little scene after the performance. She practically climbed Nick like a tree right there in front of everyone. OK, so she didn't initiate contact, but once contact was made, wow! Pike was sure the whole room would go up in flames. He'd never seen such chemistry. And certainly he hadn't meant to drive them apart. Hell, he, more than anyone, wanted to see Elsa lovesick for someone who returned the favour.

Even though he was in deep shit, he couldn't keep the smile off his face. The icy-cool Elsa Crane was behaving strangely because she was smitten. Before he could carry his line of thought much beyond the Eureka moment, the office door opened. Elsa stuck her head out and nodded him in with little more than a grunt for a greeting. Pike took a deep breath and braced himself. Grunted greetings never boded well. He followed her into the room and stood in front of her desk.

When she returned to her seat without a word, he took the bull by the horns. 'I'm sorry I went behind your back, Elsa.' He should have left it at that, but he was a master at opening his mouth and inserting his foot. 'It was right to let him do the act with Deb, though, clearly you could see that.'

She studied him with a gaze he struggled to meet, a gaze that made him shift nervously from foot to foot. 'How long have we worked together, Pike?' The total calm in her voice made him uncomfortable.

'A long time, Elsa,' he said. 'We've always been a great team.'

She came to stand in front of him. 'Yes, we've always been a great team. All of us together have been a great team. You and I built that team. And how much of that time have you been team leader?'

He braced himself. 'Never, Elsa.'

She still held him captive in her titanium gaze. 'And have I ever led this group wrongly, Pike?'

'No. No one would ever question your leadership. You're the best at what you do.'

'You were right about Nick being ready. It's true. But

the world wouldn't have come to an end if we'd given Pagan his role, given Mrs B a discount and given Nick a little more time to get comfortable with what has to be a huge situation for him to get his head around. He's being pushed like none of us ever were.'

'He volunteered,' Pike said. 'He didn't come in thinking it would be easy, and you've been the hardest on him from the beginning.'

She moved until they stood nose to nose, and he inhaled the coffee on her breath, the clean, soapy morning smell of her, and beneath that the spicy dark scent of the woman herself, a scent with which he, maybe more than anyone else at Mount Vegas, was familiar. She grabbed him by the hair and pulled him down until his forehead was practically against hers. He sucked a tight breath at the prickle of pain along his scalp. 'I don't appreciate being told what I already know, even if I owed you an explanation, which I don't. We drop it here, Pike, unless you want me to take it out on your ass in the dungeon, and trust me, as angry as I am at the moment, you really don't want that. But if you ever, *ever* undermine my authority again, I will see you below decks, and I promise the punishment'll be hard and long.' Her voice was little more than a snarl. 'Do I make myself clear?'

'Quite clear, mistress,' he said, stepping back, his eyes lowered, his heart hammering in his chest. He clasped his hands in front of his burgeoning erection. Elsa had never threatened him with punishment for any of his transgressions. She avoided the dungeon like the plague most of the time. And as much as she hated being the submissive in any dungeon act, she absolutely refused to play the dominant, no matter if it meant postponing the act. In spite of her discomfort surrounding the dungeon, Pike couldn't keep the thought from affecting his cock. He wasn't sure he'd survive

Elsa in the dungeon on the other side of the crop, but he was sure it would be an exquisite way to die.

'And don't call me mistress.' With hands that were uncharacteristically shaky, she straightened the jacket of her light linen suit and began to pace again. 'Pike, you're my friend, you've always been my friend, and I need you to be that whatever happens. I'm sorry if that blurs the lines of authority at times. Most of the time that blurring is a natural part of what makes our relationship work, but last night wasn't one of those times. I've Skyped with Rita and I know you had no choice in her request to watch Nick and Deb. Certainly there was nothing to be anything but proud of in what she saw, but going over my head with Nick Chase was way out of line. We're treading dangerous waters with him fulfilling Tanya's contract anyway, and I need my team to support me in this.'

'Rita Holly was all right with it.' Pike said.

'Yes, but she just as easily could have been against it.'

And then Pike opened his big mouth again. 'Elsa, I'm sorry. You can send my ass off to the dungeon and put my cock in a chastity belt for the next month if you want, but I don't think you're seeing too clearly where Nick Chase is concerned.'

She turned on him. 'What the hell is that supposed to mean?'

'Chase isn't a danger to Mount Vegas. In fact, I can't see him being anything but good for the Mount in general, and I think Rita's right, you should recruit him. But he is a danger, Elsa. He's a danger to your heart.'

'That's ridiculous, Pike. What happened last night after the act was just –'

They were interrupted by a soft knock on the door that caused it to swing open wide, and there stood Nick Chase.

'I'm sorry,' he said, looking from one of them to the other. 'I guess it wasn't latched. I'll come back later.'

'It's all right, Nick.' Elsa stepped back. 'Pike was just leaving.'

The tension in the room was so thick Nick could have sliced it with his Victorinox. Pike gave him a friendly slap on the back as he left, and Elsa motioned him in.

'How much did you hear?' she said, grabbing her bag and nodding toward the door again.

'Only the bit about me being a danger to your heart. I heard that bit.'

'Pike has a big mouth, and he often engages it before he engages his brain. You have the limo?'

'It's down in the parking garage, just like you asked.' Elsa had texted him earlier and asked if he had an extra limo, and if he could drive it in. He thought it a strange request, but then it was Mount Vegas, and it was nowhere near the strangest request he'd ever had.

Neither of them spoke until they were in the elevator, and then Nick said, 'Those were the Mount Vegas offices, I presume?'

'Yup. Well, some of them. We're sort of spread out all over town. I'll give you the grand tour later,' Elsa said. Then she added, 'So, did you have a good time with Tanya last night?'

He gave her a quick glance, but she didn't return it. She only stood facing the front, the look on her face neutral. 'It was OK,' he replied.

She raised an eyebrow. 'Just OK? That's hardly like Tanya – especially not a grateful Tanya.'

'Do you want a blow by blow?' he asked.

'Not in the elevator, Mr Chase.' She batted thick eyelashes at him and offered a demure smile. 'You might embarrass me.'

'Elsa –' he laid his hands on her shoulders and turned

her to face him '– I was with Tanya because you all but shoved me at her, and then she wouldn't take no for an answer.' He released her and they both quickly turned to face the door as it opened. Then he spoke from between his teeth as they navigated the crowd of people waiting to get inside. 'I would have rather been with you.' As they shoved through the crowd, he offered her a quick smile. 'But then I can see how you might have felt it better for us not to be together, what with me being a danger to your heart and all.'

'Fuck you, Nick Chase,' she said, but the corners of her mouth twitched slightly with the threatening smile.

'Any time, Elsa Crane, any time. In fact, the back seat of the limo is very roomy.'

She slipped her arm through his. 'I'm counting on it. I have a huge event for some VIPs coming up in a few weeks, and I need to put cameras in a limo. I'm working up a scene coming from The Wedding Chapel to the Cosmopolitan. It doesn't have to be time specific. If the limo scene is hot enough, I'm sure Mrs Keyser won't mind if we linger there while the driver does a few laps around the city.'

Nick stopped in front of the Lincoln Town Car. 'I have a bigger one if it'll help,' he said.

She walked around it and ran a palm along the door handle. 'No, it's just for the happy newlyweds, so I want to create a cosy feeling.' She nodded to the back door, and he unlocked it.

He admired a view of her lovely rounded backside and those delicious long legs as she slid across the seat and over against the far door. He didn't wait for an invite but slid right on in next to her. 'So tell me about this fantasy my limo will star in, and why my limo rather than one of the Mount Vegas limos.

'Mount Vegas limos are leased, as are the drivers, and we usually don't involve them in our work.'

'But mine belong to an employee.'

'Yours belong to you,' she said, smiling over at him, stroking the leather seat in between them in a way he wished she'd stroke him. 'That means not only can you drive them but you can participate in the act if need be. Plus I figured you wouldn't mind someone having sex in the back.'

He held her gaze. 'It's Vegas, Elsa. You'd be hard pressed to find a limo driver who hasn't had couples doing the nasty in the back seat. Most tourists think sex in the back of a limo is mandatory, a part of the Vegas experience. So what else?'

She sucked her bottom lip. 'Well, we're calling the fantasy *The Billionaire Buys a Virgin Bride*, and it's the most complicated thing we've ever done, though not so complex as far as the kink goes, just to put together.'

He blinked. 'Seriously? *The Billionaire Buys a Virgin Bride*?'

She shrugged. 'We get all kinds, Nick. We get all kinds. You'll see after you've been here a while.'

'So how does it go?' he asked, laying his hand on the seat next to hers.

'Well, there's a bit of feeling up at The Wedding Chapel. We're still arranging that. You know, the billionaire giving a grope beneath the taffeta to make sure he got what he paid for and then maybe letting his innocent bride feel the vigour of his manhood.' She lowered her voice, squared her shoulders, and made a cock-stroking motion above her groin that left him chuckling.

'So far I like it,' he said.

'After they say their "I dos", they're off in the limo with a little grope and play and the nervous bride begging her horny hubby to be gentle with her, but loving it oh so much when he touches her –' she nodded down to her crotch and offered him a fake shy look as

99

she nibbled her lip '– down there.' Fake or not, it got his cock's attention. She continued. 'Then it's off to the Cosmopolitan for the deflowering. The plot's simple enough, but the changes in location complicate things.'

'And who'll you get to play the newlyweds?'

'We're lucky enough to have a couple coming in from London who have agreed to do it for us. They're from the London branch of The Mount.'

Nick scooted closer. 'Didn't know there was more than one.'

'There is,' she said. 'And these two are even more VIP than Mrs Keyser, so she'll get a double treat, and so will the rest of us.'

'So what do you think?' He scooted still closer and laid his hand on her thigh. 'Will the couple have room for a proper grope in my humble limo? Shall we find out?' Before she had a chance to respond, he leant in and took her mouth. She gave only the slightest moan of protest accompanied by the smallest attempt to squirm away before she found herself up tight against the door. Then she slipped her arms around his neck and pulled him in closer.

'Mmm.' She spoke against his lips with a flick of her tongue. 'I think the happy couple will enjoy groping in your limo just fine, Nick.'

'Well, there will be all that taffeta to contend with,' he said. She gave a little yelp of surprise as he lifted her to straddle his lap. With hands at her hips, he rucked up her linen skirt until her muscular thighs rested on either side of his. He got just a glimpse of pale panties before she shifted her hips and raked her whole silk-covered crotch against his. He gasped and she let out a low chuckle.

'Thought so,' she said. 'Thought I could see some serious swelling in the groinal area there, Mr Chase.'

'And you're not easing it any doing that,' he said,

shifting his arse into the dark leather and up to meet her raking.

'Who said I was trying to ease it?' She found a rhythm that was so getting him there. Then, with her gaze locked on him, she opened the buttons at the front of her top until the lace of a matching silk bra peeked from the breach. With a catch he didn't notice until it was undone, she opened the front of the bra and eased the cups apart till he could see the rounded swell of cleavage and the tightened bud of nipple and areola. 'You like my tits, don't you, Nick?' she said.

'What? Is that a trick question?'

Still holding his gaze, she took him by the wrists, then bathed each palm with her very agile, very warm tongue, lingering to fellate several of his fingers in a way his empathetic cock totally appreciated before she guided his hands to her breasts. Her nipples puckered against his wet palms and she nibbled her lip and shivered at his cupping. 'Mmm, you feel that right down to your cock, don't you, Mr Chase?' And Christ if she didn't do some sort of grip and squeeze with her girlie muscles that felt like her pussy was kissing along the length of his cock. Astoundingly, he could feel those nibbles clear through her panties and his jeans.

The rocking and shifting intensified; her tongue did the tango with his. Reluctantly, he slid his hands away from her breasts and she moaned a protest into his mouth that quickly became a purr of pleasure as he cupped his hands under her tight arse, squeezing and kneading. Then he squirmed and shoved until he was lying in the seat on top of her, wriggling for position between her eagerly accommodating legs.

'Oh God, Nick, don't stop,' she breathed against his neck, wrapping her legs around his waist. With each shift and thrust his still-clothed cock shoved the gusset of her panties deeper into the valley of her that swelled

101

and pouted and opened, humid and undulating along his length.

He lowered his mouth to take her nipples in turn, and she fisted a tight hand in his hair to hold him to her breasts, as if he would go anywhere, as if he would want to be anywhere other than closer to Elsa Crane.

'Your butt,' he whispered, grinding particularly hard against her. 'Is it still sore?'

'Almost healed,' she said, arching up to meet his thrust. 'And anyway, who cares? What you're doing definitely takes my mind off a sore butt.'

She bit back the last word, and her whole body trembled with orgasm.

'Was that good?' he whispered, feeling his cock surge in her pleasure. 'Did you like that?'

'Mmm,' she managed, nodding her head in a wild cascade of auburn hair.

'I have a condom,' he whispered when she stopped trembling.

'Other than that stiff, raking cock of yours, I don't care what you have, just keep doing what you're doing and let's see what happens.'

He could feel her orgasm, wet against the front of his jeans. His cock jerked and strained and his balls felt like they were full of hot lead. The wetness of her panties pressed the silk against her pussy, intimating the shape of her with each undulation, driving it along the press of his jeans against his heft and creating delicious friction.

Elsa wriggled and rolled until they both nearly ended up on the floor in a wave of giggles before she righted herself and gained the upper position. 'And now, Nick,' she gasped. 'I'm gonna return the favour and make you come in your pants.'

'Elsa, no. Elsa …' She slid down along the length of him so hard and so tight that he feared his jeans would combust from the friction, and then there was no thinking, there was not even any breathing. He would come in his pants. He would come in his pants for Elsa Crane and he would be fucking pleased to do it. Which was just as well because he was way past the tipping point, and Elsa knew it.

She ravaged his mouth and thumbed his nipples. 'I want you to come now, Nick. I want to feel you spurt clear through your jeans. I want to feel your heat wetting me, burning me up.'

And how could he refuse? The limo shook beneath him as he unloaded in his jeans with Elsa squirming out another orgasm against his crotch. And God, they smelled great together! His jizz spiked with Elsa Crane's salty sweet heat would have made the best perfumers drool. Then she fell forward on top of him with a heavy sigh.

When Nick could engage his brain enough to remember how to speak, he laughed. 'Jesus, woman, if we have this much fun without taking our clothes off, I can't wait to get you naked.'

'Sadly, that's not going to happen today,' Elsa said. 'You have training, and Beetle won't be happy if you're late. You can hardly go like that though.' She eyeballed his wet crotch. Even in the just-shot-his-wad state, it made his cock surge. 'I'll have Pike come get you and show you where the showers are. I'll have him bring you some jeans too. You two are close to the same size, I'd guess.'

She was already on her BlackBerry. Once she had called her second in command, she found a packet of tissues in her bag and cleaned herself as though it didn't bother her at all, him watching. Maybe it didn't bother her, but it made him want to help her out, made him want to say fuck the training and take Elsa again while she was still wet and ready, and he was getting that way fast.

Chapter Ten

Nick was given instructions to go to the office next to Elsa's. As he walked by the suite where he'd overheard Pike tell Elsa that her heart was in danger, his own heart skipped a beat, and he found himself wanting to make a detour. His cock liked the idea at least as much as his heart did. He imagined having Elsa on the top of her big oak desk, having her on the floor and on the sofa, and … well, having her just about everywhere; anywhere would do.

But he wasn't invited to her suite. Instead, he stopped in front of the one next to it and knocked timidly. Under different circumstances, he would be excited to meet with someone as quirky and sexy as Beetle – suspecting, as he did, that fucking would probably be involved at some point. But the fact that Elsa might be in the room next door made it difficult to think of anything else. And then the door opened and, as they seemed to do on a regular basis at Mount Vegas, things took a turn toward the unexpected.

The woman who greeted him was dressed in a dowdy knee-length grey skirt and matching jacket. She could have been dressed for the role of Mary Poppins or as a stereotypical schoolmarm about to smack his hands with her ruler. Her strawberry blonde hair was scraped up off her neck and held in place by a large, black comb. Her eyes were half hidden behind horn-rimmed glasses. In spite of the frump, Nick could see that the woman beneath was no slouch.

'Mr Chase,' she said, 'Ms Beetle is waiting for you. If you'll follow me through, please.' She led him into a space done up as an old-fashioned schoolroom complete with half a dozen desks and a chalkboard. The teacher's desk at the front was empty.

'Take a seat.' The woman pointed to a place front and centre. 'I'm Miss Kandi. I'll be your teacher for today under the supervision of Principal Beetle.'

Just then, the door burst open, and Beetle marched in dressed in a black pleated skirt short enough to reveal the tops of her stockings where the garter belt held them in place. She wore no blouse beneath her tailored black jacket. In one hand, she carried a highly polished red apple, which she sat on the corner of the teacher's desk.

'Mr Chase.' She nodded a greeting to Nick. 'Miss Kandi.' But the teacher didn't get a curt nod. Instead, she got a full-on tongue-kiss and a grope of her tit that left Nick with a bulge in his jeans. His lesson had begun. 'Do take off your jacket, Miss Kandi,' Beetle instructed. 'This is Vegas, and it's always hot.'

The woman did as she was told, to reveal a thin white blouse over a black lace bra. Beetle removed her own jacket, which covered a tightly laced corset that barely contained the bulge of her breasts.

'And now, Mr Chase,' Beetle said, looking him up and down, 'it's my task to see to your education. And while you're under the tutelage of Miss Kandi and me, you'll behave like a proper student, speak when spoken to, answer all questions, pay attention in class and learn the lesson set before you, or face the consequences. Are we clear?'

She had to be kidding, he thought. Surely she had to be kidding.

'Are we clear, Mr Chase?' She sat on the front of the

desk and crossed her legs so that he got the full view of her bare pussy before she settled.

'Yes, ma'am. We're clear.'

'Good. If you'll look around, you'll notice that this isn't your typical schoolroom. This is a classroom designed to teach the Mount Vegas novice all he or she will need to know to perform to the tastes of a voyeur, no matter what those tastes might be. Your job, Mr Chase, will be to convince even the most demanding of our clients that you're exactly what they asked for, that you know exactly what they fantasise about because you fantasise about it too.' She took a long wooden pointer from the top of the desk and ran it through her hands. 'You proved that you possess some skills when you performed last night with Deb. But that was an easy task, Mr Chase. This room's the place where you'll learn to cope with the more difficult fantasies, and Miss Kandi and I are here to assist you in the learning process.' For a moment she studied him, stroking the pointer along her palm. 'You look hot, Mr Chase. But then you should be, since you just got a peek at my pussy.' An unwelcome blush crawled up his throat and over his cheeks. Jesus, after last night, he'd figured nothing would ever make him blush again. 'You'd better get used to it, because you're on the crash course and you'll be seeing a lot of pussy and cock in the next two months.' She went on with her explanation. 'This room's one of the non-hotel set-ups that Mount Vegas has throughout the city. As you can imagine, naughty students and strict teachers are a very popular fantasy. This room's well equipped with cameras for when a teacher needs to punish a student, or the principal needs to check up on a teacher.'

With that, she extended the pointer until the tip caught the hem of Miss Kandi's skirt. And Jesus, if the dowdy little teacher didn't blush and try to shove away like no one had ever done such a shocking thing to her.

106

The more she tried to pull away, the more Principal Beetle rucked up the front of her skirt until Nick would have had to close his eyes not to see the tightly trimmed curls of her pussy, as strawberry blonde as her knotted hair.

'And now show me, Mr Chase,' Beetle instructed. 'Show me what a misbehaving schoolboy would do at this point.'

Nick reacted without thinking, fumbling with the pen he had in his pocket as though he were about to take notes, then dropping it on the floor. He scrambled to his knees to pick it up, just as Miss Kandi shifted her stance and gave him a view of her heavily pouting snatch. God, could he actually catch a little whiff of horny pussy? As he reached for the pen, *whack*! Beetle brought the wooden heft of the pointer down hard across his jeaned arse.

'Sonovabi –' Nick swallowed back his words. His cock jerked in his jeans as he shoved his way to his feet.

'Oh you dirty, dirty boy.' Miss Kandi's voice was high-pitched and breathless, and the blush made her skin glow like well-fired porcelain. 'Principal Beetle, did you see what this naughty boy did? He looked up my dress …' Her lip quivered. 'He looked at my –' She dug in her pocket for a lace handkerchief to wipe her brow.

Nick now stood at the side of his desk, hands clasped in front of his bulge, head bowed in shame. He knew this fantasy.

'Is that true, Mr Chase? Did you look at Miss Kandi's lady bits?'

'Yes, ma'am,' he said, joining Ms Kandi with a hard blush in spite of the fact that this was all a game.

Beetle moved closer to him. 'It appears you liked what you saw.' She gave his obvious erection a hard stroke through his jeans, and he gasped. 'Since you've admitted to being a filthy boy, all that's left is the punishment filthy boys get.'

He didn't like the sound of that. She took him by the arm and pulled him forward to the end of the teacher's desk. There she unbuckled his belt, pulled it free from the waistband and handed it to Miss Kandi. Then she went to work on his fly.

Miss Kandi doubled his belt in half and ran the leather of it over the palm of her hand. All the while her eyes were locked on his crotch. And suddenly he twigged.

'Wait a minute. Are you going to spank me? Elsa said there'd be no spanking. Elsa said –'

'Elsa's not here.' Principal Beetle yanked his jeans and boxers down until his cock bounced free and his arse was exposed. Then she grabbed his balls and held them just tight enough to get his full attention. 'You can take your punishment and learn your lesson or you can walk out that door and not come back. All up to you, Mr Chase. You're of no use to us if you can't take a little pain when the need arises. Your fuck stick works just fine; excellent, in fact.' She gave his cock a fisted stroke. 'But every man has a cock, and every man knows how to use it for his pleasure. Maybe if he's good, he knows how to use it for someone else's pleasure. Those are just the first steps at Mount Vegas.' She held his gaze with dark, hard eyes. 'Now do you want to learn the lesson or do you want to go drive your limo and jerk yourself off?'

His pulse felt like it would explode right through his throat, and God, his dick couldn't get harder if it had to. And here he was about to get his arse beat with his own belt. What the fuck was the matter with him? And yet he sucked a deep breath and bent over the end of the desk, arse up. Beetle stretched his arms out along the battered wood surface until his hands could grip the other end above his head.

'Good boy,' she said, moving to stand beside him.

'Good boy,' she whispered against his ear, gently stroking his hair. 'Remember, people are watching you get what you know you deserve.' Then she turned and nodded to Miss Kandi, who stood behind him, holding the looped belt like someone who knew exactly what the hell she was doing.

Nick gritted his teeth and held his breath as the first blow cracked like a bullet and sent fire through his right arse check. His mind exploded in every curse word he knew – squared. Anger and frustration flashed red hot behind his closed eyes as the second smack scorched his other buttock, and he couldn't hold back a harsh grunt.

'Go easy on him, Miss Kandi,' Beetle said. 'His tight little bottom's never had the belt before.' And fuck if the woman didn't bend and kiss each arse cheek in turn. Then she spread his buttocks apart and ran her warm wet tongue up from the base of his balls all the way to his arsehole, and his cock jerked and strained in its tight bind against the desk. Before he could focus too much on what Miss Kandi was doing, Beetle curled a rough hand in his hair and jerked his head up. 'Look at me when you're being punished, Mr Chase. I want to see the look on your face while Miss Kandi spanks your bottom until you squirm.' She bent and gave him a heated tongue kiss, which he half returned, half swallowed. Then she said, 'You were very naughty looking up Miss Kandi's dress to see her little pussy, weren't you?'

'Yes, Ms Beetle.' His words grated against his throat and the world before his eyes had taken on shades of angry red.

'Good boy,' she said again. Then she nodded to Miss Kandi and Nick braced himself for the next blow, which burned over his butt like fire. He bit his lip to keep from cursing.

'Tell me, Mr Chase, did you like Miss Kandi's pussy? Tell me the truth or you'll get it harder.'

'Yes, Ms Beetle! I liked Miss Kandi's pussy.'

Another smack landed hard and crisp across his burning arse, and he understood completely why Elsa was angry with Pike. But before he could let his anger surge, Miss Kandi's hot little tongue went back to work on his butt, this time snaking in to tease his arsehole while her free hand wriggled between his legs to cup his balls. For a second, he was certain he'd shoot his wad against the side of the desk, and as he shifted into shallow breathing mode, his out of focus gaze locked on Beetle's face, the next blow came and then the next.

'Stop,' Beetle commanded. 'I think you might be enjoying Mr Chase's punishment just a little too much, Miss Kandi. Come here.' The teacher obeyed.

Beetle directed her to stand behind the desk where the chair would have been. Miss Kandi's face was flushed and her breathing was at least as hard as Nick's. 'Oh dear,' Beetle said, then she jerked open the front of the woman's white shirt and gave her tits a kneading. 'Your nipples are like bullet points, Miss Kandi. Are you having naughty thoughts about the spanking of Mr Chase's bare bottom?'

The teacher only responded with a whimper.

'Mr Chase,' Beetle addressed him. 'Would you mind running a hand up under Miss Kandi's skirt and telling me if her little pussy's wet?'

Nick's brain struggled to register what was being asked of him until Beetle reached around and lifted the woman's skirt so that he could just make out the strawberry blonde thatch against her mons. 'Do it,' Beetle commanded.

With a hand that no longer seemed quite like his own, Nick manoeuvred his fingers over the teacher's soft, tight curls and wriggled down to where her clit strained from under its hood. She moaned and bit her lip. A little more probing and he slid two fingers between her swollen folds into the hot, slippery flood of her juices.

'Well?' Beetle demanded. 'Is she wet?'

'Yes, Ms Beetle. Her pussy's very wet.' With Miss Kandi close enough that he could smell her arousal, Nick was once again breathing shallowly.

'Let me see.' Beetle slapped his hand away with a sharp whack of the pointer, then she shoved the tip of it in between the teacher's pussy lips. The woman whimpered and shivered. Nick didn't know how much more shallow breathing he could manage before the inevitable happened.

'Get up!' Beetle commanded, and Nick practically fell off the desk, cupping his cock protectively.

With one raking of her fingers, Beetle pulled the comb from Miss Kandi's hair, and it fell loose in a waterfall of rose gold, which Beetle curled around her hand. She half dragged, half shoved the woman to the end of the desk that Nick had occupied. 'Face up,' she ordered, when the teacher hoiked her skirt to assume the position. 'I'll be using your mouth.'

Miss Kandi, now whimpering slightly, did as she was told. She planted the soft pillows of her arse on the desk, wriggling and shifting until her feet, still in their plain black pumps, sat flat on the desk top, her hips tilting to give Nick a magnificent view of her sopping slit.

'Good,' Beetle said. 'Now, lie back and let Mr Chase use your wet cunny before his cock explodes.'

It was insane. It was crazy, and Nick would have never believed it of himself, but he was buried to the hilt in tight, slick pussy before Miss Kandi could even lie back on the desk. His arse burnt like fire and he didn't care; in fact, it was strange that it somehow added to the powerful need surging through him. If he hadn't been right on the edge before, he certainly was when Beetle crawled onto the desk, hiked her skirt, and squatted onto Miss Kandi's mouth. She mewled like a kitten, grabbed Beetle's arse, and

111

began to eat like a starving woman.

'You see, Mr Chase,' Beetle said, shoving the ruined front of Miss Kandi's blouse aside and clawing at the bra until the woman's tits burst over the top and into her hands. 'Sometimes lessons can be painful to learn, but if you stick to it and take your punishment when you've earned it, you get your reward in the end.'

It was hard to hear her over the whimpers and moans of Miss Kandi, whose grip was showing him no mercy. Beetle's last words barely penetrated the testosterone haze in which he found himself, with his balls bouncing, his punished arse burning, and his cock thrusting deep into tight wet pussy. How long it lasted, he couldn't have guessed, but he was way beyond going for endurance this time. He emptied his balls long and hard into Miss Kandi's tight cunt just as she thrashed out her orgasm and Beetle came all over her face. Thus endeth the lesson.

As the three collapsed onto the desk in gasps and groans, Elsa shut off the monitor on which she'd been observing the act and stared into space. She was still breathing hard herself. Her pussy was still trembling with aftershocks, and her head was still buzzing with endorphins from another Nick Chase-induced orgasm. Christ, the man had skills! It wasn't just that he knew what to do with his cock, that was a given. But when he entered a fantasy, even one staged for training purposes, he did so as though it were real, and because of that there was serious chemistry. The man was a natural. She hadn't expected Beetle to jump right in at the deep end, especially when they all knew how nervous Nick was about spanking, but he had acquitted himself very well. Again. She wished like hell she could be in on the aftercare so she could tend his wounded bottom, comfort him, tell him how well he was doing.

God, she must be getting soft. Beetle was exactly right: being able to get it up and hold a wad was only the very basics of what happened at Mount Vegas, and if Nick Chase couldn't endure a little pain, then he really didn't belong here. OK, so sometimes they went weeks without a fantasy that involved pain, but sometimes every single fantasy involved spanking or nipple clamps or bondage or some form of BDSM that would make a novice like Nick run for cover. But he hadn't. He hadn't run for cover. And she knew Kandi well enough to know she could seriously wield a belt or a cane or anything else that needed wielding.

Elsa had had multiples watching the schoolroom scene. It had been a real voyeuristic experience for her. She'd imagined herself right there in Kandi's place, spanking and teasing and kissing that lovely arse of Nick's until he could barely hold his load. Then she imagined spreading her legs and letting him fuck her. Jesus, she'd wanted to be in Kandi's shoes! But Elsa knew that Kandi, even with her strong arm, was much more gentle than she herself would ever be. And now she could see Nick's potential, now it was clear he could be a real asset to Mount Vegas, she didn't want to push too far too fast. And yet, at the same time, she couldn't keep from wondering just how far she could push him. And if he were ever truly pushed to the limits … Well, her fantasies in that direction would just have to remain fantasies, wouldn't they? Still, in spite of what she knew, in spite of the reasons why it was bad idea, God, she wanted to spend some rough time with Nick Chase. The little quiver behind her breastbone told her that he might, just might be up for it, and that frightened her even as it intrigued her.

Once Miss Kandi had gently massaged his stinging arse with lotion, and Beetle had offered him a cold bottle of water to drink, the two women had taken him through an array of sex toys that were displayed on work benches lining the wall in the classroom – from nipple clamps to anal beads and everything in between. Some of these toys they demonstrated on each other, others they just explained. After his rough initiation into the classroom, they were fairly gentle on him. Kandi, he learned, had just got back from a two-week vacation in France, which lessened the blow of Tanya's loss.

'Pike'll probably give you the tour of the dungeon tomorrow,' Beetle said, hefting a dildo that reminded him irresistibly of Horse. 'You've had enough for one day.' She gave him a teasing quirk of a smile. 'Don't look so frightened. You won't be asked to sub for Pike. But if you're going to replace Tanya then you need to be familiar with what goes on in his domain. We're not all good at every aspect of what Mount Vegas does, but we need to know what everyone else is up to because we all participate in putting together the fantasies and making them go well for the clients.'

She looked down at her watch. 'Pagan's manning the control room this evening. You'll be sitting in with him to see how we operate the voyeurs' side of things. Kandi and I are both performing, so let's grab a quick bite before it all happens. I'm starving. You up for Mexican, Nick?'

Chapter Eleven

Two nights, several more intensive sessions in the schoolroom, and an expensive haircut later, and Nick was back in wardrobe. Elsa stood next to him, dressed in the black trousers, white shirt, and tie of a dealer, and even in that she looked sexy enough to make his mouth water. Kandi wore the micro-mini flip skirt and bustier of a cocktail waitress and, dressed smart casual, he would play a middle-class businessman relaxing in the casino after a busy day. The play at the blackjack table was to end in a bet that would involve Kandi and Nick having sex in the suite of their client while he watched and orchestrated events.

'Alex Fenton will be slumming, of course,' Elsa said to Nick as Minnie put the final touches on her hair, which she wore pinned up with a tortoiseshell comb. 'He finds the rich and famous boring, finds it more interesting to see how the other half lives. He pays a great deal more for his fantasy because he wants to be in the room with the actors. He's one of only three people who get that privilege. Of course, there's a look-but-don't-touch policy, but that suits him just fine.' She turned to straighten Nick's collar. 'He won't ask you to do anything too off the wall: nothing more than a little light bondage – maybe tying Kandi to the bed, that sort of thing. Mostly he gets off on watching and calling the shots. I know you're up for it, Nick, or I wouldn't have put you in the role. But if you have problems, Kandi'll help you through.'

'I wish it were you,' he said. 'I'd feel a lot more comfortable with you.'

'Well it's not, and anyway, Fenton and I, we … don't get along very well.'

'Should I be jealous?'

'Stupid question. You work for Mount Vegas. You should never be jealous.'

Strangely, he wasn't nervous about the act. He'd do what he always did. He'd do it for Elsa. And him fucking Kandi, that was fine. He could do it. He'd done it before. That was Mr Fenton's fantasy. But once it was over, once he'd done his best to get Elsa all wet and squirming, vicariously, he had every intention of making sure he got way more from her than a winning hand at blackjack.

Most of what he knew about blackjack came from playing 21 with his aunt when he was a kid. She had been a dealer for a while. But he listened quietly while Elsa reminded him of the rules, telling him just to stand next to Fenton and act natural while the man called the shots. Elsa assured him that even at the blackjack table, Fenton would manipulate until he was in total control, manipulate for his maximum viewing pleasure. That was a part of the game he loved to play.

Elsa and Kandi left for the casino ahead of Nick. He knew by the time he arrived, Fenton would already be playing.

Elsa had barely got her table set up and finished last-minute mic and camera checks when Fenton sauntered in like he owned the place, and he very well could have, she thought.

'So lovely to see you again, Elsa.' Though he never touched her, there was always something that felt

116

physical in the way he observed people. 'You get more beautiful, more intriguing every time I see you.'

Her smile was nothing more than a spastic jerk of muscles at the corners of her mouth. She'd learned not to trust the man too far.

'Oh darling, surely you're not still mad at me for last time, are you?' He bought $100 worth of chips, and she could feel him looking her up and down and she sorted them out.

'I'm always mad at you, Fenton. That's why I'm dealing tonight, and I wouldn't even be doing that if my team wasn't all busy.'

His eyes sparkled. 'And if I hadn't insisted that you play with me.'

She ignored his remark and dealt his hand.

When he received an ace and a jack right out of the shoot, he laughed out loud. 'My, my, my, looks like it's going to be a lucky night. I'm so looking forward to it, Elsa.'

Just then Nick walked in. Elsa felt the little catch of her breath at the sight of him, at the realisation that she could have picked him out in a crowd anywhere. He came to the table, offered a smile and bought $100 worth of chips.

As he gave their voyeur a surreptitious once-over, Elsa did the same to him. Damn, the man looked good! Fenton wasn't a bad looking man – in fact, he was quite attractive, but in spite of his wealthy patina that, even at its most subtle, screamed to be noticed, it was Nick Chase she couldn't keep her eyes off. And that wasn't supposed to happen. He worked for her; he was temporary help, nothing more. She was about to deal the first hand when Kandi sidled up to the table with an empty drink tray.

'What can I get you two?'

Fenton didn't wait for Nick's response. 'Here's what I

want you to do, gorgeous.' He laid a crisp $100 bill on her tray. 'I want you to bring me and my friend here –' he nodded to Nick '– lots of nice, wet drinks and some good luck. You keep the drinks and the luck coming and I'll make sure there are plenty more of these for your efforts.' He nodded to the money.

'Of course, Mr …'

'Just call me Fenton. I'll have a Heineken and my friend here … what's your name?'

'Nick. Gin and tonic for me, please.'

'You heard Nick,' Fenton said with a flirty smile that Kandi returned in kind.

'Don't you worry, Fenton, I'll take real good care of you both.' As she walked away, Fenton rubbed his hands together and gave Elsa the onceover like she was way more than just the dealer. Of course, he loved nothing as much as wrong-footing her. He'd been doing it for a while now. She just smiled, but Nick gave him a look that could have scorched nails. Jesus, just what she needed: the unpredictable Fenton and a jealous Nick.

'All right, Fenton said, 'shall we see if we can win some money from this lovely lady?'

When Kandi returned with their drinks, Nick had just won on double-down with a bust for both Fenton and Elsa. 'You're just in time to help Nick celebrate, sweetheart,' Fenton told her, as Kandi leant over to set Nick's drink down. 'That's his third winning hand since you've been gone, and I think that deserves a congratulatory kiss, don't you?'

She blushed slightly and gave Nick a peck on the cheek.

'Oh, come on now, sweetheart. That's the kind of kiss you might give Nick's grandmother. You can do better than that.' He slipped another $100 bill onto her tray and winked at Nick.

'Well, if he really wants me to …' she said. Her

cheeks were flushed and Elsa could see her pulse hammering just below her ear as she held Nick's gaze for confirmation.

'Of course he wants you to. Unless he's gay. You're not gay, are you, Nick?'

'Nope. Not gay.'

'There, you see.' Fenton nodded to Nick, who offered his best embarrassed chuckle, which Elsa figured wasn't too hard for him to manage under the circumstances. When Kandi sat her tray down and leant in for a kiss, Nick pulled her close and dipped her low, resulting in a little squeal that was quickly subsumed in a low purr as Nick gave her a good, tonsil-deep tongue ravishing, and the people at the next table cheered and clapped. When he released her she came up with a hand on her chest and a breathless laugh. 'Wow! Nick, I think I should give *you* the tip.'

Show-off, Elsa thought, but she liked it and she could tell Fenton did too.

'You may get to before the night's over, dear,' Fenton said. 'Because I don't intend to let him keep winning, so he may need to rely on that magical tongue of his.' As Elsa dealt the cards, he addressed her. 'Technically, that should have been you kissing Nick, honey. After all you lost the most, didn't you?'

Elsa offered a tight-lipped smile and dealt. The devious fucker was already manipulating to get what he wanted, and that always made her nervous. The next few hands were pretty much a draw between Fenton, Nick, and the dealer. Elsa kept dealing and smiling, ignoring the way both men looked at her like she was lunch and they were starving. She'd just won a hand when Kandi came back to check on them.

Fenton ordered another beer and nodded to Elsa. 'Dealer just won, sweetheart, and what a dealer she is. I think you should give her a kiss.' And she did! She walked right up to Elsa and laid one on her. Elsa had to at least pretend to be a professional, so she didn't give Kandi the Nick Chase treatment, but there was enough tongue and enough groping to make sure Nick's cock paid attention – poor behaviour on her part, Elsa was sure, but she just couldn't help herself.

And, of course, Fenton didn't miss it. 'Nice one, darlin', nice one. Now I need you to do me another favour, sweet cheeks,' he said, winking at Kandi.

'Anything,' she replied with a bright smile.

'You see, hon, I think our friend Nick here enjoyed that kiss you just gave our lovely dealer maybe even more than you two did.' He gave a glance under the edge of the table. 'Can you check it out for me?'

When Kandi blushed hard and looked around the casino, Fenton said, 'Don't worry, darlin', I won't tell anyone, and –' he peeled off another $100 and waved it at her '– I'll make it worth your while.'

She moved to stand next to Nick and cautiously ran her hand down beneath the table. 'Oh, don't be so nervous, hon. He won't bite, will you, Nick?'

'Not unless she wants me to.' Nick caught his breath and sucked his teeth as Kandi's hand came to rest against the bulge at his fly.

'Well?'

She giggled. 'I think you're right, Fenton. I think he did enjoy it.' She gave him a stroke, and he gave a little grunt. And Fenton laughed.

'She's a feisty one, isn't she, Nick?'

'Can't say I don't like it though.' Nick stood still as she gave him a good groping through his chinos.

'I think our dealer likes it too.' Fenton nodded to Elsa's breasts. 'Or maybe the air conditioning's just a little too cool for her.'

Elsa let the unplanned blush slide up her cheeks. She wasn't supposed to be more than a prop in this little

120

scenario, but there was no disguising the painful swell of her nipples.

'Now then, darlin',' Fenton said to Kandi, 'why don't you go off and get our drinks, and think of some more creative ways to reward our next winner.'

'I'm not sure who actually won that hand,' Elsa said, dealing the cards.

'Well, the truth is, I like a good win-win scenario,' Fenton said. 'It's always a pleasure to see someone well satisfied.'

This time, Kandi wasn't gone very long, and she returned just in time to catch Fenton doing very well for himself with a split, beating the dealer while Nick went bust.

'Oooh, looks like you're the winner this time, Fenton.' She sat the drinks and the tray down. 'What would you like?'

'That depends,' he said with a blinding smile, 'on just how much of a wild and crazy girl you are, hon.' He peeled off a couple more hundred-dollar bills from his money clip.

Kandi's eyes were as big as the chips. Her pulse leapt against her throat and her breasts rose and fell double-time in their excited press against her bustier. 'What exactly do you have in mind?'

'Well the way I view it, sweet cheeks, is not so much as I won but Nick here lost, and since you've been treating him pretty damn fine so far, I think it might just be time for him to return the favour. What do you say, Nick?'

'Fair's fair,' Nick replied.

Elsa's heart raced as she wondered what Fenton had up his sleeve now.

He downed the rest of his beer and rubbed his hands together. 'I'm very good at observing the signs, sweetheart. You've heated up our lovely dealer, and certainly you've done a damn fine job raising Nick's temperature. And me, well …' He chuckled. 'I'm stiff just thinking about all the fun we've been having. That being the case –' he leant closer to her until Elsa was sure he could look right down the front of her bustier '– then I'm guessing you might be just a little bit turned on too, hmm?'

The blush practically exploded on Kandi's cheeks.

'Maybe you're just a little bit wet –' he nodded to her crotch '– down there. Hmmm?'

'And if I am?' Her voice was a breathless rasp.

'Well, you certainly can't do your job like that, all overheated and distracted, now can you? I'm thinking maybe Nick could do something to – you know – relieve a little bit of that tension.' He leant closer still. 'If you're worried about your boss, don't. You could say I have a working arrangement with her. What do you say, Nick?' he said, without looking away from Kandi.

'I believe in reciprocity,' Nick said, but Elsa didn't miss the quick dart of his eyes to her.

'Great, fantastic! Then Nick, the first thing I want is for you to finger your way into our hot little waitress' panties and tell me if she's wet. I'm willing to bet my Aston Martin she is. What do you think, sweetheart? Is that a safe bet?'

'I think that's a safe bet for you to make,' Kandi replied. She dropped into the chair next to Nick and spread her legs, scrunching her skirt with a fist. Nick scooted to the edge of his chair and slid his hand up her thigh, then raked the crotch of her panties aside, and she caught her breath in a girlish gasp.

'Mmm, do I smell wet pussy?' Fenton said with a tease of a smile as Kandi ground her arse against the chair and shifted closer to Nick's probing fingers. 'What do you think, Nick, can you make her come before our dealer here gets impatient and forces us back to the game?'

'Gonna do my best,' Nick said. Then he shot Elsa another glance. 'But I'm guessing as impatient as our dealer is, I might have to resort to some extreme methods.'

And then he did the damnedest thing! Nick Chase slid down under the blackjack table and in between Kandi's spread thighs. Kandi let out a little kitten cry.

'Fuck me!' Fenton gasped, making no effort to keep his hands away from the bulge growing in his trousers. 'Don't know if that's gonna do her, Nicky boy, but it's sure as hell about to send me off like a bottle rocket on the Fourth of July. What about you, hon?' He nodded to Elsa, who could do nothing but smile. Sonovabitch if Nick's tongue wasn't doing the tango all over Kandi's pussy! How the hell did he do that? OK, fair enough, he was sexy, but Elsa dealt with multiple versions of sexy every day. What made Nick Chase so fucking different? She rocked subtly in her practical shoes until she could get the seam of her trousers right where she needed it, then she damn near bit a hole in her lip as Nick's hand snaked up from under the table to cup and thumb Kandi's tits, and none too subtly either. Christ, the man was insane! Right here in the middle of the casino! OK, so they'd made arrangements to minimise observers, but still, this was completely sizzling.

Fenton squirmed and shifted, and did everything but pull out his junk and tug on it. And the look on Kandi's face – the way she nibbled and licked her lips, the way she concentrated and grimaced and sucked little gulps of breath between her teeth – had Elsa's filthy mind imagining what might be going on underneath the blackjack table. Kandi's round breasts looked like they'd explode out of the bustier with all the heavy breathing, and Elsa couldn't help but think about Nick's cock, tight in his chinos, practically bursting the seam. The thought panicked her. He had to make this last. Damn, what if he couldn't hold his load? She knew he was doing it for her, but if he blew his wad too soon by being too cavalier, she was going to kill him.

Just then, Kandi gave a little yelp and practically fell off the chair as orgasm rolled up over her.

Nick came up from under the table wet-faced and smiling like the cat that ate the cream. With his eyes locked on Elsa, he pulled a handkerchief from his pocket and wiped his mouth like he'd just had the best meal ever. 'Now that I've paid my debt, Fenton,' he said, 'shall we play some blackjack?'

Fenton laughed out loud. 'Jesus Christ, Nicolas, I don't know if I can survive much more of that. Not sure our little waitress can either, though I'm sure she'd love to try. And frankly –' he glanced over at Elsa '– I'm getting bored with blackjack when there's so much other … entertainment to be had, so how about we make another bet? This involves you too, sweet cheeks, so don't run away,' he said to Kandi.

He studied her for a moment then he said, 'Do you like nice cars, darlin'?' The smile on the man's face was completely predatory. Elsa's stomach tightened and the tension her neck ratcheted up a notch, enough to make her forget how horny Nick had just made her.

'Ooh yes. I love nice cars.' Kandi's voice was a breathy purr.

'I'll bet my Aston Martin,' Fenton said.

'Oh my God,' she gasped. 'You mean like the one James Bond drives?'

He nodded and leant so close Elsa was afraid the man would kiss Kandi. 'Only mine's nicer. What do you say? Would you like that bet?'

'Seriously?' Nick said. 'You can't really expect us to believe that you're willing to give her your car? Because I –'

Fenton raised a hand, stopping him mid-sentence. 'I didn't say I'd give her my car. I said I'd bet my car. Not the same thing.' Then he snapped his fingers and a man who was clearly a bodyguard materialised from behind a nearby slot machine. 'Alistair, can you go out to the Aston and get the paperwork, please?'

'Fuck me,' Nick gasped as the black-suited hulk, not much smaller than Pagan, gave a brisk nod and headed toward the exit. 'And what does she have to bet? I mean, is she even allowed to play? She's the waitress. I'm sure there are rules. We are still playing blackjack, aren't we?'

'Of course we're playing blackjack, Nicky boy.' Fenton smiled. 'We're just making the bet a little bit more ... interesting.

'I don't know about Nick, but I have nothing to bet,' Kandi said.

'Oh, you both have something to bet, darlin', don't you worry. You have something I want very much.' His gaze travelled from one of them to the other and then he stroked his chin thoughtfully. 'If you win, sweetie, you get the Aston Martin, and you can drive it back home tonight.' The predator showed in his eyes once again. 'But if I win –' he looked her up and down '– I get your company for the night.' Before she could respond, he added, 'I won't hurt you. I promise. In fact, I won't even touch you. I want Nick here to do that for me.'

'You're kidding me.' Nick forced an embarrassed laugh. 'You want us to ... While you watch?'

'That's right, while I watch.' Fenton toyed with his chips. 'What I want is to watch the two of you doing what it's already clear you're dying to do, what you'd probably end up doing later tonight anyway. And let's face it, wouldn't it be a lot more fun and a lot more kinky to have someone watch, maybe call the shots while you're doing it?' Fenton's smile didn't waver. 'If I win, I get the two you for the night. You're mine for whatever I want you to do to each other. If Nick wins, that means our waitress here wins – what's your name, sweetheart?'

'Kandi,' she managed with some effort.

'If Nick wins, Kandi gets the Aston Martin.'

'But what does Nick get?' she asked.

'Why, sweet cheeks, Nick's gonna win either way, isn't he? If he wins, you get the Aston Martin and, well, I suppose the two of you can fuck each other's brains out in it if you're so inclined. However, if I win, you'll get to find out if Nick can use his cock as well as he does his tongue, and all in the luxury of my very expensive suite. And me, I get to watch. There, you see, a win-win, don't you think?'

Nick and Kandi gave each other a lingering glance like they were attempting to read each other's minds, then they both nodded their agreement at the same time. 'All right. We're in,' Kandi said.

'Good, then shall we play cards?'

On the first hand, the dealer won with an ace and a ten. Both Nick and Fenton went bust. Fenton laughed. 'Guess we didn't take the dealer into consideration, did we, Nicky boy? What do you think – maybe our lovely dealer might win the Aston Martin?'

Elsa only smiled demurely and shrugged. But even she had to admit she couldn't wait to get back to the control room and see how Nick would make Fenton's fantasy all about her. Fuck, did she really just think that? Before she could dwell on it, she was dealing the next hand. She dealt Fenton two eights for a split, and Nick held at 18. Dealer had the queen of clubs turned up.

'Don't worry, Nicky,' Fenton said, 'you're going to win either way. Isn't that right, sweet cheeks?' Kandi only smiled and leant closer to Nick. When Elsa dealt a six of diamonds for Fenton's first eight, it was no surprise when he went bust with the nine of clubs she dealt him next.

Kandi gave a little gasp. Fenton chuckled. 'Looks like you're one step closer to that Aston Martin, hon.'

'Tell us, Fenton, what colour's Kandi's car?' Nick asked. 'Is it silver like James Bond's?'

'Kandi's car is still my car, and those fantasies you're having of the two of you in the back seat are as close to that car as you're going to get. ' Fenton said with a cool smile. 'It's black, by the way.' He nodded to Elsa and everyone leant close as she dealt him ten of clubs.

Kandi practically bounced off her chair and Nick chuckled. 'Tough luck on that one, Fenton. Personally I like black cars better than silver, don't you, Kandi?'

Fenton only smiled and tapped the table for Elsa to hit him again. Everyone held their breath as Elsa dealt Fenton a two of hearts.

'Oh my God,' Kandi managed. 'Oh my God! I don't know if I can –'

Fenton held up his hand. 'Game's not over yet.' He nodded to Elsa. 'I could lose it all to our lovely dealer here.'

And Elsa flipped over her second card, a four of spades.

A little yelp escaped Kandi's throat. She grabbed the edge of the table for dear life. 'I don't know if I can, Fenton. Dear God, I don't know if I can do this. I mean, I want to, but … I've never done anything like this before.'

Fenton's eyes were suddenly like ice. 'A bet's a bet, Kandi. You know that.'

The little whimper Kandi managed sounded very convincing.

'However,' he said, with a sudden bright smile. 'This was not your typical situation, was it? I mean it was a split: double the chances, double the bet.' Just then his bodyguard returned and handed him a leather portfolio. 'That being the case, I did lose one bet, therefore –' he took the portfolio from the bodyguard and handed it to Kandi, who stared at him, brow drawn, eyes wide '– the Aston Martin's all yours, sugar. Won fair and square.'

Before anyone at the table could do more than gasp, he turned his attention to Elsa. 'As for the second hand, however, the way I see it I won and the dealer lost. Therefore, Kandi, you can go back to your job several hundred dollars and one Aston Martin richer. And I'll take Nick and the dealer off to my room for entertainment.'

There was a joint inhale of breath from dealer, waitress, and Nick. For a second, it felt like the whole casino was freeze-framed around them. Elsa heard buzzing in her ears; her shoulders stiffened, anger roiled up her spine. The fucker was manipulating her again. Then the dealer completely disappeared, and it was 100 per cent Elsa Crane who spoke. 'No. That wasn't part of the deal. I'm not part of the deal.'

Fenton held her in his usual amused gaze. 'Why not, Elsa? You both work for Mount Vegas, so what difference does it make? They all work for you, and I want him and you.'

'I'm not a part of the deal, Fenton,' Elsa repeated.

'I think that you are, darling. I said there would be a bet placed at the blackjack table. I said it would involve a couple going back to my room to fuck while I watched. I didn't specify who, so now I am. I want you and Nick. Now come on, time's wasting and I'm anxious to enjoy my winnings.'

He turned and gestured them to follow with the kind of confidence of someone who had no doubt he'd be obeyed. Elsa cursed out loud, then motioned to Nick and they both followed Fenton to the elevator banks while Kandi, holding the deed to her new Aston Martin, looked on stunned.

As they got into the elevator, Elsa hissed, 'If you ever pull a stunt like this with me again, Fenton, I'll cut you off. I don't care how much money you offer.'

The man's smile was a poor attempt at contrition. 'My dearest Elsa, I promise you, I'll be a good boy from now on and not break your rules, but this –' he looked from her to Nick and back again '– well, this was just too good to miss.' When they both gave him a questioning glance, he threw open his arms and nearly doubled over with a belly-laugh. 'Seriously? Come now. I'm a real voyeur, Elsa, not one of your wannabes. I take great pleasure in seeing what no one else sees, and that means reading the signs, darlin', reading the signs. And the chemistry sizzling between the two of you, even while you were playing your parts – and quite nicely, I might add – would outdazzle the lights of Vegas.' He leant closer to her and his smile broadened. 'I don't know what's going on between you, but when we get back to the suite, with me to orchestrate our night's entertainment, I fully expect the event to register on the Richter scale.'

Chapter Twelve

Inside, the suite was softly lit and the lounge was dark leather and soft carpets. The blackout curtains were open wide and the lights of the city twinkled beyond. Nick wondered if perhaps the watcher liked to be watched. On the glass coffee table sat a bottle of Dom Perignon chilling in a bucket of ice. Fenton opened it and filled three flutes, then nodded for the pair to sit opposite him.

Nick couldn't hold back the little hiss between his teeth as his sore arse touched down. 'Have they had you in the dungeon?' Fenton asked, as Nick shifted on the sofa to find the least painful position.

'Training,' Nick replied. Elsa shot him a sharp glance and then turned her attention back to Fenton.

'A trainee,' the man said. 'This just keeps getting better and better.' He lifted his glass. 'A toast to satisfaction.' He tossed his drink back and rubbed his hands together. 'Now, Elsa, there's a lovely bottle of complimentary lotion on the vanity next to the sink in the bathroom. Get it, please.'

Without a word, she did as she was told. When she returned, Fenton nodded to Nick. 'Give the man's poor stinging arse a little care first off. I want you both in good form. Nick, lower your trousers and lean over the sofa. Let's have a look.'

Nick did as he was told. Jesus, he couldn't believe he was baring his arse for some rich bastard he'd never met before just for the opportunity to fuck Elsa Crane.

Fenton let out a low whistle. 'Youch! Bet that hurt. Belt?'

'Yup.'

'Did Elsa do it?'

'Nope.'

'Didn't think so,' Fenton said, 'or it would have been a whole lot worse.'

The sound that came from Elsa's throat was a low growl. And what the hell? Was he totally out of his fucking mind? Somehow the idea of Elsa laying hard stripes across his backside was not only appealing, but it was downright hot. His cock pointed to the sofa he was bent over.

'Elsa, if you would, please ...' Fenton nodded her toward Nick's exposed butt. 'No, wait.'

She paused before opening the bottle.

'First take off that ridiculous dealer's get-up,' he told her. 'I can't think of anything less appropriate for you to wear, my darling. I'd much prefer to see what's underneath, wouldn't you Nick?'

'I would,' Nick replied, turning to watch Elsa step out of her shoes and drag her tie from around her neck as though it had somehow offended her. Then she efficiently lost the shirt and trousers. Both men gasped their appreciation as she stood before them in tiny white lace panties and a matching bra that cupped her like hands, barely covering her nipples. It displayed very well her rounded fullness and the valley in between, the valley in which Nick would love to bury his face and linger.

'Exquisite,' Fenton said. 'Elsa, you are absolutely stunning. I've always had such a crush on you, you know?'

Nick bristled.

'I'm flattered, Fenton, but I'm not your type.' Elsa

turned her attention back to Nick's wounded arse.

'Wait. I've changed my mind.' Fenton scooted forward on the sofa and began unbuttoning his shirt. 'Elsa, forget the lotion. I'm sure your warm, wet tongue would feel much better on Nick's sore bottom. I want to see you bathe those welts and kiss them better. I want to watch while you make the man squirm with something other than pain. Perhaps not your forte, darling, but I'm guessing you're extremely versatile.'

If looks could kill, Nick was pretty sure Fenton would be way dead. And there was that little hitch again, the little jerk in his cock at the disturbing yet intriguing thought of Elsa dealing out pain along with pleasure as easily as she did cards at the blackjack table.

Nick's cock went from half-mast to full attention, and Fenton heaved a happy sigh. 'There, you see. The man likes that idea a lot, Elsa. Now, you, Nick, stay bent over. Spread your legs a little more. I want to see the reaction of your tight asshole when Elsa goes to work on those muscular buttocks of yours.'

Nick did as he asked, feeling way more exposed than he had with just his cock waving for attention.

It was uncanny how Fenton seemed to catch his thoughts like he'd fished them right out of his head. 'Don't worry, Nick. I'm not going to fuck your ass. But I do love to watch the way that filthy sphincter responds to foreplay. You'd be amazed at just how telling an asshole can be. It's nearly as much of a giveaway to the state of arousal as a hard schlong.' He waved a hand. 'Now go on, Elsa, make our Nick's poor, wounded butt feel better.'

Nick had expected to feel Elsa's anger translated into the way she touched him. He couldn't have been more wrong. First she placed strong hands on each of his hipbones and drew him back until he could feel the feathered humidity of her breath low on his spine and down the parting of his buttocks, like a warm breeze over his anus. Then she pressed a very soft, very tender kiss where his back met the swell of his buttocks and, Jesus, he was undone! Somewhere a long way off, he heard Fenton sigh. Another kiss settled at the intimation of each butt cheek and he felt her breath travel the valley in between before her tongue pressed flat and wet just where his left thigh ended and the swell of his arse began. Then it slid like warm silk all the way up and over his buttock. Nick shuddered, shivered, fighting a feeling somewhere in his chest that migrated down low in his belly then rested tight and urgent against his heavy balls.

'Oh God,' he cried out. 'Elsa!'

'I know,' she whispered as the next laving of her tongue came up his right arse cheek. 'I know, Nick.' She reached around him and sheathed his cock in her fist, pressing her thumb hard against the head, which was already slippery with precome. 'Just hold it. Hold it all down low and tight, and I promise you, it'll be so worth the wait.'

There were ten stripes across his arse. Five on each cheek. Nick had counted, Nick had felt every single one of them as though they had been branded into his brain as well as carved into his backside, but this, this was far more intimate, far more frightening and, God, he didn't know how he'd be able to hold back the flood, but he wanted to, he needed to for Elsa. He shivered as another long lap of her tongue traversed his backside, ending in a tiny nip of a kiss that he felt all the way to the crown of his head. Christ! How could he endure? How could he survive Elsa Crane unleashed against his wounds, unleashed against the depth of his need? He hadn't even known that need was there until Elsa.

The next trail of her tongue curved back on itself and shivered teasingly down the crack of his arse, accented with a little press just above the gripping of his anus, and this time *he* grabbed the head of his cock, thumbed it as though he were holding on for dear life, and that's exactly how it felt.

'Elsa,' he whispered. And, honestly, her name was the only word in the English language he could recall when the tongue kisses were joined by the tip of her little finger worrying its way into his arsehole ever so slightly.

Nick heard Fenton's fly opening, heard the man gasp and curse softly. But none of that mattered. None of that existed at the moment. He was lost in the hypnotic lavings of Elsa's tongue. Ten long, leisurely, unbelievably tender laps, while her finger wriggled and teased just at the boundary of his grudging anal knot.

'Will you hurt me, Elsa?' It took all of his breath and all of his brain to ask.

'She will if I tell her to.' Fenton's interruption felt like a slap. 'And you'll hurt her if I say.'

Nick had the sudden urge to do a little hurting of his own to the man watching. But Elsa's stroking of his flank calmed him; it focused him on her, on her touch, on her scent, on the thick heaviness of her breath as it spilled down his spine and over his arse. He didn't give a shit about Fenton. He was there for Elsa; nothing else, no one else.

'Your ass feels better, doesn't it, Nick?' Fenton didn't wait for an answer. 'And now, I want you to take off Elsa's bra.'

As Elsa turned her back to allow his efforts, he was stunned by how empty he felt without the small intrusion of her finger. He made an awkward attempt to unhook her bra, then she laid her hands over his and guided him. As he released her, he followed the waistband around to cup her fullness and the hitch of her breath was almost a little sob as his thumbs found her plumped nipples. She leant back into his embrace and turned her head to offer him her mouth, her throat, the cradle of her collarbone and, God, he was in heaven, with his cock pressed up tight above the pillows of her bottom, with her well-muscled arms lifted to stroke his hair, to pull him closer to her.

'Yes,' Fenton whispered, 'I was right about the two of you. Raw heat. Nick, pick the bra up and bring it with us to the bedroom. You'll need it.'

Nick hoiked up his boxers and trousers, holding them over his arse just enough that he could walk, then he followed Fenton and Elsa.

The bed was an enormous four-poster with room for the whole Mount Vegas team to wallow about. With a flick of a switch, the room was flooded in soft strains of R&B, but before Nick could take in more of the surroundings, Fenton spoke. 'Elsa, I want you face up in the middle of the bed. Good, that's good. And now, Nick, I want you to take that lovely bra and tie Elsa's hands.'

When he balked, Elsa nodded her consent.

'Oh, and for fuck's sake, Nick, lose the trousers and boxers.'

Nick did as he was told, then followed instructions that resulted in Elsa's hands tied to the bedframe, wrists together, arms stretched above her head.

'Now then, Nick, I'm assuming that Elsa's been calling the shots so far in your relationship, and even if she didn't give you the welts on your arse, she gave permission. I know what a controlling bitch she can be.' Before Nick could respond to the insult, Fenton continued. 'But for tonight, I want you to take control, Nick.' He pulled a straight-backed chair close to the bed. 'As you can see, Elsa Crane is helpless before you. What I want you to do is torture her.'

'What?' Nick came up off the bed. In his mind, he already had a stranglehold on the bastard, but Fenton raised both hands and offered a back-pedalling laugh.

'It's not what you think, Nick. There'll be no whips, no belts, no flails. Nothing so unsubtle. What I want you do is see just how much self-control our Elsa has when you pleasure her.'

It was the moan from Elsa's throat that surprised Nick, the look of – was it panic? – that crossed her face. Fenton's chuckle was positively wicked. 'Oh yes, Elsa Crane, you are going to lie there completely helpless and let Nick have his way with you while I watch.' He nodded to Nick.

With his heart racing and his brain barely able to believe what he was about to do, Nick placed a plump white pillow under Elsa's arse, then he shimmied her lace panties down over her hips and off. With them, he lashed one of her ankles to the bedpost. Fetching her tie from the lounge, he bound the other with that. It was hard to concentrate around the tug of his heavy load, but he secured her spread-eagle, the heavy swell of her pussy displayed atop the pillow like some extravagantly expensive piece of jewellery in one of Vegas's exclusive boutiques. Then he practically fell tongue-first into the delicious breach of her, slick and sticky and sweet for him.

Christ, her pussy was wet for him! That did things to him. It wasn't like he didn't know how to make a woman moist when the rare opportunity arose. But somehow making Elsa Crane wet for him, just for him, was a whole different level of foreplay. And as much as he wanted to unload into the heat of her, he wanted to revel in her own desire, to bask in her need, her need for him. His tongue took the lead, dipping and lapping between her labia while the rest of him, on an almost uncanny level, tuned in to the way she breathed, the beat of her heart, the heat of her skin, the blush crawling over her breasts, the stippling of her areolas as her arousal grew.

The rich, midnight scent of her flooded his nostrils and sharpened his own ache. Just when she found the rhythm that he knew would get her there, just when her little grunts and mews intensified with purpose, he gave her clit a nip and pulled away. She growled her frustration, making a worthless effort to raise her pubis off the pillow to get closer to him. He turned his attention to the impatient bulge of her nipples, giving each a hard suck and a sharp bite between his front teeth.'

'Fuck,' she whispered. 'Oh fuck, Nick! Fuck.'

Oh yes, she wanted. She needed. 'I know, Elsa,' he whispered. 'I know.' He ran his tongue down between her breasts and over her belly to penetrate her navel in sharp little thrusts, and he felt the shiver climb her spine.

'How long can you hold it, Elsa?' Fenton's voice sounded like it had been rubbed with sandpaper, breathlessly forcing its way into the room. 'I want to know, darling.'

Fenton was only background noise as Nick kissed and nipped down over Elsa's mons, resting his chin for a moment in the soft spring of pubic curls, looking up her body at the rounded rise and fall of her. Then he continued his migration south to the place where she needed serious pressure, serious tongue action. There he breathed only whispers of kisses before opening her engorged, dark folds with two fingers to see the deep, tight hole, shimmering in her mother of pearl juices, juices that were there to accommodate his cock, to ease his penetration, to welcome him into her anxious depths. And Christ, he so wanted to go there now, but instead, he swirled a finger and then two into the silky wet of her, and her moan was belly-deep, animal harsh as every muscle of her tightened, gripped and strained toward him.

'You want to get closer, don't you?' he whispered against her clit, and she jerked and whimpered. 'You want to get closer to me.' He slid his fingers deeper into her tight grip and nibbled on her labia. 'I want you closer, Elsa. I want you more than close; I want to be inside you.'

Her response was a convulsive sob.

'No whispering, Nick. If you're talking dirty to our Elsa, I want to hear.'

Nick ignored him, going down deep into her once again, then wriggling and thrusting his fingers while he slurped and licked and nibbled his way up over her clit. She tasted of salt and metal, of honey and butter melted on hot bread. She tasted of everything that would sate a man's hunger while driving him insane until he could totally devour her. Then, just when she found her rhythm, just when the labouring of her breath, the grinding of her hips assured him she was close, he pulled back again. She sobbed and cursed and struggled against her restraints as he nipped and licked his slow way down her thigh, then he sat back carefully on his haunches, making sure that he was in her line of sight. He ran his open palm up between her drenched folds until she bucked off her pillow and whimpered, until his hand glistened with her juices. Then, with his eyes locked on hers, he began to stroke his cock, easing the friction with those lovely juices, thrusting into his fisted grip, imagining how her tight pussy would feel around him. It was his rhythm she caught, breathlessly grinding and humping as best she could in her bound position, her pussy gripping and releasing, gripping and releasing, darkening the pristine pillowcase with her flood.

'How long can he keep it up, Elsa?' Fenton's voice rasped into the orgy of heavy breathing. 'How long can you hold back? I've always wanted to know. I've always wanted to watch your control shatter.'

Nick gave her just enough time to catch her breath, just enough time to plateau before he began another tongue dance across her slippery, tasty, fragrant pout. Her head lolled from side to side, lips parted, breath coming in desperate gasps. Her breasts rose and fell and undulated beneath the high rise of her nipples and, God, she was the most beautiful sight he'd ever seen.

He pulled away and slid up her body until he straddled her lovely, perspiring face, then he pushed his cock into her mouth. She took him with such enthusiasm that she gagged and sputtered, before he cradled her head, fingers tangled in her hair, and guided her until she got used to the length of him. Then she opened her throat and worked her tongue and drew him in until he was caught up, until he was almost lost in her, until he almost forgot his role in this whole fantasy. With an effort that felt as though it ripped him open, he pulled out and slid back down until his mouth met hers, until his fumbling fingers found their way back to her slit. He strummed her clit with his thumb and tugged at the swell of her labia until she half moaned, half cried into his mouth.

'Nick, fuck me. I need you to fuck me, I need you to …'

The deep-chested moans coming from Fenton told Nick that he wasn't going to hold out much longer. 'Fuck her, Nick. I need you to fuck her,' Fenton managed between gritted teeth, doing battle with his cock like he was riding a bucking bronco, making the chair skitter and shake beneath his arse.

Nick was ready, more than ready. He could barely remember his own name, so lost in Elsa Crane was he, so enthralled by every curve, every slope, every rise of her. He shifted and manoeuvred, feeling her hard nipples graze his as he swallowed her words down into his throat. 'Fuck me, Nick. Please. I need you to fuck me.'

Running a hand over her soft curls and opening her with a couple of fingers, he positioned himself. Then he whispered against her ear, 'I won't fuck you, Elsa, but I will make love to you.' Then he took his weight on his knees and let his desperate cock lead the way. A single thrust. That was all it took, and he was sheathed deep and tight in the pillowed jewel case of her pussy. That he could contain himself at all was stunning. That he had any control of any kind seemed an impossibility, caught and captured inside her body as he was. And yet he held himself, held his load, held everything back in the leaden weight of his balls until he could take her with him. He could sense the building of her need, need that felt like it would burst her bonds and devour him whole. With each thrust, Elsa writhed and growled helplessly beneath him, unable to do anything he didn't allow. She grabbed at his cock from her depths and sucked at him in a grip that made him surge and tense and thrust and rake against her. It was a grip that demanded everything of him, even bound as she was, until all of his senses overloaded. As orgasm exploded over her body like a living thing, he fumbled to free her hands, tossing the bra aside as her arms encircled him, her fists clenched tight against his upper back, as she buried her face against his neck and howled. The constricting spasms of her release sent him over the edge, and he spilled himself into her, spilled himself in harsh, oxygen-deprived grunts, spilled himself into the warm, tight depths of her while she held on as though her life depended on it. From his beleaguered chair, Fenton unloaded his wad across the plush pile of the carpet.

Under the circumstances, Nick couldn't imagine that they would doze, let alone fall asleep, yet they did. He had a vague recollection of Pike undoing the rest of Elsa's bonds and gently laying a blanket over them. Then, with his still cock deep inside her, Elsa curled her body around him. Nick was sure he must be dreaming at that point. Surely falling asleep with Elsa Crane wrapped around him had to be a dream.

140

Chapter Thirteen

It was Beetle who delivered the breakfast trays from room service, settling them quietly on the dressing table. But it was the weight on his chest that roused Nick from sexy dreams of Elsa Crane to the flesh and blood reality of the woman wrapped around him like a second skin. The softness of her hair tickled his chin, her breasts pressed up tight against his chest. With a surge of testosterone, he realised that his hard cock was still buried in her fist-tight grip, and the wet stickiness against his thigh was a reminder of how hot last night had been. The shifting of his hips was almost an involuntary thing, a thing that caused Elsa to moan and grip even in her sleep. Nick's balls tightened at the thought that Elsa might actually be dreaming of him.

When Beetle saw that he was awake, she placed a finger to her lips, nodded to the trays, and left. There was no sign of Fenton. At some point the blackout drapes had been drawn, cocooning the room in heavy shadows. Elsa moaned again and wriggled in his arms, the clench of her pussy causing him to grunt and catch his breath. He was torn between ravishing her where she lay, filling her dreams with sexy heat, or just lying there with his cock nestled inside and watching her sleep. He slid a hand down her back to rest on the swell of her bottom, and from her dream space, she ground her pubis against him. He held his breath, trying not to wake her and willing himself not to hump like some damned dog after a bitch in heat.

She had never answered his question – if she would hurt him. Somehow she didn't have to. Hell, the woman didn't even look harmless in her sleep. She was totally a take-control sort of person, and last night must have been hard for her. Fenton had known that and had delighted in taking away her control. Nick's cock surged again as he thought about what might have happened if it had been him tied to the bed and Elsa given free rein to torture him. How would she have done that? Would it have involved pain? Would he have seen her differently in daylight if she had administered pain with his pleasure? He became aware of the subtle ebb and flow at the place of their joining, almost thrusting, but not quite, almost humping but not quite. Surely she had to be awake. He stroked her hair and kissed the top of her head, and she sighed.

'I smell breakfast,' she mumbled into his nape.

'I smell us,' he said, cupping her arse and sliding a finger down between her buttocks to stroke where her labia splayed around his cock.

'Mmm.' She sighed. 'I need to come, Nick. Think you can handle that?' She gave his cock a pussy squeeze that couldn't have been tighter if she'd fisted it, and he sucked breath between his teeth. Then he rolled with her until she was beneath him and she wrapped her legs around him and groaned. 'Oh God, yes! I don't need foreplay, I don't need finessing, Nick, I just want you to fuck me. We both need it.'

She bit back the last word, because, really, she was preaching to the converted. It wasn't Fenton calling the shots this morning. Early morning awkwardness and need dictated a quick thrust and ride down into the expensive bedding, every sleep-stiffened muscle clenched and all breathing suspended. Nick thrust, and

Elsa gripped. They grunted and strained out their orgasms in a matter of minutes, then collapsed in a heap until breath returned along with thoughts of something other than fucking.

Elsa broke the connection, shoving him to one side in a warm, wet flood against his thigh as she pushed her way to the edge of the bed. She reached for a towel that someone had thoughtfully placed on the bedside table and began to clean herself.

'Where's Fenton?' Nick asked, finding a towel on his side too.

'Probably gone back to his room.' She tossed the towel and headed to the breakfast trays. Shoving a piece of bacon into her mouth, she munched, then brought the tray back to the bed and settled it onto her lap. Nick did the same. 'This wasn't his suite,' she said. 'This was rented for his fantasy. And since he so blatantly broke the rules and the suite's paid for, I guess the team figured we might as well enjoy it.' She cocked her head. 'Funny, though. I've never fallen asleep after an act before.'

'I'd imagine not,' Nick said. 'Certainly not if it involved having your ass beaten.'

She offered him a smile that was more like a grimace. 'My ass doesn't often get beaten, Nick.'

He studied her for a moment over his coffee cup. 'You don't like not being in control, do you?'

'No. I don't.' She shoved a forkful of eggs into her mouth and swallowed without chewing. 'And Fenton knows that.' It was then they both noticed the hotel stationery envelope addressed to Elsa propped on the dressing table next to the mirror. 'No doubt it's from Fenton.' She sat her tray aside and shuffled out of bed again to grab it. 'Probably an apology for fucking with last night's act, an apology he doesn't mean.' She opened the envelope. 'Fenton always gets exactly what he wants, but he has a helluva lot more fun getting it when he's sneaky about it.'

'Then it's not the first time he's pulled a stunt like that?'

'He pretty much does it every time, and I pretty much tell him I'll never work with him again no matter how much he pays, and he pretends to be contrite, and I pretend to believe him. Then the next time he wants a fantasy, he pays Mount Vegas an obscene amount of money, and we plan everything out and brace ourselves for whatever the man throws at us this time.'

As she sat down on the bed and flicked open the folded letter, he reached over and stroked her thigh. 'I like what he threw at us this time.'

With Elsa, a growl and a grumble at Fenton's fucking with their act would have been as likely as a grab at his cock, but what he got was nothing. As she read the note her brow wrinkled, her lips tightened and thinned as though whatever words she wanted to speak, she held back.

'What is it? What did he say?' Nick asked, leaning over for a peek.

'Nothing.' Elsa shoved the note back into the envelope. 'The man's an idiot. He thinks he knows it all.' She stood and began gathering her clothes from where they were strung across the suite, and Nick felt his stomach knot.

'Elsa? What is it? What's going on?'

'I've gotta go,' she said, leaning forward to ease her breasts back into the bra she'd just picked up. He followed her into the living room where she shoved into her trousers and blouse. 'It's a busy day.'

'Surely not too busy for breakfast and a quick shower?'

She exploded. 'Damn it, Nick! You're not the boss. Don't tell me what I need.'

She grabbed her bag and her shoes and practically ran

for the door, leaving Nick wondering what the hell had just happened.

Elsa was blessedly alone in the elevator. She hated to be seen like this. It wasn't so much that she looked like she'd had a wild night. Lots of people in Vegas looked that way before one in the afternoon. It was that she felt shell-shocked, like her skin had suddenly become too thin to protect her, too thin to hide behind. She wouldn't let the letter get to her. Fenton was an idiot. He didn't know anything. He didn't understand anything.

She took a taxi over to the main offices of Mount Vegas, and since it was early, she made it up to her suite unseen. Once inside, she locked the door and practically fell into the chair behind her desk. She grabbed for the half-empty bottle of water in her bottom drawer and downed it all before she dug the letter out of her bag, opened it and reread it.

My dearest Elsa,

You were stunning, as always. I never doubted for a moment that you would be. Somehow I feel as though this time I should pay you double for letting me see so much more of Elsa Crane than you've ever allowed me to see before.

You and Nick are amazing together. I was totally taken aback by your performance. Though of course, it wasn't a performance, was it? Love and sex, in those wild, frantic, early stages, when a couple can't get enough of each other – when, in fact, they may not yet even know that they are in love – are the most powerful experiences for a watcher. They offer so very much more than just a good, voyeuristic orgasm. And though I'm very jealous that someone else finally won your heart, I can hardly hold it against you now that I've seen the two of you together. I hope you've been able to be honest with him about your situation, darling. Nick seems like the kind of person who would understand.

Thanks again for another wonderful experience.

Love,

Alex Fenton

The man was an idiot, she reminded herself again. He didn't know anything about her or about her heart, and Nick Chase didn't deserve to be dragged into the middle of all of this. He especially didn't deserve any of the craziness she could offer him.

She shoved back from the desk, stripping as she went, and padded across her private lounge to the bathroom where she pushed into the shower, willing herself not to think about Nick Chase. And yet there was a part of her that regretted washing his scent off her body, regretted washing away the remains of their passion. Her insides quivered with muscle memory and she leant back against the tiles and relived the whole experience, even as she warned herself not to.

Nick left the hotel, stunned. He'd showered quickly and managed to retrieve his clothes from his locker in the Mount Vegas wardrobe suite unseen. Fine with him. He wasn't in the mood to talk to anyone. Twice he'd attempted to call Elsa so they could have it out. But he'd lost courage before his BlackBerry could ring through. It was just as well. He was too angry over the way she'd fled to do anything but make matters worse.

He spent the drive home trying to figure out what had happened. What the hell was in the letter that had set Elsa off? In a surge of jealousy, he wondered if Fenton and Elsa were lovers. Fenton seemed to have intimate details about Elsa that a lover might have. But then this was Mount Vegas, and intimacy was a relative term.

Nick pushed his way into his house, trying to force his thoughts away from the letter and Elsa's response to it. He had his own business to tend to, he reminded himself. He needed to touch base with Lou-Ann, find out how things were with the new driver, set a time to meet over the monthly expenses.

In the kitchen, he went through the motions of making coffee. He had just flipped the switch on the machine and grabbed a Pop Tart from the cupboard when Tanya appeared from the living room, and he nearly dropped his breakfast. 'Tanya!' he exclaimed. 'Are you all right? What are you doing here?'

'Hello, Nick. I'm sorry that we invaded your house, but I still have key that you let me borrow, and since this is important, I thought that you wouldn't mind.'

'We?' Nick managed, instead of the curse that was right on the tip of his tongue over the invasion of his much-needed privacy.

'Come.' Tanya took him by the hand. 'There is someone that I would like you to meet.' She led him into the living room.

There, in front of Nick's bookshelf, stood a man who could have passed for a bouncer except for the suit even Nick could tell was expensive.

'Mr Chase, I'm Detective Victor Havers.' It was then Nick noticed the man was handling one of his pyritic ammonites.

'Please put that back.' He spoke without thinking and grabbed it away. 'It has sentimental value.'

The man offered an apologetic smile that didn't seem very apologetic at all. 'Sorry, Mr Chase, or do you prefer Dr Chase?' Before Nick could respond, he continued, 'I've always found fossils fascinating. What is it … palaeontology, right?' He ran his finger along the shelf where some of Nick's favourite fossils were displayed. 'I'm sure you can understand how it would appeal to me, digging up the dead and trying to uncover their secrets. It's just forensics, Mr Chase, isn't it? And sometimes there's not much left to go on at the end of the day, but

147

there's always something fascinating about it. Yes, fascinating.' He dragged his gaze away from the fossils to settle on Nick. 'And interesting to me that a palaeontologist would end up here in Vegas driving a limo.'

The skin prickled along the back of Nick's neck. 'Man's gotta make a living. Why are you here?' After what had happened with Elsa this morning, he was struggling with his manners.

That didn't seem to bother Victor Havers. He only smiled, just before he dropped the bomb. 'I'm here because we need your help to bring Elsa Crane and her Mount Vegas gang to justice.'

Nick shot Tanya a quick glance, doing his best to keep his surprise, and his anger, under wraps. 'As far as I know, Elsa Crane hasn't done anything that warrants the police's attention.' He hoped his voice sounded more confident than he felt. Elsa had secrets, he was sure of it. And what Mount Vegas was doing might be very unconventional, but Elsa wasn't the kind of person who would be on the outs with the law, was she?

Havers plopped down onto the sofa without being asked, and nodded to the recliner. 'Sit down, Mr Chase,' he said, as though he owned the place. Tanya sat down next to him, but Nick remained standing.

The cop's smile had congeniality plastered all over it, and yet for some reason, Nick couldn't quite buy it. 'Tanya told me about her contract, which I'm sure you know is not a legally binding document, therefore it's unlikely she would ever actually get her bonus.'

'Well, good, then. I'll turn in my notice at Mount Vegas and get back to my life,' Nick said.

'No!' Tanya practically jumped out of her seat. 'Nick, you mustn't do that. You are in good position to help me, to help the police get to the bottom of the situation with Elsa Crane and the Mount Vegas.'

'Rich people paying a stupid amount of money to watch someone else play out their sexual fantasies. I hardly see how that's a threat to the American way, Detective Havers,' Nick said.

'Mr Chase –' As Havers leant forward and clasped his hands in his lap, Nick couldn't keep from noticing a gold band with a chunky diamond on his sausage-sized ring finger. 'Surely you're not naïve enough to think that fantasies are all the Crane woman and her gang deal in.'

'And surely you're not naïve enough to think I'd believe you without more evidence than what you've given me so far,' Nick replied.

'Nick, has Elsa told you anything about the big event happening in few weeks' time with the people from London?' Tanya asked.

'You mean the fantasy for Mrs Keyser? Yes, Elsa's mentioned it. Why?'

Havers took over. 'We have reason to believe that the whole act is a cover-up for a drug deal going down at that time, a big one. And as for the English folks coming in – well, they're just a distraction. We suspect mob connections.'

Try though he might, Nick couldn't imagine Elsa would have any sort of connections with organised crime. And he certainly couldn't imagine Elsa or any of the Mount Vegas gang involved in dealing drugs. There was a strict "no drink or drugs" policy on all Mount Vegas acts, no matter what the fantasy called for. Even last night's champagne toast was barely a touching to the lips, and the drinks in the casino were all non-alcoholic, except for Fenton's. Nick had never seen any evidence that anyone used drugs and as far as he could tell, even after hours, the drinking was minimal at Mount Vegas. People were too busy fucking. It surprised him more than a little that he had absorbed so much of the Mount Vegas philosophy so quickly, and that he believed it.

Something definitely didn't feel right.

'Go on, Havers. I'm listening,' Nick said.

The detective scooted forward on the edge of the sofa and undid his jacket so Nick got a glimpse of his holster. 'No doubt in the short time you've been at Mount Vegas, Elsa Crane has run a clean ship. She hasn't had time to trust you yet, but the fact that she's let you into her tight little circle at all says it won't be long.'

'So what is it you want from me, exactly?' Nick asked, wishing Havers would just go away and leave him alone.

'Details, Mr Chase. We want details. The police are planning a raid. We know some of the details from Tanya, but the dates and times of the operation hadn't been nailed down when she was dismissed so unfortunately. We figure Elsa Crane got suspicious of her and that's the real reason she let her go. So now we need someone from the inside who can give us those details, and everyone else within Mount Vegas seems loyal to a tee. All we really need from you, Mr Chase, is dates, times, and places. That sort of thing. Of course, any other information you can give us would be an added bonus. You'll in no way be involved in our operation, and there won't be any risk to you personally.'

'And what about your bonus?' Nick asked Tanya. 'What about your mother's surgery?'

'Oh, we'll see to Tanya's mother, Nick. There are charities and support groups that will help her get what she needs. And the fact that Tanya's helped the police out won't go amiss. Of course, we'll see that your name and reputation are kept out of the papers when the news breaks, as it inevitably will. Wouldn't want anything bad reflecting on your business, now would we?'

In the kitchen, Nick could hear the coffee machine

150

gurgling out the last of the brew into the pot. The only other sound was the quiet hum of the air conditioner. He was pissed off at Tanya for inviting herself and Havers right on in and making themselves at home. Plus, for some reason he couldn't quite put his finger on, he really didn't like the guy. 'I'll need more to go on than your word, Havers. The Mount Vegas team has been nothing but good to me, and I have no evidence that any of what you're saying is true.'

Havers shifted in his seat and rubbed the bridge of his nose, and Tanya squirmed on the sofa next to him. Then he heaved himself to his feet and buttoned his jacket. 'I certainly can't force you to help us, Mr Chase. However, I would suggest you don't take too long in making your decision, because Elsa Crane and her team are going down. The real question is are you going down with them?' With an exaggerated effort, he extended his arm and looked at his watch. A rather nice watch, Nick noticed. Then he said, 'I've got to go.' He pulled a card from his pocket and laid it on the coffee table. 'Here's where you can reach me.'

With that, he motioned Tanya to follow him as he headed for the door, leaving Nick standing in the middle of his silent living room.

Once they were gone, Nick tried to call Elsa, but only got her voicemail. He left a brief "we need to talk" message and cursed Tanya out loud. He poured himself a cup of coffee, slopping it over the counter as he did so, and did his best to swallow a Pop Tart whole. Then he plopped down at the kitchen table and called Lou-Ann for the latest. After all, he still had a business to run, and it was still the limo service that paid the bills.

'Hey, handsome. Just about to call you,' came his dispatcher's voice over the phone. 'The new driver's amazing. And hot. That makes him very popular with the ladies – and with the dispatcher. Oh, and he can drive too,' she added. 'I suppose that's a plus.'

Nick grunted into the phone. 'Well, glad that figured into his evaluation somewhere.'

'Oooh, somebody didn't get enough sleepy-time last night, did he, Mr Grumpy Bear?'

'Never mind my sleepy-time, Lou-Ann; any other news I should know about?'

He heard her shuffling papers. 'Do you know an Elsa Crane?'

Nick sat up straight and felt the muscles in his stomach tighten. 'What about her?'

'Don't know how she did it, or why, but she's been sending some pretty substantial clients, repeat clients, in our direction. Business is hopping. So have you got a hottie on the side you're not telling me about? Hmm? Is that why we're not getting our Zs?'

When Nick made no attempt to fill her in, she heaved a disappointed sigh into his ear and said, 'Oh Nicky, sometimes you're such a stick in the mud. Whoever this Elsa Crane is, I love her, and if business keeps up like this, the woman may just be responsible for getting me a much-deserved raise.' Nick could hear the noise of the radio in the background calling for a limo to the Paris Las Vegas hotel.

'And there was me thinking you worked for me because of my studliness,' he said.

Lou-Ann's laugh tinkled over the phone. 'Studly you may be, Nicky dear, but your sex appeal doesn't pay my mortgage, does it?'

When Nick hung up he tried to call Elsa again, but there was still no answer, so he turned his attention to the laptop to find out what he could about Mount Vegas.

For the first time since he'd encountered the whole crazy team, he wondered why he hadn't thought to do a search at the beginning. Had Elsa really dazzled him that much?

The search for Mount Vegas wasn't difficult. The home page was a picture of Las Vegas at night, taken from the upper floors of one of the exclusive hotels, Nick would guess. In bold san serif lettering, beneath the Mount Vegas logo, were the words *Where there's always a room with a view*. The "about us" page simply read *Exclusive entertainment for imaginative people*.

'You got that right,' Nick said out loud. Beyond that, everything was password protected except for the "contact us" email address. That was it. There was no way beyond the initial pages without a password. Nick had grown up in the Vegas area and knew it intimately from driving limos. He knew that, even though prostitution was illegal in the city, the sex entertainment industry was a staple in Vegas. There was something for people of all tastes and kinks. And yet, until Nick met Tanya Povic, he'd never heard of Mount Vegas.

He Googled Elsa Crane and came up with nothing. He frowned at the screen and scratched his stubbled chin. The nature of their business meant that Mount Vegas had to be discreet, but still, very few people didn't have at least some kind of electronic footprint these days. Yet there was no Elsa Crane on Facebook, Twitter, G+, LinkedIn – at least, not the right Elsa Crane. Perhaps she went online under a different name. Lots of people did, but there was no way of knowing without asking her.

He Googled Tanya Povic and quickly found her on Facebook and Twitter. With a little shiver he realised that other than Tanya, Elsa was the only person from Mount Vegas whose last name he knew. He couldn't Google anyone else, and Tanya's profile was hardly helpful. There was a mention of some modelling she had done, but in Vegas, modelling could mean almost anything. There was no mention of her working for Mount Vegas.

On a hunch, he Googled *Mount London* and, after wading through dozens of useless hits, he came across an exclusive club in London simply called The Mount. It appeared to be legendary for both discretion and gossip – one feeding off the other. There were claims that it was everything from a secret sex cult to a hub of white slavery to a place where clients paid a fortune to eat exotic animals. All that was really certain was that it was an exclusive restaurant and dance club for which it was next to impossible to get reservations, and equally impossible for normal folks to afford.

A little more searching brought him to a magazine called *Talkabout*. The magazine faced bankruptcy after its editor had given the OK to a false story about The Mount being a sex cult, then had laid the blame for the article at the feet of Rita Martelli, who had been working for the mag under an alias.

Nick released a low whistle. He remembered the papers being full of stories and speculation about the disappearance of the Martelli heiress. That had been several years ago now. In fact, he remembered a news story about her resurfacing out of the blue. She'd just stepped out of a limo one night in front of an exclusive London club and waltzed right on in with the paparazzi going crazy all around her. He Googled the story and, sure enough, the sudden reappearance of Rita Holly Martelli was at The Mount.

Nick wasn't sure if the *Talkabout* magazine story was linked to the heiress' return or not, but with threats of lawsuits from both the Martelli matriarch and The Mount itself, the magazine had no choice but to sell or close. The result was a buy-out by Holly Enterprises, created by Coraline Martelli, head of the perfume giant, and the magazine was now owned and run by Rita Holly Martelli herself.

Rita Holly Martelli? Where'd he heard that name

before? Hadn't she been the one who had watched, long distance, his first performance with Deb for Mrs Bromley? Didn't Pike call her Rita Holly? But why would she have any rights to watch at all? Or was she one of the big clients? Certainly if she were the heiress to Martelli Fragrance she could afford the services of Mount Vegas. He would see Pike in just a little while, and Pike never seemed quite as tight-lipped as Elsa. Maybe he could find out a little more.

'Yup.' Pike led the way down a stone staircase that, if Nick hadn't known better, could have easily been in a medieval castle in England somewhere. 'Same Rita. Really stupid exposé written by her former boss before he learned the hard way who she was and that her mother owns half the world.'

'So what does she have to do with Mount Vegas? I mean, is The Mount a franchise or something?'

Pike laughed. 'I suppose that's one way of looking at it. There's a connection, yes, and Mount Vegas is a relatively new branch of The Mount.'

'And this Rita Holly Martelli is coming to Vegas? Why?'

'Oh, she and Elsa have some business to conduct,' Pike said. 'And you have a dungeon to explore,' he added, changing the subject. 'So pay attention or I'll rack you.'

Business to conduct. That could mean anything, Nick told himself. It certainly didn't mean drugs and organised crime shit. As far as he knew, the Martellis weren't involved in anything but perfume. Not that he would know one way or another. Coraline Martelli had a reputation for being a ruthless businesswoman, but then ruthlessness didn't equal criminal.

Nick was strapped, still fully clothed, to the St Andrew's cross when his BlackBerry rang. Giving him a wicked smile, Pike pulled the device out of his front pocket, with a little more groping than Nick felt was absolutely necessary, and looked at the display. 'It's Elsa,' he said, holding it up to Nick's ear.

'Nick, I need to see you in my office as soon as Pike's done with you.' No greeting, no how are you, no last night was really good. God, Nick would never understand the woman.

'I'm sort of tied up right now,' Nick said, glancing nervously at Pike, who ran a vicious-looking crop up the inside of his leg. He'd always considered himself to be pretty comfortable with his sexuality, or at least he thought he was, but as Pike moved the crop up to his crotch and trailed it over the tell-tale bulge in the front of Nick's jeans, he wasn't so sure.

'Then tell him to untie you and send you up. He can play with you some other time.' She hung up.

'She wants me in her office,' Nick said without growling.

'If I didn't know Elsa, I'd say you were trying to get away from me.' Pike shoved the BlackBerry back in Nick's pocket, once again lingering just a little longer than necessary.

'I'd probably be safer with you in the dungeon.' Nick watched as Pike hung the crop back in place and began to unbuckle the cuffs.

'I'd like to say that her bark is worse than her bite, but I wouldn't want to lie.'

'Jesus –' Nick ran a hand through his hair when Pike released his wrist '– I'd at least like to know what I did. I mean, one minute we're enjoying an intimate breakfast together in the hotel suite and the next she's making sure the door doesn't hit her in the ass on the way out.'

'You make her nervous, that's all.' Nick could feel Pike's hot breath against his crotch as he knelt to undo the ankle cuffs. 'Elsa doesn't like it when she's not in control, and she wasn't last night.'

'Is there something going on between her and Fenton?'

'Fenton would like there to be, but Elsa's not interested. There, you're free to go –' Pike held him in an uncomfortable gaze '– at least for the moment.'

This time Nick did growl, but as he turned to go, Pike stopped him with a palm on the flat of his chest. 'Don't hurt her. I get really, really mean when anyone hurts her.'

Nick didn't reply. He didn't know what to say. He didn't know what to think. He couldn't imagine there could be much worry about him hurting Elsa. He couldn't even get her to stick around long enough for breakfast and a cup of coffee.

Chapter Fourteen

From the inside of Victor's Lexus, Tanya looked out over the deserted gravel pit. All of its silent earth-moving equipment looked like sleeping dinosaurs in the darkness. She shivered, but not from the cold of the desert at night. 'Victor, why have you brought me to this place?'

'I need to fuck, Tanya, and this place gets me hard as a petrified brick bat. How about it, hon? A little sex al fresco?' Victor got out of the car and nodded her to do the same.

'Is not a very pretty place for sex al fresco,' Tanya observed.

'What is it they say? Beauty's in the eye of the beholder. I wonder, has the Mount Vegas team ever done an act in a gravel pit?' he asked.

'Not that I know of, they haven't.' She rubbed her arms for the warmth she really needed at the moment. 'Most of the people like the city with all of its big windows and bright lights for their fantasies. And if they do it outside, they want nice location, you know, gardens, grass, trees.'

'Pity,' Victor said as he motioned her around to his side of the car where he sat down on a large, flat-topped rock and patted the place for her to sit next to him. 'I've done a few acts in gravel pits,' he said as she moved cautiously to join him. ''Course my gravel pit performances aren't very glamorous, and they can get rather ... messy, but I am a cop, after all, not someone who fucks for a living. Still –' he wound a strand of her hair around his finger and toyed with it '– I could very easily imagine you and Nick Chase together here, after hours, doing a little private act just for me. What do you think?'

This time he fisted her hair and pulled her into a tight kiss while she struggled to push aside fear that rose like a bitter taste at back of her throat. Just when she was certain his kiss would suffocate her, he pulled away and sighed happily. 'Your Mr Chase and I are like two sides of the same coin, Tanya. Mr Chase digs up ancient bodies –' he leant in very close to her ear '– and I bury not so ancient ones.'

Tanya swallowed back the cry that threatened and tried to control the way her heart pounded like drum.

'Your Mr Chase might discover all kinds of things buried in places like this, don't you think, Tanya? If he knew where to look, that is. And assuming he was in any condition to look.'

'Victor, please. I promise, I will convince him to help us.' No matter how hard she tried, she couldn't keep her lip from quivering. The flood of terror that she felt was thick and nauseating and she struggled to control herself.

'Oh, don't look so distressed, Tanya –' He ran a thumb over her lip, and she flinched as he groped at her breasts through the thin tank top that she wore. 'Your Mr Chase is a law-abiding citizen. You said it yourself: he's a conservative sort, not wanting to rock anybody's boat. When push comes to shove, he'll come down on the side of the law and hand Mount Vegas and Elsa Crane over to me on a silver platter. All you have to do is ease him in that direction, Tanya. Can you do that?'

She was afraid that her heart would leap out of her mouth when she spoke. 'I will do. You know that I will,

Victor. I will see that he does what it is you ask.'

'Good.' He straightened his jacket and looked out over the deserted gravel pit. 'Yes, this would be a very good place for an act. It's just so isolated and private, isn't it?' He lifted her until she was sitting on his lap. Then he shifted so that she sat on one knee, giving him room to unzip his trousers. 'My cock gets stiff just thinking about all the fun I could have at night out here with you and Nick Chase. Does it make that little cunt of yours wet? Hell why am I asking? Your cunt's always wet, you little slut.'

He pushed her skirt up and dragged the crotch of her panties to one side. Then, with her still seated on his lap, he lifted her enough so that he could slide his cock up inside her. She tried not to cry out. He was thick and heavy and didn't bother with the foreplay. She spat on her hand and pushed her fingers in for a quick stroke of him to ease his way into her straining pussy. But in spite of her efforts to control herself, a cry escaped her throat when he grabbed her tank top by the hem and tore it all the way up her back so he could shove it off her shoulders, leaving her topless with her breasts bouncing each time he thrust. He cupped and kneaded her in his large hands, and his gropes became harder and more painful the closer he got to his orgasm.

This time, Tanya didn't even pretend to come. With cold fear prickling her skin, she bounced up and down on his lap with his hot breath against her bare back until he grunted and cursed, and she knew that he had come. He pushed her off his lap and used her torn shirt to wipe his wet cock, and then he threw it back at her.

And once he had caught his breath, he said to her, 'I'm a patient man, Tanya, but my patience has limits, and I'd advise you not to push those limits. Convince Nick Chase that Elsa Crane's a notorious criminal and her organisation needs to be brought down.' Then he took her chin in his hand and kissed her hard. 'Don't worry, sweetheart, I'll do what I can to help you make sure Mr Chase remains a law-abiding citizen. In the meantime, you can use that wet little pussy of yours to influence his decision. We men – well, we're always pushovers where wet little pussies are concerned.'

He gave her another hard kiss, then he made her ride home topless and shivering in the air conditioned Lexus.

Kandi was in the reception area of Elsa's office when Nick arrived. She was dressed in a black power suit and her hair was done up in a chignon. She looked like she could be the CEO of a big company. 'Elsa's expecting you. Just go on in. And Nick –' she flashed a bright smile '– it was really hot last night.'

'Did you keep the Aston Martin?' he asked.

She nodded. 'I don't know what the hell I'm gonna do with it. I'm more a Corvette sort of girl.' She offered Nick a wink. 'Just my bad luck, isn't it? Elsa gets the sexy guy and I'm stuck with some prissy-assed car.'

'I feel your pain,' Nick said as she nodded him toward Elsa's office.

Inside, Elsa sat behind her desk tapping away on her laptop. 'Did you bring the limo?' she asked without so much as looking up. Jesus! She acted as though nothing had happened between them. How could she be so damned cold?

'I did,' he said, trying to keep his voice neutral. 'Pike says the installation of the cameras shouldn't take long.'

'Good. He told you we'll need it tomorrow night?' She gave a few more quick keystrokes, then palmed the laptop shut. She moved to sit on the arm of the sofa next to him, looking way too good in a curve-hugging minidress in a floral print that caressed her body. Why did she always have to look so good when he was angry at her? 'I need you to drive for that act tomorrow night,

161

Nick.'

'I know, Pike told me. That's fine. That's easy enough.' When she squirmed and then eased down onto the sofa next to him, he asked, 'What are you not telling me?'

'You'll be driving Pike and me.'

'I've had lots of people fucking in the back of my limo, Elsa. You're just two more.'

'Good. That's good, then.' He was disappointed that she ignored his little dig, even more disappointed at the possibility that she might not have even noticed it. She continued. 'It's a frequently requested fantasy, but …'

'But what?'

'Well, this time the chauffeur'll be doing more than driving.'

Nick folded his arms across his chest. 'Such as?'

'Well, at first he'll just be watching, doing a bit of choking the chicken. Then he'll drive the couple to an area of the parking garage we've got cordoned off over at the Tropicana, and there, he'll join the party.'

'OK, so I drive the two of you around Vegas while you go at it in the back of my limo, and I watch and play with my junk. Then Pike and I both do you in the parking garage. Got it.'

She shifted on the sofa and ran a finger down his arm. 'We can do it that way, and we will if we have to. But that's not exactly the fantasy. You're elected because I've got no one else who can drive a limo. Pagan's our chauffeur when we have limo fantasies, but he's been specifically requested in a bodybuilding fantasy in one of the hotel gyms. Kandi didn't see the logistics problem until it was too late.'

'So?' Nick could feel the nerves in his stomach tingle. 'What exactly is the fantasy, then?'

She held his gaze. 'Mr Pickford wants to see Pike and me do the limo driver together.'

162

Nick's pulse did a drum roll, and he grabbed onto the sofa as though he feared it would eject him. 'Then Pike is going to …'

She nodded. 'While you fuck me. If you're OK with that.' Then she added, 'Don't worry about any damage to the upholstery or the carpets. We'll have your limo fully detailed for you afterwards.'

'Oh, I'm so relieved to hear that,' he said, rolling his eyes. For a moment he was sure neither of them was breathing, and he really didn't see much point in saying he'd never done it with a man before. Surely she knew that. And of course he wasn't OK with it! How could he be OK with it? He was scared shitless. Someone would watch him taking it up the arse – his virgin run, no less! And Tanya might not even get her bonus! And he didn't know what the truth was about Mount Vegas! And the cops were after Elsa and what the fuck was he still doing here?

'Nick?' Her voice was little more than a whisper. Her deep blue eyes locked on him. 'Are you all right? Because you don't have to go through with it if –'

'You said guys doing guys turns you on?'

She blinked, then offered a cautious smile. 'I did. Yes. It does. And you and Pike together – well, it would be amazing.' Her pulse fluttered against her throat and her chest rose and fell as though it were struggling to escape the sundress. 'If you can't … if you're unable to let Pike do it when the time comes, then you can both just fuck me and we'll give Mr Picket a discount and it'll be OK. Honest.'

'I'll do it.' The words were out almost before he knew it, then he added quickly. 'But I'm doing it for you, Elsa, not for Mr Picket, not for Pike. I'm doing it because it turns you on.'

Before she could respond, he laid a finger across her lips. 'And don't think this means you're off the hook for the way you ran out this morning, or for any of the other shit we need to talk about.'

'Nick, I –'

He stopped her words with a hard kiss and, even in all his confusion, he was hopeful when she returned it, her warm, expressive tongue reintroducing itself to his. She pulled away far sooner than he wanted, then stood. 'I have to get ready for tonight's act, and since you and Pike'll be in the control room, maybe you can get him to talk you through your part.' She bent and kissed him again, and nodded him toward the door.

He left the room knowing, even as he mentally kicked himself for the fact, that he wouldn't back out, that he would do this for Elsa, and that if he couldn't get some clear idea in his head as to what needed to happen next, he might be joining Elsa and Pike and the whole Mount Vegas crew in prison before very damned long. And yet, in spite of Detective Havers' visit, he still couldn't bring himself to believe they were doing anything wrong.

Chapter Fifteen

Nick thought he'd be jealous when things got hot and heavy between Elsa and Pike in the back seat of his limo, but what he got was turned on. OK, he could have been imagining it, but every so often, he was sure he could catch Elsa's gaze darting toward the mirror. He knew it was all part of Mr Picket's fantasy, that the woman and the man in the back deliberately get the limo driver hot. But this was more. This was Elsa returning the favour. Yes, he could be imagining it, but that was his fantasy, wasn't it? By the time Pike had pulled aside the scoop top of her halter dress and nursed noisily on first one and then the other of Elsa's exquisite breasts, Nick had his fly open and one hand fisted around his cock while the other rested on the steering wheel. He knew there was a camera showing the driver's response to the back seat action, and it was a testament to how far down this kinky road he'd gone that it didn't bother him at all that someone – a man, even – was watching him jerk off.

In the mirror, he could see Elsa squirming in the seat until her skirt was up over her hips. Pike yanked the crotch of her panties to one side. She offered Nick a teasing smile and spread her legs, sliding down farther in the seat. He got a tantalizing view of her heavy pout before Pike splayed her with his hand and thrust his long middle finger into her. She whimpered and bore down, then they both giggled like naughty schoolchildren and shushed each other. 'You'll make me wet his seat,' Elsa whispered, just loud enough for Nick to hear.

'Hell, you'll be squirting all over the floor once I get your G-spot all warmed up,' Pike said.

Nick was sure he could see the moisture puddling beneath Elsa's bottom and running down the edge of the seat already. His cock felt like a lead weight between his legs. He eased off on the stroking, afraid if he didn't Elsa wouldn't be the only one squirting all over the floor.

'Mmm,' Pike sniffed. 'I bet he can smell you. I bet he can smell how horny your little pussy is. Bet his cock's as stiff as mine.' Nick could see him thumbing her clit. 'Bet he'd love to stick it up your hot, pouty cunt.'

'Oh Christ! Oh fuck! I'm coming,' Elsa hissed, then she shuddered until her tits bounced, and braced her stiletto-shod feet against the floor, arching and writhing. Nick could hear the wet stroking of Pike's fingers scissoring inside Elsa's slit, and he thumbed the tip of his cock to hold his wad. Damn, he was beginning to understand why voyeurism was such big business for Mount Vegas.

'I'm gonna make you come until you can't walk straight, you filthy little thing,' Pike said. Elsa was fumbling to release Pike's cock. For a second, Nick felt fear course up his spine at the sight of the man's straining erection, thick and pale like marble in the ambient light. Nick's anus clenched involuntarily and he faltered for a moment in his stroking, until Elsa leant down and took Pike's dick into her mouth, all the way into her mouth, and Nick was thumbing himself again. Hard. As if that weren't bad enough, Elsa scrambled to reposition herself in the stretch limo so that she half stood, half squatted in front of Pike, head down in his lap, thrusting and sucking while her arse rose to perfect view in Nick's mirror, her sopping pussy clenching and releasing just above the beaded hard-on of her clit. Pike reached around to spread her bottom, to pull her open so the dark of her hole was exposed, dilated and gripping, in Nick's view, and Nick couldn't hold back a moan.

Elsa pulled away from Pike long enough to ask, 'Driver? Driver, is your cock hard?'

'Sorry, ma'am,' Nick said. 'But it's really difficult not to be … excited. You two aren't very subtle.'

Both Elsa and Pike laughed. 'No we're not,' Pike said.

'Wanna join us?' Elsa turned so that her breasts were right in his line of sight.

'No, I couldn't, really. It's against the rules and –'

'We'll pay you for your time, won't we, sweetie?' she said, turning back to Pike.

'What, you mean like a ménage?' Nick said.

'Yeah, a ménage,' Pike replied, as though he'd just thought of the most brilliant idea. 'Not an opportunity we get too much out in Iowa, ménage in a limo.'

Nick was already pulling into the parking garage at the Tropicana. 'Oooh, do hurry,' Elsa whimpered. 'I want to see that hard cock of yours, driver. What's your name? No, don't tell me. It'll be more fun for all of us if we don't know each other's names. Tell me, driver, do you have your cock out?'

'Not room for it in my jeans,' Nick said. 'Not with you two carrying on like that.'

Elsa giggled. 'Afraid I did get pussy juice all over your seat, and I think there'll probably be some jizz, maybe lots of jizz before too long. Would you like to jizz my pussy?' She wiggled her bare bottom at him. It took him two seconds to park and throw open the back door. Elsa had gone back to work on Pike's cock and Nick slipped in beside her and began to finger her wet pussy. She moaned around Pike in response.

'You two married?' Nick asked.

Pike practically guffawed. 'Are you kidding? We just met at the bar last night. Found out we're both here for the same thing – and I'm not talking the casinos.'

'Well, there's plenty of that to be had here in Vegas,' Nick said, then grabbed his penis in his fist and shoved it up into Elsa's pout. She mmmphed her approval around Pike's cock.

'She's tight, isn't she?' Pike said. 'And holy fuck, I've never seen anyone so slippery. You like that, don't you, driver?'

Nick only grunted and nodded in response. Elsa ran an exploring hand back to cup his balls and stroke his thigh. They were all scrunched in the back, way tighter than need be, but Nick was humping Elsa hard and she had Pike way down her throat with him hunched over her like he was afraid she might desert her post.

'Let me have some of her pussy juice,' Pike said, and Nick pulled out just enough for Pike to scoop his fingers through Elsa's wetness, then buried his cock to the hilt and continued thrusting.

'She's like wet silk, isn't she?' Pike said.

Nick mumbled his agreement. Though he knew it was coming, though he was expecting it, when Pike pushed his wet finger up against his anus, he froze.

'It's all right,' Pike breathed. 'You're OK with that, aren't you, buddy? It doesn't mean anything. Just means the three of us are filthy horny, just means we want to enjoy each other fully. Doesn't it? Isn't it OK?' He gave his slippery finger a little wriggle, and Nick released a shaky breath.

'I've never … I mean, I don't mind or anything … it's just that …'

'Hell, man, I haven't either,' Pike said. 'But it's Vegas. We got all night, buddy, and I promise you we'll compensate for the fares you'll miss. And we'll pay you too.'

They all laughed nervously and Nick relaxed.

'That's it, that's better. You'll like this. I can tell,' Pike said. 'We'll all like this. Just relax your little asshole and let me make it feel good.'

'I want to see! I want to see!' Elsa gasped, releasing Pike from her mouth. She pulled herself off Nick's cock and turned to face him. There was a mad scramble in the seat with Nick suddenly sandwiched in the middle. Elsa positioned herself half seated with her back against the far door, one leg up over the back seat and one pressed hard against the back of the front seat, all inviting-like. Nick ploughed into her, feeling shivers down his spine and Pike's breath against his arse crack just before he felt the man's tongue lap at his pucker, and he nearly went through the roof.

'Oh fuck! Oh God,' he gasped. 'No one's ever … I don't know if …' And hell if he could formulate a sentence.

'It's all right. It's all right,' Elsa whispered against his ear.

Nick felt like he was on both ends of the seesaw at once, with Elsa's tight, velvety grip milking his cock for all it was worth each time he thrust and with Pike behind, easing his finger past the tight sphincter into untouched territory. And Nick couldn't say he didn't like it. Nick couldn't say shit at the moment because his brain was offline and his body was losing control.

'We're gonna make this good,' Pike whispered. 'We're gonna make this so good for all of us.' Then he squirmed away and Nick heard something ripping, heard something squirting, and felt cold wetness on his anus. 'We found some of this super-glide lube in a really nasty sex shop, gonna make your little pucker all slippery and ready for me and my cock all slippery for you.' He shoved two fingers into the cool slick.

Before Nick knew it, Pike was scissoring his anus,

stretching and probing. And all of the things he felt, all of the anticipation and dread and fear and arousal, all of them surged together up his spine, down his belly and into his cock, thrusting into Elsa's heat.

She pulled him down to her and kissed him over and over, her fists curled against his upper back. 'It's gonna be good, sweetie. It's gonna be so good. I think it's so hot what you two are doing. You'll make me come so hard. My poor little pussy won't be able to stand it.'

Maybe she was trying to distract him, because they both knew that what he now felt up tight and slippery against his hole was Pike's substantial cock. And somewhere in the back of his brain, he thanked his lucky star that it was Pike's penis and not Horse's that was about to initiate his butthole.

Pike laid one large hand on his lower back, almost as though he were trying to calm him. He probably was, actually. Then he slid it down to part Nick's butt cheeks while his other hand guided his penis home. 'Just relax now.' Pike's voice was tight with arousal, his breath controlled with effort. 'I'm gonna push into you now, just relax.'

'Do it! Just do it.' Nick gasped, bracing himself for impact, impact that was slick and grudging and stung and burned like fire and felt like it reached all the way up his spine.

'Jesus that's so hot, that's so damned hot, that's amazing,' Elsa said. And just as Pike made his first real thrust and Nick felt like he was being assaulted by a battering ram, she whispered against his mouth. 'You're amazing.' And suddenly, the burning and the blunted ploughing gave way to wild, intense fullness, and he *was* amazing! He would be amazing for Elsa Crane.

At first the three of them were awkward and off balance, sliding and hunching over the seat, nearly falling onto the floor. Then they caught their stride. Nick

170

seesawed forward into Elsa's outrageously hot pussy, then back onto Pike's hard penis. He decided the man was aptly named. And then the rhythm changed so that all forward thrust buried itself into Elsa's receptive opening, with Pike following Nick in hard. And then all backward momentum pressed and impaled itself onto Pike's drilling cock. Nick wasn't exactly sure when it happened, but he knew it had. At some point they were no longer roleplaying. They were themselves, so much themselves that he feared the two could read his thoughts. Nick feared the two could see right through him. And even as it frightened him, in the scheme of things it seemed like the logical progression of the trust they needed to have in each other, of the place they needed to go together if they were to do this.

Tension built until Elsa tumbled into orgasm that began with a tremor up through the grip of her pussy and then rocked and shuddered through her whole body. It was Elsa's orgasm that laid the foundation, which sucked the two men in and down and over the edge. The first shudder of Pike's cock up inside Nick felt like a heartbeat, harder and harder, faster and faster, and the hard grip of his stomach muscles shoved Nick forward deep as he unloaded into Elsa's hungry, convulsing depths. The smell of sex filled the limo and the sounds of grunts and moans were muffled tight against each other. The windows were steamed with their body heat, and the strange sense of comfort washing over Nick was something he would have never expected as they collapsed onto each other in the back of the limo, slipping and sliding across the seat. And, strangely, Nick found that he welcomed Pike's kisses as easily as he had Tanya's or Deb's or Beetle's. In fact, he welcomed Pike's body next to his on the seat. But it was Elsa's breath he felt like his own, Elsa's heartbeat he felt shuddering against his palm, and Elsa's words that filled his brain.

'You are amazing.' Those words were not a part of the act. Nick didn't know how he knew it. He just did.

Chapter Sixteen

This time, Nick didn't make excuses when the whole Mount Vegas gang descended on the suite in the Tropicana with its enormous Jacuzzi and two orgy-ready bedrooms. The equipment had been packed away by the time Elsa, Nick, and Pike got to the suite and Beetle and Deb had ordered enough room service to feed half the hotel. Deb launched herself at the three of them in a group hug. 'You brought him along this time,' she said to Elsa, planting a huge, sloppy kiss on Nick's surprised mouth.

'Contractual obligation,' Elsa said, offering him a smile. She knew she should keep her distance. There were plenty of people for her to play with tonight. Deke was back to full strength and would be doing his first act tomorrow night. Horse and Pagan had just done a very filthy guy-on-guy gym scene and Deb and Kandi had taken over the dungeon. Beetle and Deke had run the control room. Really, her plan was just to get Nick involved with the rest of the gang and then quietly slip away. It would be better that way, no matter how much she wanted to stay for a little one-on-one. But Nick wasn't that easy to palm off, and when everyone else headed toward the feast spread on the table and the kitchen countertop he pulled her aside into the soft lighting of the entranceway. He took her mouth like it was the feast, like he would settle for nothing less, and she might have pulled away if she'd been any less hungry for him. She should have pulled away. And yet when he touched her it was like being drawn to magnetic north.

'Food can wait, Elsa,' he said. 'I want you right now. I want you bad.'

'Nick, please.' She made a half-hearted effort to push him away as his hand found its way inside her top, palm cupping her weight, thumb sweeping her nipple. 'Nick … please,' she repeated into his mouth. 'Nick, please.'

'Please what, Elsa?'

He nibbled at her ear, then at the soft spot low on her nape that sent shivers down her spine, sent a flush of wet heat rushing below her belly. And all the sensations, the delicious, frightening, disturbing sensations Nick Chase always aroused in her seemed to converge beneath her breastbone, grabbing at her breath, making her insides quiver like she walked in high places, like if she fell the fall would be desperate and terrifying. But then again, Nick Chase could almost make her believe that if she fell, she could fly.

His fingers slipped up under her skirt, into the residual slickness of his own release mixed with hers. He tweaked her, parted her, and she came. Christ! Could it really be that easy for him to take her, to control her? He didn't give her a moment to contemplate. Somewhere above her ragged breathing, she heard the zip of his fly and, in a move that was so nearly effortless she could have believed herself lost in a dream, he lifted her onto him. He shifted and grunted and impaled her.

'Elsa,' he whispered against her neck. 'Dear God, Elsa. I can't get enough of you.'

'Grub's served,' someone called from the kitchen. Someone else shushed the voice and said something about leaving them alone.

It happened quickly, like a lightning strike, like a gust of wind at the height of a storm. He thrust, his hands cupping and kneading her arse. She gripped, her legs curled around his waist, her face buried against his mussed hair. Then they were freefalling into each other's release as though they hadn't just come a little while ago in the limo, as though they had never come at all until this moment. And when it was finished, when the tremors that shook them passed, and Nick's lips settled once again to hers, the smell of food came back to them, and the sound of their friends, the people Elsa cared about, came back into focus, and he settled her onto her feet with a smile that did things to her. 'There. That's better, isn't it?' He said. And it was. It really was better.

There were backslaps and hugs and kisses all around as Elsa and Nick joined the party. 'Here's to another job well done,' Deb said raising her glass. Everyone toasted.

'I hear Mr Bernard was very pleased with the cock play in the gym,' Deke said, addressing Pagan and Horse.'

'As well he should be.' Horse practically inhaled a fajita. 'Those weights were fucking heavy.'

Pagan offered him a wicked smile. 'Why, thanks, buddy.' He adjusted his junk, barely covered in a pair of dark cotton shorts. 'I like to think so.'

Horse flipped him off and everyone laughed.

'I'd like to make a toast,' Pike said, standing up and raising a glass of red wine. 'To the popping of Nick's ass cherry. Well done, Nick! I was definitely up for it, and you were … open to new experiences.'

In the wave of laughter and the toast and backslaps that followed, Nick found himself feeling strangely comfortable with these people, and when Pike leant over and gave him a full-on tongue kiss to the cheers of the whole team, he returned the favour, even being bold enough to give the man's junk a good groping. Of course, it didn't hurt that Elsa was watching, that the scent of her was still all over his body, that the feel of her still trembled along his skin like some sort of magic spell. He liked it here. He liked it a lot.

Then the unwelcome thought of Detective Havers and Tanya shoved its way into his head. No. He was as certain as he was of his own name that neither Elsa nor Mount Vegas would be involved in any of the things Havers spoke of. There was no doubt. He leant close to Elsa and pulled her head onto his shoulder, then whispered into her ear, 'We need to talk.'

She pushed away as though he had given her an electric shock. 'Nick.' She glanced around the room at everyone else still ploughing through the food like ravenous wolves. 'Nick, please.'

He stopped her words with a kiss. 'Do you know a Detective Victor Havers?'

Her shoulders stiffened. She shot another glance around the room. 'We can't talk about this here,' she said.

'Then where?'

'Come on.' She jerked her head toward the door. 'You haven't been drinking. Are you fit to drive?'

When he nodded, she rose and said, 'You all are lovely, and I'd fuck you all in a heartbeat as I'm sure our dear Nick would too, but I'm pulling rank. Don't party too hard. I'll see you tomorrow at the Elara.'

They left to the cheers and catcalls of the rest of the team.

In the parking garage, she joined him in the front of the limo. 'Where to?' he asked.

'Just somewhere out of town. I'm not in the mood to go back to my office. Has Havers been to your house?'

'Yes. He and Tanya.'

She blew out a breath and ran a hand through her

176

hair. 'Right, then we really shouldn't go there either. Chances are good the bastard's having you watched. Probably has you bugged. The fucker's a slimy rat, and he's dangerous. Tell me what happened.'

Nick headed out toward Red Rocks. It was his automatic response, even if he wasn't going home. Elsa stared out the window as he told her about his encounter with Havers and Tanya, and when the lights of the city were behind them, he found a side road, pulled onto it and shut off the engine.

'Elsa, I want to know what's going on, and I want to know about The Mount.' When she didn't answer, he asked, 'Is Mount Vegas involved in something illegal?'

He heard her sigh in the darkness. 'Mount Vegas is involved in exactly what you've seen. Though what we do is not actually illegal, the area in which we operate is grey. You're no doubt aware that while prostitution is legal in the state of Nevada, it's not legal in the city limits of Las Vegas or anywhere in Clark County.'

'What Mount Vegas is doing isn't prostitution,' Nick said.

'True. But what Mount Vegas is doing has to do with sex, and anything that has to do with sex, no matter how consensual, no matter how above board, is suspect. Sadly, that's just the result of Western civilisation's religious roots. No getting away from it. We've all been socialised by it whether we like it or not. And the fact that money changes hands for anything to do with sex is always frowned upon. Because it's Vegas, there's as much hearsay and myth as there is truth behind the seamier side of the city. And Nick, I would have never allowed you to take over for Tanya if I was putting you or your business at risk legally, surely you know that?'

'Then what is it Havers thinks he has on you and Mount Vegas?' Nick asked.

'Can we talk about this outside?' she said. 'I need

some fresh air. It feels like I've been cooped up for days.'

Nick pulled a blanket from the trunk and helped her up onto the hood. Once they were comfortably reclining against the windshield, looking up at the Milky Way stretching across the night sky, he settled the blanket over them and pulled her close. 'Tell me.'

She snuggled against him. 'Mount Vegas makes a ton of money, Nick. A ton of money. And we do it offering a service that's totally unique. Though we've tried to keep it all as discreet as possible, good news gets out. In our case, no matter how hush-hush we've been, what happens in Vegas hasn't stayed in Vegas. And though we're still one of the city's best kept secrets, our business grows by word of mouth, and not all of our clients are as discreet as we'd like them to be. That's just due to the fact that we're really, really good at what we do.

'The police have been aware of Mount Vegas almost from the beginning. That was important for us, important that they understood that grey area in which we operate, and really, Nick, a lot of Vegas operates in a grey area, doesn't it? So though they know about it, like all police forces, Vegas has its share of cops on the take. Havers runs a protection racket. He keeps his clients safe from … well, from him and his thugs. His fee depends on just how lucrative the business is. The more vulnerable a business is, the easier it is for him to put the hurt on them. Mount Vegas is not all that vulnerable, so he's had to find a different way in. Planting drugs, lots of drugs, usually does the trick when all else fails. Oh, some have tried to hold out against him. Businesses have burned to the ground. Family members have ended up dead, people have disappeared. No one holds out for long.'

'Jesus,' Nick said under his breath. 'And he wants

Mount Vegas.'

Elsa nodded. 'He wants Mount Vegas. And though everyone knows that about Havers, no one can prove anything. And because of his connections, no one can touch him. No one would dare. The fact that Mount Vegas has no roots in organised crime and has no connections with any of the powers-that-be in the area, in any area that could tarnish our reputation, and the fact it's a cash cow hasn't been missed by people who can do us real harm.' She raised herself up on one elbow and he could feel her looking down at him. 'That's the truth of it, Nick. We've known that we'd have to fight this battle from the beginning, so we've come into the world with our backs against the wall and we've learned to keep our eyes and ears open and dodge the bullets. We've made friends where we've been able to and slipped under the radar where we had to in order to make sure it was clear we weren't horning in on anyone's turf. It hasn't been easy, but we've managed it, and we've thrived.'

She shivered. Nick pulled her back down against him. She settled in close and continued. 'I know that you've probably got more reason to believe Havers than me. He's a cop and I'm … well, I'm someone you still don't know if you can trust. But I'm telling you the truth. I swear it.'

'I don't like him,' Nick said without a thought. 'And I got the feeling that Tanya was – I don't know, scared of him.' When Elsa didn't respond, he said, 'Do you think he can really do what he says, bring down you and Mount Vegas?'

'Oh, I'm sure he'll try. And you say he plans this during the big act we'll be doing when the London folks are here?'

Nick nodded into the darkness. 'He says that's all just a cover-up. Elsa, if he can pull this off, will we all end up in jail?'

'Quite likely, Nick. Though not from the truth, we won't.'

Once again there was a long moment of silence. 'Elsa, I did a little research. Rita Holly Martelli and The Mount in London all seem to be connected to Mount Vegas, and obviously they are if Rita Holly's coming here. What exactly is The Mount, and why do I get the idea that it's way bigger than Mount Vegas and a London dance club?'

Elsa sighed. 'You're too nosey for your own good, Nick Chase. You know that?'

'I tend to be that way when there's a possibility of me getting my ass carted off to jail.'

She shook her head. 'No. You've always been nosey.' She lifted her face to his and gave him a lingering kiss, and he moaned softly and pulled her on top of him, feeling himself harden under her body. She could so easily make him forget everything but the feel of her, the need for her. Perhaps she sensed it. She gave his bottom lip a nibble and laid her hand against his chest, creating enough breathing space for his brain to kick back in. Then she took a deep breath. 'Nick, I'm going to ask you to do something for me, and I need you to trust me enough to do it without questioning.'

'Ask first, and then I'll decide,' he said, feeling a knot tighten in his gut.

'I need you to go along with Havers. I need you to tell him exactly what he wants to know.'

'Jesus, woman, you don't want much, do you?'

This time she curled her fist in his hair and pulled him into a toe-kinking kiss that had his cock's full attention and nearly had him forgetting his own name. 'I want everything. I want absolutely everything.'

'That much is clear,' he breathed into her mouth. 'You could convince God to give you heaven and the devil to give you hell. What choice could a mere limo driver have?'

'A mere limo driver, my ass,' she said, smiling down at him. 'Doctor Nicolas Chase. I know about your research in the Valley of Fire and the Muddy Mountains, and I know you spent time working in the John Day Fossil Beds out in Oregon. Just because you're no longer openly involved with a university doesn't mean you're just a limo driver. You're not the only one who's nosey.'

'That was another life, Elsa. A man has to make a living. I'm no more fit for academia than I am to be driving limos. One's too political; one's just mind-numbing.' He ran his hand up under her skirt to cup her, and she caught her breath. 'Maybe I'm fit to be your sex slave. What do you think? I think I could be good at that.'

He felt her stiffen and pull away and he held his breath, wondering if he'd lose her again, wondering what he'd said.

But she relaxed back into his arms. 'You don't really want to be my sex slave, Nick. I'm a very strict mistress.'

'And why is it that the thought makes my cock hard?'

She laughed and he felt her breath against his ear. 'Your cock has been hard since the moment I met you. I don't think it takes much.'

'It takes more than you think, Elsa. More than you think.'

'So will you do it? Will you do what I ask as far as Havers is concerned?'

'All right.' He twirled a strand of her hair around his finger. 'And if it all goes to hell, do you think they'll allow us conjugal visits in prison?'

'I might be able to arrange it,' she said with a soft giggle. 'I have connections, you know?'

For a long moment they lay in silence, his hand stroking her bottom, his cock pressing in delicious

181

discomfort against the weight of her body. Then he spoke. 'Tell me something.'

When she made no response, he continued. 'I Googled Mount Vegas and though I found it, I didn't find out anything I didn't already know. I Googled Tanya, and though there wasn't a lot about her, I did find her. As for the other Mount Vegas folks – well, it embarrasses me to say I don't know their last names, and their nicknames turned up nothing, but Elsa, you're un-Googleable. Why is that?'

She tightened her embrace, almost as though she were afraid of losing *him*. He liked that thought. It was always the other way round. She kissed him, this time lazily and leisurely, and when she pulled away, she slid out from under the blanket and off the hood. She stood looking out into the desert, then she inhaled as though she'd only just now remembered to breathe. 'It's because I don't exist, Nick. I don't exist. And now you'd better take me back to the hotel. We've got a busy day ahead of us tomorrow.'

Before he could get over the shock of what she'd just said, or even ask what the hell she meant, she was already settled back into the limo and buckling her seatbelt.

The closer they got to Vegas, the more frustrated he felt. She sat next to him, staring out the window into the darkness, lost in her own thoughts. She'd told him she didn't exist. How the hell could she not exist? The very thought disturbed him somewhere deep inside. Her people clearly adored her. She was outrageously competent. Havers certainly knew who she was, and he wanted her brought down. Men like him didn't want someone brought down unless they were frightening, unless they mattered, unless they existed. She existed! She damn well existed and the way she constantly jerked him around was another testament to that existence. He would find out what the fuck was going on no matter what he had to do to manage it.

As resolved as he was, he didn't confront her on it. It would do him no good at the moment. There might come a time when she'd trust him enough to tell him what the hell was going on, but in the meantime, he'd just have to find out on his own.

At the Tropicana, they took the elevator in silence, and he left her at the door with a lingering kiss, not wanting to leave, yet knowing that she needed space. He needed space too.

'You'll do what I ask, then … about Havers?' she said, holding him in a gaze that was a fortress.

'I said that I would,' he replied.

Relief flashed across her face. She kissed him again and turned without saying goodbye.

It was only when he got out of the limo in front of his house that he noticed her BlackBerry lying in the middle of the seat. He probably wouldn't even have noticed it then if it hadn't rung. He picked it up, thinking it would be her letting him know she'd left it behind.

But the melodic female voice on the device wasn't Elsa's.

'Sorry to bother you, sweetie, but I just couldn't wait to hear how it went tonight with Nick and Pike. Dying to know details.'

'Hello?' Nick said. 'Who is this?'

There was a pause, but Nick could still hear the woman breathing. 'Um, who is *this*?' came the reply. 'What are you doing answering Elsa's phone?' Then there was an excited squeal that made him hold the phone away from his ear. 'You're Nick, aren't you? Nick Chase? Wow! It's so good to finally meet you. I'm Rita Holly. I'm a friend of Elsa's.'

'From the Mount in London, Rita Holly Martelli, that Rita Holly?' He spoke around the rapid staccato of his pulse.

'That would be me,' the woman said. 'I see you've done your homework, and if I'm guessing right, and I usually do, then our Elsa won't be happy that you've done it so well. Hold it, is she there?'

'Nope. She left her BlackBerry in my limo.' Nick shut the door and leant back against the hood. 'Hardly my fault, is it?'

The laugh she offered him was positively wicked, and Nick liked the woman already. 'Certainly not your fault. Though the fact that you're there with her phone and your limo and she's not – well, that might just be your fault. Is it?'

'I only wish I knew,' Nick said.

'Mmm. Well, Elsa can tend to be a bit flighty. Bit secretive too, but then that's a part of what makes her so hot. My, my, she's getting careless, isn't she, not taking her BlackBerry with her? But I can imagine you were distracting her, weren't you, Mr Chase?'

'Might have been,' he said.

'Which raises a plethora of juicy new questions I'm dying to ask you, Nick – it is all right if I call you Nick, isn't it? I already feel like we're old friends.' She went on without waiting for his answer, 'Now I'd advise against continuing this conversation on Elsa's BlackBerry and risking her substantial wrath, which, no doubt, you'll get anyway, but let's not make it worse. Why don't you give me your number and let me call you back, because I think you and I have a whole lot to talk about.'

Chapter Seventeen

Elsa had watched the sun rise over the mountains, a view she could see clearly from the upper floors of the Elara. She hadn't slept. Pagan had delivered her BlackBerry to the front desk a couple of hours ago, no doubt not happy that she'd sent him to get it, but she didn't want to face Nick right now, and she didn't want company.

Now it was almost lunchtime and she had kept herself busy planning out the acts that were scheduled for the next two months. She palmed her laptop closed and stood to pace in front of the window. After Nick had left, she'd taken a taxi and checked in to one of the suites at the Elara. It was her favourite hotel when she needed to be alone, when she needed to think. She supposed it was because the Elara was the first hotel she had taken refuge in, what seemed like a lifetime ago now. For three days, she'd been afraid to leave the suite. Then for another three days she hadn't left it because she'd been planning and scheming how she would survive. She was a little bit like God, she thought to herself with a tight smile. On the seventh day, she became Elsa Crane. She left the room and discovered Vegas. Of course, that took a whole lot more than one day. But it was a good beginning.

And all that time, while she was becoming Elsa Crane, Nick Chase was right there, sharing her city, knowing it, in some ways better than she ever would, down to its prehistory, down to a past even more ancient than that of The Mount. Nick and Elsa, all that time together in the same city. For a second, she wondered how the space could have possibly been big enough for them both to live their lives and not be drawn to each other like giant magnets. Or perhaps they repelled each other instead.

She supposed it said something about her that she took her refuge in a generic hotel suite rather than choosing something more upscale, rather than buying a place and making it her own like Pike had done. She came into Vegas without an identity and sometimes she wondered whether she would always be that way. There was power in walking the city's streets unseen, unnoticed. Oh, she could be noticed if she wanted, but she learned, she planned, she schemed, she observed when she was unnoticed. She got lost in the throng of people who had come with dreams of winning their fortune; lost in the throng of people who had come with the idea of hooking up. She walked unnoticed amid the people who'd eloped, the people who were having affairs, the people who were just ordinary Las Vegans trying to make a living in the madness. Elsa knew them all, watched them all, became familiar with them all. Alex Fenton was wrong. He wasn't the ultimate voyeur. She was. She was the one who saw what no one else ever did and made it work for her. She was the true observer, keeping herself distant, unnamed, unnoticed, above it all.

And then she met Nick Chase.

She settled back at the laptop to work on more fantasy plans, to keep her mind off Nick Chase and what she had inadvertently pulled him into. And what he had not so inadvertently pulled her into. She was interrupted by a knock on the door. No doubt room service delivering lunch. She was still thinking about *not* thinking about Nick when she opened the door, and there before her, looking way less jetlagged than Elsa would have thought possible, was Rita Holly.

Elsa stood stunned, making little fish gasps at the woman who was already a legend in The Mount, the woman who until now, she had never met in person.

Rita offered her an amused smile. 'Well, are you going to invite me in or just let me stand here in the hall looking silly?' Before Elsa could do more than just step out of the way, Rita added. 'I know, I know, uninvited guests are a pain in the arse, sweetie, but after my little conversation with Nick last night, I felt it was time we talked. So I took the Martelli jet, had a nice nap over the Pole, and here I am.'

'Nick? You talked to Nick?'

'I certainly did. And why the hell he isn't here with you is beyond me. But since he isn't, then maybe it's time for a serious talk, just the two of us.'

Just then, room service arrived. 'Mmm, that smells great,' Rita said, sniffing. 'I'm famished. Can you bring me one of whatever that is quick before I starve, and here's for your troubles.' She handed the waiter a wad of money, to which the raised eyebrow cued Elsa that it was more than enough to get the job done. The waiter quickly deposited the tray on the table and left.

Elsa forced a smile that she hoped would pass for welcoming as Rita sat down next to her and nabbed a French fry from her plate. She didn't want company, and she didn't want prying. Pike knew that when she was at the Elara, she was off limits.

As if Rita had read her mind, she said, 'Oh, don't blame Pike. He didn't tell me where you were. I just figured it out. Remember you told me this was where you hang out when you need to think. Now, Nick and I had a very interesting conversation last night on your phone while you should have had him locked in this suite, fucking his brains out. First of all, Nick asked lots of questions about Mount Vegas and The Mount, in general, and I answered them.'

'You did what?' Elsa felt as if her chest would explode. 'You had no right. It wasn't yours to tell.'

Rita held her in a steady gaze. 'First of all, as your superior in The Mount, I had every right. Secondly, as your friend, surely you know I would never violate your trust and what's yours to tell.'

The sense of relief Elsa felt was so great that she found herself fighting back tears.

'I've petitioned for Nick to be given access to the archives of Mount Vegas and The Mount in general, if he wants. We both know he belongs in The Mount, and I see no further reason for us to keep secrets from him.' She snitched another fry. 'And don't give me that bullshit that after he finishes Tanya's contract you'll be happy to let him walk. I know that's not true.'

Elsa scrubbed a hand over her face and stared down at her untouched club sandwich. 'No. I don't want him to leave when Tanya's contract is up. But it doesn't matter what I want, does it? My role here has always been to bring Mount Vegas up to speed, to build it and its reputation until it's ready to join The Mount as a full-fledged coven.'

'Oh, give me a break, Elsa! I know the sales pitch. Hell, my mother wrote the fucking sales pitch. You're here because you want to be. You love what you do and you're good at it and so's your team. You built Mount Vegas with a different twist, a vibrant twist that no other coven or potential coven has. Even when Vivienne was in control in London, do you know why she disliked you so much?'

Elsa shook her head.

'Because of your purity of purpose. She could find no fault in you no matter how hard she tried, and you were too far away for her to interfere with what you were doing, like she did with me. Plus I personally think she was afraid of you. I know I am.' Rita leant forward across the table. 'But your walls have been breached, sweetie. Might as well admit it and enjoy. And about damn time, that's all I can say.'

'My love life is not your business, Rita, no matter how good a friend you are.'

'Of course it's my business. You're a sister in The Mount, and Nick can't go back to where he was any more than you can. So it's time you deal with it. And anyway, that's not why I'm here.'

They were interrupted by another knock and the waiter delivered a tray for Rita, who took it and returned to the table. 'Eat your lunch, Elsa. You'll need all your strength for what's ahead of you.' She sat down and met Elsa's gaze across the full tray. 'Nick told me about this Havers bloke. He also told me that you told him to go along with the man's plan. Now I think it's time you fill me in on all the details.'

In the Beginning: The Story of Mount Vegas and How It Came To Be a Fledgling of The Mount

By Alexandra 'Beetle' Crane Marcus, historian, Mount Vegas.

There was a woman in Vegas making waves. She was a dangerous woman, who had no alliances and took no sides. She quickly became a powerful woman. She gave people their sexual fantasies, a look through the scope at their deepest desires, at their most erotic thoughts. There was a woman in Vegas who showed people the sex they wanted to see, the sex they wanted to experience, but were afraid to, and her name was Elsa Crane. No one knew who she was nor where she came from, but she gave Vegas a secret that everyone whispered about and everyone wanted. She drew people to her, competent

189

*people, people who could see her vision and who wanted
to become a part of it. She caught people's attention –
powerful people, people who knew about sex and the
human heart. First she drew to her Pike Harrison
Danes, of the Houston Coven of The Mount. He was sent
to her by the High Council to recruit her, to draw her
into the family she didn't know she had.*

*Together, and with the blessing of the Roman High
Council, Elsa Danes Crane and Pike Harrison Danes
laid the foundations for Mount Vegas. And from that
moment onward, the eyes of The Mount have been upon
the work of Elsa Danes Crane and the vibrant
organisation that she heads.*

Nick still couldn't get his mind around it. The Mount
really was a sex cult – a really ancient sex cult! His
imagination conjured erotic romps in the Corinthian-
pillared back rooms of the Roman Forum and in the high
towers of mediaeval castles. That would be good for
more than a few jerk-off sessions, he was certain. But
what really stunned him was that such a sex cult's power
and influence could be so subtle that no one even knew
about it, and yet so enormous that it was literally global.

No wonder *Talkabout* magazine was brought to its
knees. It was telling the truth, but then again, from what
Nick could see, it was a truth so preposterous no one
would believe it, and the magazine's editor had to leave
the country in disgrace. Rita Holly had given Nick
permission to look at the Mount Vegas archives, for
which Beetle was responsible. The Vegas branch of The
Mount was only a few years old and had not yet attained
coven status. Rita assured him that they weren't
witches – or at least some of them weren't. He wasn't
sure if she had been joking or not. When he had asked
Rita about Elsa, asked her to tell him why she claimed
she didn't exist, Rita told him it was Elsa's story to tell

when the time was right. He wished she'd given him a more comforting answer. However, she assured him that if he wanted to know more about The Mount, they could Skype. He figured Elsa would be furious when she found out, but he hadn't seen Elsa. She'd sent Pagan to collect her BlackBerry, and he had told Nick that he'd be doing an act with Beetle tonight, and it was complicated.

So now, here he was playing pool, which he was lousy at, wearing skinny fucking jeans, which he was uncomfortable in, and hanging out in a seedy bar he hadn't known existed until tonight. He was being watched hungrily by two men sipping Coors Lite long necks and leaning on the bar, making sure he could see their junk through their jeans. It wasn't actually a gay bar, Beetle told him. It was the kind of place where if you hung out long enough you were likely to hook up no matter who you were or what your tastes were. Another of Vegas's best kept secrets. He was beginning to think he didn't know his native town very well at all.

He leant over the table, lined up his shot, and scratched. Again. He wondered if the top of the table was going to hold up under his assault until Beetle arrived. One of the men at the bar raised his bottle in Nick's direction and blew him a kiss. Feeling stupid, Nick took a bow and turned back to the beleaguered table just as Beetle sauntered into the bar, gave a look around the room, then settled her gaze on him.

'Here, let me take care of that for you,' she said, grabbing a cue and coming to his side. He'd seen her in full drag when they were dressing in wardrobe, but he was still astonished at just how well Beetle pulled off the act. She wore a light jean jacket over a plain white T-shirt, one that fit loosely over her tightly bound breasts. It was clear through her snug black jeans that she was sporting a package. It was a soft cock, he'd been told, made for women who dressed in drag, made for women who wanted to know what it feels like to walk with a cock between their legs. They called it packing. She rubbed it up against his hip as she leant over the table. 'Let's start over, shall we? I'll rack the balls.'

She walked like a man, and the cadence of her voice would have passed for male. Her short, dark hair was styled like a man's. Even the fake five o'clock shadow on her cheeks looked real. If Nick hadn't known that it was Beetle leaning over him, fondling his thigh, he'd have thought some man was coming on to him.

Beetle ordered two beers, which they didn't drink. She seemed to know her way around a pool table much better than he did. But it was hard to pay attention to the game when their real game was to feel each other up and, fuck, if the cock in her jeans pressing against his thigh didn't feel as real as his own. Only his was getting hard. How could it not be when her hand snaked under the edge of the pool table to stroke him through his jeans?

The game devolved into groping and rubbing and teasing with the pool cues. And when Beetle's tongue found its way into Nick's mouth, he braced himself for what was coming next. 'Don't think I can wait much longer.' She spoke against his lips. 'I want to fuck your ass. You'd like that, wouldn't you?' She gave his cock a hard stroke.

As the groping and fondling heated up, Beetle stuck a finger inside Nick's belt and pulled him out behind the bar into an alley next to the trash bins. Then she shoved him forward against the wall and cranked his arm up behind his back. All of this he knew would happen, yet the adrenaline rush of being so handled shocked him, and the thrill of it went straight to his cock. Beetle pulled a bandana from her pocket and tied it over his eyes.

'Wait a minute,' he said. 'What the hell are you doing?' He didn't have to fake the nervousness in his voice. Though loss of control seemed to be the norm since he had been with Mount Vegas, it still made him uneasy, still tightened his throat and made his pulse race.

'I'm making it better,' Beetle said against his ear. 'Trust me, you'll like it.' Then, while his back was turned and his eyes covered, Beetle lowered her jeans and removed the soft cock. Though he couldn't see, Nick knew that she then pulled a cock-shaped dildo from the inside pocket of her jacket and fitted it into the strap-on harness she already wore. With rough hands, she yanked and tugged at Nick's skinny jeans and tiny undershorts until his arse was bared and his cock sprang at full point. She shoved and rearranged him until his back hole was exposed. Though it was still tender from last night, it was no less ready to play as she slathered him with lube. 'Oh, you want this so bad, don't you, slut?' she whispered in his ear, and her fingers went to work on his anus. He nodded and grunted and cursed out loud when she pushed the dildo home, not lingering to caress and dilate his opening as Pike had. But the hot fire quickly turned to that different feeling of fullness he had never known before last night, and he soon forgot the discomfort.

Then Beetle reached around him and began to stroke his cock while she thrust. 'Fuck, slut, you're filthy, aren't you? All hard and heavy and ready to jizz the wall for me, aren't you?' She shoved in hard, and Nick swallowed a curse. 'Aren't you?'

'Yessss,' he hissed between his teeth. And then the tables turned. It was when his hand strayed to reach for Beetle's hip to pull her in tighter that the fantasy unfolded. Nick's fumbling fingers found the strap and followed it down to the base of the harness and the anchorage of the dildo.

'What the fuck?' He yanked off the handkerchief and pushed Beetle off, throwing her against the wall where she cowered. 'What the hell are you playing at? Shit! You're not a guy.'

'I'm sorry, I'm so sorry,' Beetle gasped, suddenly sounding almost little girlish. 'I only wanted to know what it felt like, what guys feel when they ... when they do it to another man.' Her words ended in a little yelp when Nick shoved up her shirt and found the clasps that held the binding in place. He ripped them free, resulting in a swirling spiral of cloth as he yanked and pulled until her small, pale breasts were exposed in the amber glow of the streetlight. She sucked in a harsh breath as he squeezed them and pinched her nipple.

Then he kissed her on the mouth, hard and long and brutal, and they both came up gasping. 'So did you like it?'

'Oh God, yes! It was good. It was great. It was the hottest thing ever,' she said, her words coming out in breathless little puffs.

'But it didn't take care of this, did it?' He shoved a hand down between her legs, down below the strap-on, and fingered open her pussy. 'Shit, that's got to be the wettest cunt I've ever felt. Tell me, bitch, do you like it both ways? Cuz I figure you do.'

Beetle nodded and whimpered as he gave her clit a hard pinch.

'I like taking it up the ass,' he said as his fingers fucked her wildly, making the strap-on bounce and sway beneath its decoration of binding cloth. 'But I like to stud a bit of pussy now and then, and yours smells ripe and ready to be fucked.'

With that, he turned her to the wall, spread her legs with a press of his knees, and buried his cock in her cunt, with her keening, 'Oh God, oh God, oh God!' Her tight little breasts bounced like jelly and her arse slapped back hard against him each time he thrust into her.

'I'm gonna make you come, slut, then I'm gonna

unload in your filthy little cunt.' He thrust hard. 'It's all your fault, you and your girlie cock. I've never had a good pegging before, and I'm a sucker for new experiences, aren't you?'

Suddenly she convulsed and shivered all over. 'Oh Christ, I'm coming! I'm coming!'

She came so mightily it felt like she was having some kind of seizure. Her muscular body was small, but powerful, and it was all Nick could do to hold on to her. Before he could regain control, before he knew what was happening, she pushed back hard, then pulled herself off his cock, twisting out from between him and the wall. She grabbed his arm as she did and pinned it up behind his back again. He growled and felt his shoulder pop with just enough tension to make him think twice about struggling. And fuck, before he could catch his breath, she was up in his arse again, deep and hard. He had been warned that the woman was a mixed martial artist, and he made a mental note never to make her mad.

'I like it both ways, cunt,' she breathed in his ear. 'But right now, I want to see you jizz the wall while I fuck your ass. I bet those balls are heavy down there between your legs, all full and distended.' She offered a sigh. 'Sadly, there's no way for me to know what that feels like, is there? So I'll just have to experience it vicariously.' She gave the weight of him a cupping and a squeezing, then she manoeuvred herself just so the rake and thrust of the dildo was maddening against his prostate. He ground back against her in his struggle to get more while she cupped his balls and kneaded. 'Show me how you jerk off,' she demanded. 'I want to see how a real man takes care of his cock. Show me. Help me get you there.'

He spat on his palm and thrust his erection into his fist, shoving at it like it was a hungry snatch while Beetle ploughed his arsehole like she was riding a pogo stick.

195

'Come for me, slut,' she huffed against the back of his neck. 'Come for me.' He thrust and jerked, and Beetle humped and pushed. He could feel the brick abrading his forearm in his efforts to protect his face from Beetle's woman-handling, yet the harder she thrust forward the harder he thrust back. Jesus, the woman was driving him crazy!

The last sane thought he had before his cock erupted in spurt after spurt against the wall and Beetle bellowed out another orgasm was how hot Elsa would get watching this mixed-up gender-bender they'd just pulled off. The image of her finger-fucking herself in front of the computer screen, watching Beetle peg his arse, the image of her tugging at her nipples and grinding against the furniture in the control room, made his orgasm sweeter and hotter as he and Beetle collapsed in a heap. He tugged his jeans up enough to protect his bare arse from the gravel as Beetle settled onto his lap in a flurry of tongue kisses while she continued to stroke the strap-on, still wet with lube that smelled of strawberries.

'I think your ass is going to be very popular,' she whispered in his ear, once they were sure the cameras were off and the act had ended.

He gave his softening dick a stroke in empathy with her attention to the strap-on. 'Possibly, but I'm hoping my cock will be even more so.'

Her laughter was a warm against his neck. 'Trust me, your cock is already the toast of Mount Vegas, and beyond.'

Chapter Eighteen

There were greetings all round when Nick and Beetle got back to the Elara.

'So Nick, how long before that asshole of yours is ready to play with me?' Horse said, adjusting his junk in his shorts.

'I stretched it pretty good for him tonight,' Beetle said. 'It won't be long until he'll be begging you to ride him, Horse.' She gave Nick a kiss and slapped him on the back.

'If you're looking for Elsa,' Pike said, handing Nick a beer and a slice of pizza, 'she had something important to attend to. Sorry, stud.'

Nick ate his pizza without tasting it and tried to participate in the conversation and the recap of the night's events. Deke and Kandi had had a stealth fuck in the canal down at The Venetian. Pagan and Deb had gone at it in a dressing room at Caesar's Palace. But it didn't seem right without Elsa. Something important to attend to, Pike had said. What the hell did that mean? He wondered if she were avoiding him. Jesus, the woman drove him crazy. But he laughed and joked and even settled into the hot tub with Deb and Deke. He figured it would be easier here than it would be at home alone.

As Pike settled in next to him, he asked, 'Where does Elsa live?'

'If I told you that, she'd have to kill you. And don't be

so long-faced. You know, it's not always about you.'

He was showered and dressed and just ready to head home when the email came. Though he'd been invited to crash in the hotel suite, he didn't feel like sharing a bed tonight unless it was with Elsa.

The email was from her.

You were amazing tonight, Nick. Sorry I missed you afterward, but there were things I needed to take care of. I also wanted you to have the attached information to give our mutual friends when they ask for it. After that, we relax and enjoy the fireworks.

He couldn't hold back a shiver as he scrolled down to find the details for Mrs Keyser's big event. He wished he could feel so sure about watching the fireworks. He wished Elsa would just tell him what the hell was going on. He didn't like the not knowing, and Havers scared him.

Nick had just returned from a morning meeting with Lou-Ann and his limo staff and was halfway through his second Pop Tart when Havers showed up with Tanya at his side. He'd called Havers in the morning before his meeting and left a message with his answering service. Then, as an afterthought, he called Tanya too.

They were both dressed to the nines. He would have expected that of Tanya. He figured she was looking for work and had to keep up appearances. And though Nick wasn't fashion conscious, he'd seen enough conspicuous consumption in Vegas to know expensive clothing when he saw it, and after what Elsa had told him, he understood why Havers could afford to dress so well.

He opened the door and let them in. Tanya kissed him on the mouth as though they were lovers. 'You have some news for us,' she said, not waiting for Havers to speak.

Nick led them upstairs to the kitchen, feeling like a

stool pigeon in spite of Elsa's insistence.

'That coffee smells great, Mr Chase,' Havers said. 'I could use a cup.'

Nick bristled when Havers nodded to Tanya, and she went about making the man a cup of coffee like it were her kitchen, or even worse, like it were Havers' kitchen and she was his fucking maid. Two sugars and lots of milk, Nick noticed. Tanya knew how the detective liked it. As he watched her set the coffee in front of the man and settle in the chair beside him, Nick was pretty sure Tanya knew how Havers liked lots of things besides his coffee.

Havers took a sip and offered a satisfied sigh. 'You do make good coffee, Chase. Tell me, did you learn that driving limo or digging fossils?'

'I learned it from working long hours, and needing caffeine,' Nick replied.

'Beats the hell out of the battery acid down at the precinct, that's for sure.' Then Havers straightened his tie and studied Nick for a long moment, absently twisting the heavy gold ring around his finger. 'I'm assuming you've come to the conclusion that it's wise to be on the right side of the law in this situation.'

Nick bit his tongue, reminding himself again that he was doing what Elsa asked. But Christ, it worried him. This man was dangerous. This man could bring down Mount Vegas. This man could hurt Elsa. He downed his own coffee for courage and ignored the Pop Tart, which he no longer wanted. 'I'm driving the limo for the event you're talking about, Detective Havers, so I got the details early enough to plan my route. I'm in a position to give you the information you need.'

'That's good, that's great,' Havers said. 'To tell you the truth, I wasn't sure we could count on you, Chase, but Tanya had faith you'd come through.'

Nick ground his teeth. Tanya was a real hero, all

right. She'd certainly pulled him in. Though he couldn't fault her for that when it meant he got to know Elsa. And suddenly he missed her desperately.

'I have to decide on my route first,' Nick said. 'And because of the nature of the client's fantasy, it's possible I could be driving around a little bit. You do know that the people involved from London are VIPs with Mount Vegas?'

'Them, I don't care about,' Havers said, waving a beefy hand. 'They have nothing to do with what's going on with Elsa Crane as far as we know.'

Nick wondered if Havers had any idea that one of those people was the Martelli heiress.

'It's Elsa Crane and Mount Vegas we want. The London folks, as far as we can tell, are just a cover-up the Crane woman is using to pull off the deal. She wants full attention on them. What I really need to know is where I'll find Elsa Crane and her gang while this is going on. My people have never been able to pinpoint them when the time comes. We know what they do, and we know that they set up control rooms in whatever hotel they deem best for the occasion, but we've never managed to catch them in the act.'

Nick found that very difficult to believe. Vegas wasn't that big. But he would do what Elsa had asked him with no questions. At least for now.

'Well, you won't have that problem this time.' He stood and refilled his coffee cup. 'They'll be in the Cosmopolitan. I can't give you the room number until the day.'

'Great, fantastic,' Havers said. 'I have to catch them in the act, as you know, so timing is everything. But with the information you've given us we'll be able to shut down Crane and her gang for good.'

'Look,' Nick said. 'I've never seen anything else going on but what's supposed to go on, so I can't help you there. I have no idea what you're looking for. I'm not in the inner circle.'

'Oh, don't you worry about that, Chase. We know what we're looking for and exactly where to find it. All we really needed were times and locations. That was the missing piece of the puzzle. And now we have that information, we can get rid of this scourge on our fair city.'

Nick nearly gagged on his coffee. Did the man really think him that naïve, that stupid? But he forced a smile. 'Always glad to do my part.'

'You've made a wise decision, Chase,' Havers said, coming to his feet and offering Nick his hand. Nick returned the shake with little enthusiasm. 'I'll be in touch if I need anything else.' He nodded to Tanya, who offered Nick a quick glance over her shoulder as she followed him out the door.

It was Nick's first time to run the control centre, which had been set up at the Paris. It was a low staff night because two of the scheduled acts were simple masturbation scenes – one calling for a man with a large cock. That act starred Horse, of course. And the other starred Kandi, playing with herself in a hot tub. The final act was a one-night stand with Deb picking up Deke. All three were simple one-set fantasies that Nick could cut his teeth on in the control room. Pagan would help him out if he had trouble; otherwise, the big man was curled up on the sofa reading a romance novel. Who knew?

There had been no sign of Elsa, and no word from her other than the terse thank you she had posted back after his meeting with Havers and Tanya. In fact, no one seemed to know where Elsa was, and that made Nick nervous. He reminded himself for the hundredth time that it wasn't always about him. Whatever was going on with Havers had to weigh on her. Add to that the responsibility of running Mount Vegas, and he couldn't expect to be the only thing on Elsa's mind. He certainly felt like she was the only thing on his and it pissed him off a little to think she might not have allocated him quite so much time for obsessing over as he had her.

The acts were all going well. In Nick's head, he kept replacing Deke and Deb with Elsa and himself. He would love nothing more than to have no agenda with her other than to return to a hotel room together and make love all night – make that all weekend. No, make that all week! Every once in the while, Pagan would peek in and ask how it was going. It was a slow night and a chance for people to have a much-needed break.

The two masturbation scenes had just finished and Horse and Kandi were in the kitchen ordering room service while Deke pleasured Deb in the bathtub using the shower massage. Nick was involved in the last minute wrap-up of the scene, ignoring his hard cock, making sure the ending happened like planned and everyone was out and all cameras off before he headed into the kitchen to join the feast. He heard the commotion outside the bedroom and just assumed it was room service arriving. Then he heard Horse say, 'Elsa, what are you … Oh my God! Look what the dogs drug in!'

Nick shut down the cameras and called in the all-clear to the room where Deke and Deb were. Then he turned to find Elsa standing in the doorway next to a woman he recognised from a certain late-night Skype session.

Elsa offered a smile. 'Nick, I'd like you to meet Rita and Edward from The Mount in London.'

Before she could say anything else, Rita Holly swooped in and grabbed him in a bear-hug. 'Nick Chase! I meet the legend, at last.'

Over Rita's shoulder, Elsa offered him a shrug. 'They

came early.'

'We decided we wanted a little holiday,' Edward said, giving Nick a hearty handshake.

'Nick, this is Leo,' Rita said, as a man who was almost as well muscled as Pagan but a little older and a lot darker came into the room. 'Leo's our resident voyeur in London, better known as the Zookeeper. He's hoping you can fit a very special fantasy into your schedule for him.'

'Is pleasure,' Leo said, and Nick detected a Slavic accent very similar to Tanya's.

'He's one of our High Council members and one of my very favourite people,' Rita said.

Just then, room service arrived with enough food to feed half of Vegas, with Deb and Deke following right behind. They had barely settled in when Pike and Beetle showed up to join the party and greet the London contingent.

No one was subtle in their efforts to push Elsa and Nick together. Once they were all settled and scarfing down food, Pike asked around a mouthful of tamale, 'Is this about Mount Vegas's status?'

'Of course is about the Mount Vegas status,' Leo answered. 'But is also about a holiday and chance to catch up with good friends.'

Chapter Nineteen

Leo had insisted that the rest of the Mount Vegas team keep his fantasy a secret from the participants. An exception had been made, Nick was told, for the High Council member to participate in his own fantasy. He had a reputation as a voyeur with a very specific kind of kink, and he was well-respected in The Mount.

Nick was collected by Pagan and Pike, who were dressed in dark green coveralls with logo patches over the breast pockets that simply read *The Zoo*. He was told he'd be working with one other Mount Vegas member and that during the entire act, he was not to speak, and he was to do exactly as Leo told him. If he disobeyed either one of these directives, he would be punished. That was all he knew. He was ushered to a remote part of the car park where a black van awaited with the rear door open. There he was stripped of all his clothing and ordered into the back, into a cage the size of a large pet carrier, which Pike then covered with a heavy blanket, leaving him in darkness.

It felt like they drove for a long time, and in his darkened cage, he had no idea where they were going. It was only when he was released in front of a cabin with the night sky's diamond sparkle spread overhead that Nick realised he was with Elsa. She didn't seem happy. But she was as naked as he was, and happy or not, Elsa Crane naked always got his cock's full attention.

'Oh, they are here! My lovely pets are here.' Leo burst from the cabin rubbing his hands together. 'And look at the two of you –' he ran a hand up Elsa's hip and stroked her breasts '– so exquisite and so ready to play.' He cupped Nick's balls and caressed the length of his erection. 'But then I hear our Nick is always ready to play, isn't that true, darling Elsa? Oh, and look how lovely he blushes. He doesn't want me to know he wants to fuck you, darling. But he is healthy, virile pet. Of course he wants chance to mount you and ride your lovely wet pussy, and you are wet for him, my beauty, aren't you?' He lowered a hand over her mons and gave a gentle probe. 'Of course you are. So wet.' He nodded to Pike and Pagan, who placed matching blue rhinestone-studded collars around Elsa and Nick's throats. 'Thank you, gentlemen. You have been most kind,' he said to them. 'Now come along, my darlings, come into the house so that we can play. It will be lovely. You will see.'

He turned to the cabin. Nick gave Elsa a quick glance, which she returned with a shrug, then padded off behind Leo.

The cabin was rustic, but comfortable – only one large room with a small kitchenette and a huge bed. The adjoining bathroom had an enormous Jacuzzi. The small dining table was spread with cold meats, cheeses, bread, and fruit. 'I know that pets get very hungry when they are allowed to play freely, and you are here to play, my darlings, and pets do so enjoy the playing. Now –' he snapped his fingers '– onto the carpet by the fireplace, both of you. Sit, sit! Get comfortable.' Leo clucked his tongue as they plopped down cross-legged. Oh my darlings, don't be nervous. Leo only wants to watch you enjoy yourselves.' He looked from one of them to the other, then scratched his chin. 'Is clear that you both need to come quite badly, but you are new pets with still

205

so much to learn. Perhaps is that you don't know each other so well, and you are shy. Perhaps that is why so nervous. My darlings –' he stepped closer '– pets get to know each other through their noses and with their tongues, and then once they know each other, once they are comfortable, then they can fuck.'

When they gave him a blank stare, he plopped down onto the carpet next to them. 'Here. Is like this. Come here, Elsa. On your hands and knees now. Is good. Is a good girl. Now open your legs so that Nick can see your little wet pussy, so that he can smell you and taste you.'

Nick could see the blush crawling up Elsa's throat as she did what the man asked. His stomach fluttered at the sight of Elsa Crane blushing, and his dick responded by stretching closer.

'That is good girl.' Leo moved forward to stroke her flank as though she were a flighty horse. 'Now come here, Nick, come and get to know our Elsa, get to know how much her little pussy needs your cock.'

Feeling a blush burn up over his own cheeks, feeling as though his heart would leap from his chest, Nick positioned himself on hands and knees behind Elsa. It wasn't so much that he was drawn into the man's fantasy as he was drawn into the scent and the sight of Elsa spread there before him, so open, so ready. On hands and knees she offered herself in a submissive position, the position of an animal in need of sexual relief. He felt the rise of his own animal lust as he moved closer, inhaling deeply, burying his face in the cleft of her. At first contact her body twitched and she gasped and shuddered and eased back closer to his breath, closer to the lap and plough of his tongue.

'There you see, Nick, the poor thing needs your cock so badly. She needs you to mount her and make her feel better. You can taste her need, can't you? You can smell how much she wants you to fuck her. And look at your cock, how it stretches to get closer to her, how your balls are so heavy for her.'

Stating the obvious in such a different way only amplified Nick's need for Elsa, and as she wriggled back closer to his mouth, and her breath came in tight little gasps, he figured Leo's dirty talk was having the same effect on her. As he watched them in rut, Leo unzipped his trousers, sat back against the love seat and began to stroke himself.

'Oh, you are both such lovely pets, so strong and potent, and you both need to come so badly, don't you, my beauties? Now mount her, Nick. I think that you won't need to convince her. Put your lovely penis up inside her where she's all wet and hungry for you, then you can both come and you will both feel so much better, so much more relaxed.'

Nick really did feel like an animal, taking Elsa from behind, an animal mating with the fittest, most powerful female, and as he thrust home, she thrust back against him and growled and grunted in a feral response.

'Is good,' Leo gasped. 'Is so good, now both of you can come. You are ready and you need it so badly. Once you have had the release and then some food, then we will be at our leisure to play.'

Leo was right. It only took a few thrusts and Nick filled her with his need, a need that was desperate and overwhelming. It hadn't been that long since he'd come. But he knew, and he had a sneaking suspicion that Leo knew as well, that it wasn't the sex he and Elsa craved so much as it was each other. He wished Elsa knew that.

Leo came into a white handkerchief, and when he had wiped himself, he disappeared into the bathroom and brought back a towel. 'Now let me clean you up, my darlings, now that you feel better. Then we will have something to eat, and then maybe a bath.' He tisk-tisked. 'Pets can be so messy when they fuck.'

Once Leo finished, it was time to eat. They sat on the floor next to the table by Leo's chair and, as crazy as it seemed, he fed them from his hands – melon, peaches, strawberries dipped in chocolate, chocolate that dripped onto Elsa's nipples and Nick's belly, chocolate that had to be licked off. Elsa had softened and warmed to the game, offering playful nips and naughty smiles and rubbing her cheek against Leo's thigh. She was radiant and relaxed, like Nick had never seen her.

'You are such lovely pets,' Leo said, offering each of them a nibble of bread and honey. 'You see how much more you are yourselves when you are pets. Is good? No?'

Elsa laid her head on Leo's thigh, and Nick moved to hunch his body over hers so that he could do the same, but still touch her.

Leo stroked her hair and then Nick's. 'We forget how to play. We forget how to just be ourselves. Is lovely when we remember again. Is lovely when there is no agenda.'

And he was right. It was, indeed, lovely. Once they'd been fed, they made love once more under the watchful eyes of the Zookeeper, who then bathed them, which turned into a splashy pool-party of a romp that devolved into laughs and giggles and more playful sex. When, at last, they were tired from their play, they curled around each other on the foot of the bed, after Leo crawled down between the sheets. Nick had no idea who else was watching them, if anyone, and he didn't care. As he pulled Elsa into a possessive spoon position, he couldn't help being grateful to the Zookeeper for the most intimate time he'd ever had with Elsa Crane.

Leo woke them, long toward morning. He was freshly showered and dressed. 'My fantasy is over now, darlings.' He nodded them into the bed and pulled the blankets up over them. 'You stay and sleep. You are tired from your play.' He kissed each of them gently then left.

'Sonovabitch! They took our clothes.'

Nick awoke to find Elsa standing naked in front of an empty wardrobe, and just when he braced for her anger, he realised her shoulders were shaking. For a frightening moment, he thought she was crying. But then he heard a soft snort that erupted into a giggle, followed by an actual belly laugh.

'They took our fucking clothes! We're naked, in the desert, with no transport, Nick.' Still cackling, she moved to the refrigerator and opened the door. 'But we have a whole fridge full of gourmet food. And coffee! Really good coffee.' She turned to face him with tears rolling down her cheeks. 'We hit the jackpot! We hit the fucking jackpot! Maybe they'll leave us alone. Maybe they'll forget where they put us. Come on, I'm starving.'

Still trying to get his head around the sight of Elsa Crane laughing hysterically, he watched her lovely backside as she moved about making coffee. But he couldn't stay away from her for very long. He threw back the covers and moved to stand behind her, his cock stretching toward her in muscle memory.

She reached behind her and gave him a grope. 'Put that thing away until after I've eaten.' She flipped the coffee maker on and turned in his arms. 'Then I'll happily fuck you senseless. In fact –' she leant into him and raked a sloppy kiss across his mouth '– I'm looking forward to it.'

They sat close to each other at the table, eating the leftovers of last night's feast, even feeding each other tasty morsels with sticky fingers or with sticky lips. Nick was outrageously hard. But he was so much more than just aroused. He was happy! Fuck, he couldn't remember ever being this happy. So when Elsa deliberately missed his mouth with a morsel of strawberry raked through cream cheese and licked the residue off of his chin and then his chest, he curled his fingers in her hair and held her there against the hammering of his heart.

In a move that totally surprised him, she shoved in between him and the table to sit on his lap and, though his cock was quick to respond, damned if his heart wasn't quicker. Her kiss was long and lingering, tasting of coffee and strawberries, and the scent of lavender from the bath didn't hide the scent of her with which he'd become so familiar. The scent of sleep still lingered on her skin, and beneath that was the scent of lust that was the core of the woman, the scent of wildness that lent itself perfectly to being a pet. Her sigh was a deep shudder. 'I could get lost in you, Nick Chase. So easily I could get lost in you, and that scares me.'

He pulled her close, feeling as though he could never get close enough. 'If you get lost in me, I'll always find you, Elsa Crane.'

She stood so quickly that he wondered if he'd said something wrong, and everything in him tightened at the thought of losing her again. Instead, she paced in front of the fireplace. Then she turned to face him and plopped down on the rug, not unlike she had when Leo was there.

'There were sand hill cranes. They were migrating out across the prairies of Nebraska when I ran away. They were beautiful, powerful, and they could just fly away, whenever they wanted. That's how I became Elsa Crane. And Elsa – well, I just liked that name.'

Hardly able to breathe, Nick came to sit next to her and took her hand. To his delight, she didn't pull away. 'Edgar Terrill, he was my husband.' She raised a hand as though clearing a chalkboard. 'He's dead now. I was Elizabeth Harold Terrill. I married him for security mostly. I was 19 and he was 40 and he was loaded. He fancied himself a dom, but really he was just a bully. He …' She took a deep breath and pulled her knees up tight against her chest. 'He beat me, I mean really beat me. He liked to humiliate me by making me take pictures of what he did with other women in his dungeon. It was an amazing dungeon. He had the money to do it up right.'

'Fuck,' Nick, whispered, fighting back the urge to take her in his arms, to protect her, fighting back the urge to kill a man who was already dead. He sat still and listened, not wanting to spook her, not wanting her to feel threatened.

'I got good at taking pictures, making videos, at making them look … like he wanted them to look. I got good at telling him what he should do to make the pictures better. When I did that, when he was pleased, he left me alone. And because he was pleased, he let me spend my days researching BDSM sites and sex sites, researching anything that might make his little dungeon excursions better.' She shook her head and her fingers tightened around Nick's hand. 'He didn't want me out of the house unless we were together. He controlled every aspect of my life, and he thought … he thought I was such a little slut, such a little pervert that I was happy to stay at home locked away, that I was happy to research sex sites and how to take better pictures, better videos, find better ways for him to show what a sex god he was.

'I got good at what he left me, that's what I did. It was all I could do.' She looked up into Nick's eyes. 'So one day I convinced him to let me tie him up. I'd been researching Shibari at the time, and I'd promised to show him what I'd learned. I told him his women would think it was sexy, what I would show him. I tied him spread-eagle between two pillars in the basement. And then I –' she took a deep breath '– and then I beat him.'

Nick said nothing. He wasn't sure he could even

speak around the rise of feelings he could barely get his head around.

'No, that's not right. I didn't beat him. I tortured him. I used all of those instruments he'd either used on me or I'd videoed him using on his women on him. At first, he screamed at me and called me names, told me he'd kill me when I released him. So I gagged him.' She looked up at Nick. 'I could have just beaten him and left, but the thing is, Nick, he got hard. And I got wet. I found I liked doing to him what he'd done to so many others, what he'd done to me, and that I had way more finesse at it than he would ever have.'

'Jesus,' Nick whispered.

She laughed softly. 'It gets better. I made him come. And then I made him hold it until I wanted him to come. And when he was quivering all over, when I knew he would die holding it in order to obey me, I let him come. Nick, I'd never felt such power, such control. I don't know how long I was there. I had only planned to give him a good, hard thrashing and leave. But when he was too exhausted to go on, I left him shackled to the bondage bed. I already had my bags packed. I'd figured out how to hack his bank account, so I withdrew enough to get me well on my way. I bought a used car from a disreputable dealer, paid cash, and then I just drove.'

She smiled up at Nick. 'No, I didn't kill him, if that's what you're thinking, and I didn't deliberately leave him there to die. Though I heard later that it took him a while to recover. I knew the names and numbers of the women he had me make arrangements with. I left a message for one of them to come after I was gone. Plus, I knew the maid who always cleaned up after playtime – she played sometimes too. I knew she'd be down soon enough.'

'And that's how you ended up in Vegas?' Nick pulled a blanket from the bed and settled it around her shoulders.

'I had enough money to get me started, keep me from starving. For the first three days I was afraid to leave the hotel room, afraid Edgar would find me. But the more time passed, the more sure I became that wasn't going to happen, the more I explored Vegas. I created a new identity, I surfed the net, I schemed. I didn't know what to do at first, but then one night at a casino bar, I heard a couple of men talking about the sex they'd seen through their telescopes at night from the hotel room windows. They both regretted that people weren't more creative.

'So I bought the equipment I thought I'd need, hired a few people I'd met working in the casinos who I thought would be up for it, and put my plan into action. I'd done several fantasies and was pulling in enough to pay the bills when I met Pike. He had insights, ideas, connections. It was only later that I learned he was a member of The Mount in Houston, and that he'd been sent to me because someone in Houston heard about what I was doing.'

'And what happened with Edgar?'

'I angsted for a long time, not sure if I'd killed him, worried that I had injured him, and yet knowing that I'd done everything right.' She pulled the blanket tighter around her. 'Mostly I worried that I'd liked it so much, that I had fantasies about keeping him there bound in the dungeon, using him to learn, to push my boundaries, and his. And then I'd wake up in a cold sweat from dreams that he had found me and he was going to carry out his promise and kill me.

'Then I got the divorce papers. They came via a very circuitous route. It was no fault, with a hefty settlement. Definitely not like Edgar. It was only later I learned The Mount could be very persuasive. He died last year. Heart failure. He left me everything. The man had no heirs, and though I can't imagine him wishing me anything but the worst, there you go. Pike said maybe he was grateful that I helped him find his inner submissive, but I think it's more likely that someone at The Mount … suggested he leave the money to me.'

Nick scooted close and took her into his arms. 'So it's over and yet you still tell me you don't exist.'

'I owe The Mount a lot, Nick. They've taken care of me, helped me heal. And for me to be given the responsibility of beginning a new coven in Vegas is an honour I can never repay. I came here as no one. I stayed no one all this time to protect myself, and until Mount Vegas is given coven status, I'll continue to be no one. And no, they didn't ask it of me. I felt it was best. That's all.'

'And what happened with Edgar is why you never take up the role as dominatrix in the dungeon?'

She stood and sipped from her now tepid coffee, holding the blanket around her like a robe. 'I wanted to kill him, Nick. For weeks before it all happened, while I was planning, I had dreams about doing just that.' She turned to face him. 'And they weren't nightmares. Oh, Pike's tried to get me to do acts as the dominatrix, but Beetle's good in the dungeon and so is Deb when she needs to be. Better to keep me out of there. Better to let someone who knows their limits take control. How do I know what kind of monster I'll unleash if I turn myself loose in the dungeon at Mount Vegas? How do I know if I'll be able to control myself? I couldn't bear it if I hurt those I love, those who trust me.'

'Elsa –' he took her into his arms '– it was your control that kept you from killing Edgar. Surely you can see that. It was your control that pulled you back from the brink.'

She slipped her arms around his neck and buried her face against his shoulder, and the blanket fell away. He pulled her close, feeling her next to him like another part of him, a part he'd discovered only recently, a part he

214

hadn't known was missing until he found her. That she had told him her story, that she'd made herself so vulnerable to him, was something he still couldn't settle his mind around.

His cock was just beginning to stretch and press against her when there was a brisk knock and Rita and Leo stepped inside. Leo pulled a suitcase in one hand and had a garment bag thrown over his shoulder.

'Sorry to interrupt,' Rita said. 'We gave you as much time as we could. I wish it had been more.'

Elsa lifted her mouth to Nick's and settled a soft kiss on his lips. 'It's all right, Rita. It was enough.'

'Sometimes is our animal nature that can help us get in touch with what it is that's really important,' Leo said. 'Now come. You will bathe. I have brought clothes, and then we will go back to the Mount Vegas offices and talk.'

Chapter Twenty

'Not a good time, Nick.' Elsa looked up from her laptop and then glanced over her shoulder toward the living quarters behind her office.

'Well, that's just too damn bad.' He shook his BlackBerry at her. 'What's this message about Pagan driving the limo instead of me for Mrs Keyser's fantasy? That's not in the plan. That's not a part of the deal. Now what the fuck's going on?'

She offered a half-hearted chuckle and pushed back from her desk, shutting the door to the living area as she did so. 'What, are you afraid you'll miss seeing our billionaire grope his virgin bride? OK, I know Rita looks good, but I'm not too bad.'

As she rounded the desk, he pulled her into his arms and gave her mouth a good hard tongue-lashing until her knees were weak, until she clung to him breathlessly. 'You know I'd give the hottest fantasy you can muster a miss if it meant spending time with you, Elsa, so stop playing with me. What the hell's going on?'

'Look, I'm sorry. We'll talk about this later, but not now.' She shrugged him off, then took his hand and guided him toward the door.

'Don't fob me off,' he said, jerking away from her. 'I have a right to know.'

She worried her lip between her teeth, and shifted from foot to foot, struggling to hold his gaze. 'Look, I just … this is not your battle, Nick. You've already been pulled in too deep as it is. I never intended for you to get involved. I never imagined you'd volunteer to fulfil Tanya's contract, and I just think it's better if we do it this way. Now, really –' She looked over her shoulder toward the door to the living quarters. 'You have to leave. I'm very –'

'That's bullshit. This is as much my battle as it is anyone's, Elsa, and you know it. I'm not leaving until we get this straightened out.'

'Damn it, Nick!' It's not your fucking call. I can kick your ass out of this organisation as easily as I did Tanya's, and I will if I have to. I want you safe! I don't want you anywhere near Mount Vegas tomorrow night.'

'Elsa –' he took her by the shoulders and forced her to look at him '– that's not going to happen. If you keep me from driving, I'll be mad as hell, but I'll be right there with you and the rest of the gang in the control room. So deal with it.'

'Elsa, if it's not too much trouble, I need you to come and look at …' The door to the living quarters burst open and Tanya stepped out. She stopped mid-sentence when she saw Nick still holding onto Elsa's shoulders. For a second everyone froze, and the room was awash in prickly silence.

Then Nick stepped back, looking from one of them to the other. 'Would someone mind telling me what the hell's going on?'

Tanya said nothing. She only nodded to Elsa, who blew out a heavy breath and rubbed the back of her neck. Then she held him in her clear blue gaze. 'Tanya's working for Mount Vegas, Nick,' Elsa said. 'She's helping us bring down Havers.'

Nick managed to get the sofa under his arse before he dropped like a stone. For a moment, he sat looking from one to the other feeling like he'd just fallen into the

217

Twilight Zone.

Tanya broke the deafening silence. 'I was the way in.' She sat down in the chair across from him.

'What do you mean the way in?'

'She broke the rules on purpose, that's what she means.' Elsa took the seat next to Nick. 'We knew Havers had plans to bring us down and then give us a choice of going to prison for something we didn't do or paying the huge price for his protection services. We just didn't know how he would do it or when, so we decided to be proactive. We had Tanya very conspicuously gambling away lots of money, we had her having sex with people she wasn't supposed to. We made sure one of those was Havers. We knew he'd love nothing more than to get his claws into an insider from Mount Vegas.'

'I was the perfect insider for him,' Tanya said. 'I am alien here in this country and, shall we say, I have sketchy past. That means I am expendable in Havers' eyes. That means he would never think of me as being a danger to him. I have too much to risk.'

'Christ!' Nick ran a hand through his hair and glared at first one of them then the other. 'And me?'

'You were only supposed to be Tanya's last fuck, the straw that broke the camel's back.' Elsa said. 'We knew who you were and that you were a nice guy. What we didn't know, what we could have never suspected, was that you would follow Tanya on in, that you would volunteer to fulfil her contract.'

'And we had to let you do this because Havers had men watching me that night.'

'Fuck,' Nick whispered. 'And the part about your mother needing surgery?'

'My mother is dead, Nick, for a long time now. It was excuse I used to make my … situation seem more heartbreaking. That I have a gambling problem that I would try to pay off with sex is not so unusual here in Vegas.

Everyone has hard luck story in Vegas. When you volunteered to fulfil my contract, we all believed that once you saw what it is that it would mean, then you would go away and be none the wiser for it.'

'But you pursued me,' Nick said. 'You asked me to come back, to talk to Elsa.'

'It was Havers. He insisted that I do that. I still didn't think that you would, and I wanted my situation to look real. Havers was already watching me most of the time. If he had suspected for one minute that I was lying, it could have been bad. He saw us together, and then I stupidly told him that you were offering to rescue me. He then pushed me to use you.'

'When you came back –' Elsa continued the story '– we thought what you saw, what I offered you with Beetle and Deb would frighten you off.' She looked down at her hands folded in her lap. 'Though I have to confess that by that time I wasn't too anxious for you to leave.'

'We. You keep saying we. Does that mean that all of Mount Vegas is in on this little game?' Nick said.

'No,' Elsa replied. 'Only Tanya and me. I didn't want anyone else at risk. I've got friends as well as enemies in the police force, and places considerably higher than that. The fewer of my people who knew, the better. To them it just looked like Tanya kept fucking up. That's all. And the London folks know only because you told them. Honestly, we had no idea that Havers would try to involve you. That was never part of the plan.'

'So all of this has been a lie then.' Nick stood and wiped sweaty hands down his jeans. The weight in his chest felt like lead. 'You were just toying with me all the time.'

'No, Nick.' Elsa stood and reached for his hand. 'I was never toying with you. I would have refused you completely if I'd known Havers would get you involved.

219

And as for the rest, you have to believe –'

He jerked his hand away. 'Believe what? That any of it was any more than just another good act for the client? Tell me, Elsa, why should I believe that? Why should I believe any of what you say?' She reached for him again, but he stepped back. 'Never mind. It hardly matters now, does it? Get whoever you want to drive the damn limo. Just return it when you're done.' He turned and left.

'You must go after him,' Tanya said. 'You can't let him go thinking such a thing.'

Elsa felt like she'd been gutted, but she didn't move. 'Let him think what he wants, as long as it keeps him safe.'

With hands that were way steadier than she felt on the inside, she picked up her BlackBerry and sent an email to all of the members of the Mount Vegas team informing them of a change of venue for the control room from the Cosmopolitan to the Bellagio. Nick was included on that list, though she figured he probably wouldn't show up anyway, and it was just as well. This would keep everyone safe, and that's what mattered now, keeping her team safe.

'Is not right, Elsa, you letting him think that you have used him so. He's good man,' Tanya said.

'That's right. He is a good man, and he doesn't deserve to be caught up in this.'

'It seems to me that the man loves the Mount Vegas as much as we all do, and that he should have some say in what he deserves.'

'I didn't ask for your opinion, Tanya, and there are already way more people involved in this mess than I ever intended. I want it over with and I want my people out of harm's way. Now, if you'll excuse me. I've got a fantasy to plan.'

Tanya didn't move. She stood with her shoulders squared and her gaze locked on Elsa. 'And I am also one of your people, in case you have forgotten this. What I have done I have done out of love for you, for the Mount Vegas. It has not been easy for me to do this thing that you asked of me and to let the people I care about think bad things of me, but I did it. And is nothing that any one of us wouldn't do for you, Elsa. And Nick, maybe Nick even more so. You are not God, and sometimes even Elsa Crane needs help.' Then she turned and left.

When she was gone, Elsa locked the door behind her, then laid her head down on her desk and wept.

The day of Mrs Keyser's fantasy dawned bright and clear. Elsa went through the motions of helping set up the control room and making sure everything was ready, of joking and laughing with the London folks as they got ready for their big performance. Nick was noticeably absent, just as she had planned it, though there was still a part of her that had hoped he would defy her, that had hoped perhaps he cared enough about her …

Best not to go there, she reminded herself. What was done was done, and she should have known better than to involve herself with him any more than she was involved with any of the rest of the team. Her lapse in judgement had caused them both pain, caused her way more grief than she would have ever thought possible.

Once everything had been sorted and organised, she made the excuse of an urgent meeting and left her team to do what they did best. Then she made her way back to the Cosmopolitan to make sure that the original control room was set up the way she wanted it. It was one of seven rooms in hotels around the city that Elsa maintained permanently for Mount Vegas use. They were all registered under different names, names that changed randomly throughout the course of the year so that no one would suspect anything. That was a holdover from her days of not knowing if Edgar would show up to make good on his threat. It worked well for what Mount Vegas did too, helping to maintain the anonymity they needed and the discretion their clients demanded.

She arrived at the Cosmopolitan with one medium hard-sider suitcase and a hefty briefcase. Within the two bags, she had all the equipment she would need. Once inside, she checked the room to make sure everything was in order. First she set up the scope. And then she went to work on the rest, setting up the bedroom she used for the control room just as she always did, with a few minor changes.

She showered, dressed and prepared herself, all the while struggling to focus on what was ahead of her, what had to happen for this nightmare to come to an end, struggling not to focus on the pain below her sternum she felt at Nick's absence. Once she was ready, make-up perfect, hair perfect, room perfect, she settled in to wait. This was where Havers would find her when he came for her, as she knew that he would. If things went badly, if the man had more influence than she thought he did, then the rest of her team would be safe and unharmed, and they wouldn't face prison or … worse.

Chapter Twenty-one

Nick arrived just in time to view Edward on the control room monitor, dressed as the billionaire, with Rita Holly as his innocent virgin bride. They were at The Wedding Chapel.

'You have lovely breasts,' Edward half growled, tugging the front of his bride's white off-the-shoulder gown down until the swell of her nearly spilled over the top, thumbing her nipples through the thin fabric as he did so.

Rita whimpered, 'Oh please, sir, not here. I feel so exposed, and it's a church.'

She yelped as his hand found its way up under the taffeta and began to stroke.

'What, do you think God wouldn't approve of a man fondling his woman?

She shivered at his touch and shifted her hips ever so slightly. He offered a whisper of a laugh. 'Good girl, you left off the panties just like I told you to.' He moved in closer and lowered his face to bite the top of one breast and she gasped. He chuckled into her cleavage. 'You like that, don't you? It makes you wet, doesn't it, darling? You may be a virgin, but you're still a little slut. That's what makes you worth the money I paid for you. Oh yes, you're a slut, with your little clitty so tight and hard.' He nibbled her ear. 'Do you even know what your clit is, sweetheart? Do you know where it's at? I like the thought of teaching you just exactly where everything is, and how to make it feel real good.' He guided her hand to the bulge in his trousers and she blushed and quivered.

'Where the hell have you been?' Pike hissed over his shoulder at Nick. Everyone shushed him as Edward guided his virgin bride's hand inside his fly to feel, for the first time, what a man felt like.

Nick ignored the question. 'Where's Elsa?'

'She said something came up that needed dealing with,' Beetle replied. 'Grab a beer and get in here. Rita and Edward are amazing.'

Before he could tell them he thought Elsa was drawing Havers away from the rest of Mount Vegas, the newly married couple and their driver were suddenly surrounded by police. All three were forced up against the side of the limo, spread-eagle, while Edward cursed at the officers. 'What the hell's the meaning of this? Do you know who I am? How dare you accost my wife and me on our wedding day? I want to talk to your superiors.'

While they were frisked by uniformed officers, two more officers searched the vehicle. 'What the hell's going on?' Edward shouted.

'What the hell is going on?' Pike repeated on the other side of the monitor. 'This is not the way the act is scripted.'

'Where the fuck's Elsa?' Nick's voice rose above the murmuring of the spectators. 'She's in danger. I've got to get to her.'

'I don't know where she is,' Pike said. 'She didn't tell me. There are often things that come up she has to take care of. Some of our clients won't speak to anyone but her. Nick, if you know what's going on, you'd better come clean.'

'It's Havers. He's staged a raid. I imagine he's planted drugs in the limo and plans –'

Pike grabbed him by the throat and shoved him up hard against the wall, rattling the equipment. 'You knew about this? You fucking knew about this and didn't tell me?'

Nick shoved back. 'Get the hell off me. Yes! I knew about this, and Elsa made me promise to keep it quiet. Now shut up and listen. Elsa's in danger.' He suddenly had everyone's full attention. 'There has to be some place she'd go,' he said.

As the police search continued on screen, Beetle spoke up. 'She's trying to protect us. Crazy woman! She's never changed the control room venue on us before. The control room's the heart of the fantasies. It's the first thing that's ever set and it's written in stone until the night's over. We should have guessed something was wrong. The Cosmopolitan. That was where we were supposed to be.'

'Room 2017,' Pike added just as the door opened and Tanya burst in.

'Tell them what's going on, Tanya,' Nick called over his shoulder. 'Elsa set us all up. I'm going to find her.'

The room erupted in chaos, but Nick didn't care. He was already in the hall and racing toward the elevator. He had to get to Elsa before Havers did.

The knock on the door, though completely expected, still made Elsa jump. On the monitor, she watched the police frisk Rita and Edward and Pagan, searching for the drugs they wouldn't find. Her people were safe. They would all stay safe. She turned down the volume and moved to the door like she was moving in a dream.

'Hello, Elsa. Surprised to see me?' Havers stood in the hall, dressed in his expensive suit. The heavy diamond in his ring caught the light in the entryway and flashed bright. 'I'm sure by now you've seen that your people are being searched, and I don't have to tell you

225

that the officers will find exactly what they're looking for.' He unbuttoned his jacket to expose his gun holster – for her benefit, no doubt. He nodded toward the control room. 'Shall we watch the fun?'

She stepped aside, and Havers walked in. 'Good girl. I like a cooperative woman, and if you want this evening to end sweet, then you're going to have to be extra cooperative. Are we clear?'

'Very.'

'Good, then let's have a look. Where is everyone? I figured we'd have a party.'

'We're only running one fantasy tonight, so I gave everyone the night off.'

'What a considerate boss you, are, Ms Crane. No wonder they all love working for you. Tanya tells me your people are quite loyal.'

On the control room monitor, the search continued. The limo was being practically torn apart and the cops had done everything but cavity-search its three passengers.

Havers stepped forward, and glared hard at the monitor. 'What the fuck?'

Elsa said nothing.

When the police had given up on their search of the car, the virgin bride spoke over her shoulder. 'If you're looking for the cocaine that was planted in the trunk of our limo – well, the cops already found that. The other cops. You know? The good cops?' She offered them a dainty smile. 'So you lot might as well go have coffee and doughnuts because it's all been sorted.'

'What the fuck's going on?' Havers said.

'False alarm, detective. My people don't mess with drugs. The whole damn police department knows that. Oh, and the man who planted them – Bridger, I think was his name –he's not ratting on anyone yet, but the night's young, and I know the lovely officers from

226

Internal Affairs who are interrogating him. I'm confident they'll get a full confession,' Elsa said, eyes still glued to the crazy scene on the monitor. Rita, Edward and Pagan now leant back against the limo and watched while the supervising officer confirmed what Rita had just said.

Havers glared at the goings on around the limo with his hands thrust in his pockets, then he chuckled softly. 'That –' he nodded to the screen where Pagan was helping the billionaire and his bride back into the limo '– none of that matters, you know. First of all you're assuming Bridger will live long enough to get interrogated. Dangerous business, police work. Many a good cop lost in the line of duty. Secondly, you're the one I'm after because you're the one in control. It's that loyalty that Tanya spoke of I'm counting on, sweetheart. So if you want to stay out of trouble and stay in one piece in my town, then you're gonna have to pony up like everyone else does, like your Tanya's doing.'

'Ah, you want to extort money from me.'

Havers shrugged. 'Call it what you want. I prefer to think of it as a little insurance policy for your organisation and the safety of its employees.'

'That must be how you afford that big hunk of jewellery –' she nodded to the ring '– and if I'm not mistaken, the suit's tailored. Can't afford many of those on a cop's salary.'

'Let's just say my pension plan's a little better than most on the force.'

'I'm sure it is, but I already have insurance, and I know how to take care of my people.'

Havers turned on her so quickly that she hadn't seen it coming. She gasped as he grabbed her by the hair and pulled her back tight against his shoulder. 'I don't think you quite get the picture, Elsa. The deal is simple. If I get my percentage, you and your people and your property stay safe. If I don't –' he jerked her until she thought her neck would snap '– then I can't vouch for anyone's safety and, really, Vegas can be such a dangerous place. Here's the way this is going to work. I get 15 per cent for keeping you and your people safe, along with certain other fringe benefits.' He shoved a hand inside her tank top and groped her breast. Then he looked around the room. 'Since we're here alone, well, I don't see why we can't start off now with some of those extras.' He thrust his clothed cock against her bottom. 'You know, as a token of good faith.'

She relaxed into his grip to ease the pain in her scalp and allowed him to guide her to the other bedroom.

Getting a key card for the room was a testament to the quality of Nick's training at Mount Vegas and to his ability to sweet talk if necessary. Plus the receptionist recognised him from the previous time he'd been at the hotel with Elsa. Thankfully, the woman let slip that Elsa was already upstairs. He had just taken a gamble that she would change the venue to protect everyone and face Havers alone. Jesus, the woman was infuriating, and he loved her for it.

He had been up all night thinking about what had happened and, in the end, it had been simple. He couldn't just walk away from Elsa Crane. He knew her heart. That was the truth of it. He knew her heart, whether she wanted to admit it or not. She had trusted him with intimate secrets. She had let him in. And if she were trying to protect him and her people, well, he'd have done the same thing in her shoes. And damn it, she wasn't getting rid of him that easily. Mount Vegas was the closest thing to a family, to a place to belong, that he'd had in a long time, and it was worth fighting for.

There was no alternative but to use the electronic card key and risk being heard. He gritted his teeth and let the card click as it slid home. Then he pushed the door open. From the control room, he could hear the sounds of sex, and he knew that, in a nearby room, the billionaire was now devirginising his bride, and she was liking it plenty. But the control room was deserted and his heart stopped. His breathing stopped. Sweat trickled under his armpits, and the back of his neck went clammy.

Dear God, had Havers already got to Elsa? Who knew what the bastard would do? What if he'd taken her somewhere? No one would ever know. It was then he heard a gasp come from the other bedroom followed by a little yelp. Then he heard Havers say, 'I hear the beds here are real comfortable. Not that I'm concerned with comfort, Elsa – at least not yours.'

Relief nearly drove Nick to his knees even as every muscle in his body tensed. He moved silently to the second bedroom, barely daring to breathe. There he peeked around the corner to see Havers give Elsa a hard shove onto the bed. The man was about to undo his fly when Nick tackled him from behind, and Elsa came up off the mattress like a cat pouncing, calling Nick's name as the two men tumbled to the floor. But before Nick could pin him, Havers pulled a gun, and everyone froze.

'That was stupid, Mr Chase,' he said, breathing hard as he pushed his way to his feet and gestured to Nick to do the same. 'You just lost your helpful citizen award. The law doesn't look kindly on people who assault police officers.' He motioned Nick over next to Elsa.

'You all right?' Nick said, keeping his eyes on Havers and the gun.

'Elsa's just fine,' Havers replied. 'Though I would imagine she's really disappointed that you interrupted our fun. Never mind. There'll be plenty of time for me to pork the bitch later.' Nick bristled and Havers chuckled at the response he'd clearly hoped for. 'We were just discussing the … benefits of Elsa allowing me and my team to protect Mount Vegas. You see, Elsa, Nick here's a perfect example. He finds himself at gunpoint, and without my protection. Now, if Mount Vegas were under my protection, he would be under my protection too, but as it is – well, if I were to shoot him right here and now, especially after he's assaulted me and all, and if he were to die on the way to the hospital …' He raised the gun and took aim. 'The police force would not only understand, but they would completely sympathise.' He cocked the gun. 'You see how a simple monthly insurance payment can save lives, Elsa?'

'All right!' Elsa stepped in front of Nick with her hands up. 'All right, I'll do what you ask. I'll pay you the money, just put the gun down.'

Havers lowered the gun slightly. 'There, you see, Chase. She can be cooperative when it suits her.'

The electronic door lock sounded like a gunshot in the charged atmosphere and the faltering in Havers' attention was all Nick needed. He dived at the man and the gun went off. He heard Elsa shout his name just as the bullet shattered the light fixture overhead. In his peripheral vision, Nick caught a glimpse of Tanya. As Havers rolled and bucked, Elsa stomped his wrist with a sharp stiletto. He yowled and cursed, and the gun fell away from his grasp. She grabbed it up, and Nick rolled off him just as Tanya nabbed him in the neck with a stun gun. He convulsed, gurgled, and went limp. Almost before it could all sink in, the room was flooded with police.

'It's all right now, Ms Crane.' A policeman took the gun gently from Elsa's hands and gave her arm a reassuring pat. 'Everything's under control. It's all right. We have everything we need.'

Tanya launched herself at Elsa, smothering her in a hug that could have cracked ribs. Then she stepped back and looked expectantly, first at Nick, then at Elsa, and Elsa came into Nick's arms with a little sob. She held on to him tightly while the cops cuffed Havers, and Nick

230

was very all right with that.

'Are we all going to be in trouble?' he asked as two of the policemen dragged Havers to his feet.

A squat cop built like a fireplug answered with a jerk of his head. 'Only one in trouble here's Detective Havers. Thanks to Ms Crane and Ms Povic, we've got all the evidence we need to finally bring him down.'

Nick looked from one of them to the other. Elsa lifted onto her toes and kissed him. 'I specialise in voyeuristic experiences, remember?' She nodded to the control room. 'This was just one more.'

As they left the hotel suite, Fireplug Cop leant in close to Elsa. 'Ms Crane, I don't suppose there's any chance of us getting our hands on a copy of that act you were just recording? Some of us would like to know what happens with the billionaire and his virgin bride.'

Her laughter was a sound from heaven to Nick. 'I don't think Mrs Keyser would mind at all,' she said, 'especially when she knows nothing about this little fantasy.'

Nick raised an eyebrow. 'You mean it was all a set-up?'

'Oh, it's Mrs Keyser's fantasy all right. We just happen to be acting it out two weeks early. I didn't expect Rita and Edward to show up so soon and, well, there's no keeping a secret from Coraline Martelli's daughter. That being the case, it looks like the two of us might still get our chance to play the billionaire and his bride.' She batted her eyelashes delicately.

Back in the suite at the Bellagio, the three of them were overwhelmed with hugs and backslaps, and especially from the bride and groom, still dressed for their nuptials. Pike shoved his way forward and group hugged all three of them. 'Welcome back, Tanya. We missed you.' Then he turned his attention to Elsa. 'Don't you ever, ever pull a stunt like that again and then keep it from us or I'll have you in my dungeon whether you like it or not.' He folded her in a hug that lifted her off her feet, then he gave Nick a meaningful nod toward the empty bedroom. Nick didn't have to be told twice. He grabbed Elsa by the hand and marched her to the only place in the suite that wasn't crawling with Mount folks.

Before she could say anything, he scooped her into his arms and kissed her long and hard. 'I don't care,' he said, when he finally pulled away. 'I don't care that you kept this whole thing from me – well, I do care, but it doesn't change the way I feel.'

'Nick, I –'

'I don't want to hear excuses. I know everything was a ruse to help the cops bring down Havers and his gang, and I understand why you couldn't tell me. I do. But the rest of it, the rest of what's happened between you and me, is real and you can't tell me it isn't.' He took her face in his hands and forced her to meet his gaze. 'I love you, Elsa Crane, and it took nearly losing you to make me realise that.'

'No!' She pushed his hands away and stepped back. 'No, you don't love me. You can't possibly love me. If you really knew me, you wouldn't say that. You couldn't.'

'What, because of your past? Fuck, we all have pasts and I don't care. All I care about is now. All I care about is us.'

'But Nick, I –'

There was a soft knock on the door and Leo stuck his head in. 'I'm sorry to interrupt. I know is not a good time and you two have been through rough night, but you are needed. If you would please come.'

Elsa didn't try to pull away when Nick took her hand. In the lounge, everyone had settled on sofas, chairs, and the floor – all with plates and drinks, and the feeding frenzy was on. Rita, still dressed in her bridal gown, sat between Edward and Leo on the sofa. She smiled up at Nick and Elsa. 'I like the dress. Thought I'd wear it a little longer for fun.'

'You look good in it,' Elsa said.

'I know the two of you've had a rough night,' Rita said, 'and you deserve a break. Well, I promise you'll get one soon.'

From somewhere, Pagan and Pike produced a couple of chairs for them, and they sat. Rita nodded her thanks and continued. 'What I have to say is too important to put off, especially after all that's just happened.' She came to her feet and stood in front of Elsa and Nick looking more like a priestess than a bride. 'Nick, you know that people who petition for membership into The Mount have to undergo an initiation. We talked about that the other night. I hope you want to be a member of The Mount, because the Mount definitely wants you.'

'I'd like that. Very much.' Nick spoke around the lump in his throat. He hadn't realised until Rita had asked him just how badly he did want membership into The Mount. 'I'd like to be a permanent part of Mount Vegas, if they'll have me.'

There was a spontaneous eruption of applause and cheering from the assembled crew. 'And there's your answer,' Rita said. 'The decision hasn't been taken lightly by any member of the Mount Vegas Council, but they all agree your place is with them and you're an asset that'll very much enhance Mount Vegas.'

'What do I have to do?' Nick asked, feeling Elsa's fingers curl around his in encouragement. 'For my initiation, I mean.'

'We've also discussed that.' This time it was Elsa who spoke. 'We've all agreed that there's nothing we could put you through, as far as an initiation goes, that would prove your worthiness more than what you've

233

already done, for us and for Tanya. So the membership's yours if you want it.'

There was another round of applause and then Rita cleared her throat to get everyone's attention again. 'There's one more very important matter to discuss and that's the elevation of Mount Vegas to full coven status.'

The room was suddenly silent. Even the clink of cutlery on porcelain stopped. Nick wondered if all breathing stopped too. Rita continued. 'We all agree, as do the High Council members in Rome, that the time has come for Mount Vegas to take its place as a fully-fledged coven.'

There were cheers and whistles, and Nick nearly pulled Elsa out of her chair in his enthusiastic kiss. Then Rita raised a hand for quiet. 'There is one more thing.' She moved to kneel in front of Elsa's chair, taking her hands and looking up into her eyes. 'And this is not so much an initiation as it is a moving forward, an opportunity to heal old wounds and a favour for me, Elsa.'

Elsa glanced nervously around the room. 'Ask me what you want, Rita. I can hardly refuse you.'

'You can, sweetie. In this case you can. But I'm hoping that you won't.'

'Ask me.' Elsa's voice was barely more than a whisper. All colour drained from her cheeks.

'I want you to do an act for me, for us –' She nodded to the rest of the room. 'I want you to go into the dungeon, Elsa, and I want you to take Nick as your sub.'

The room was dead silent. Elsa's pulse jumped against her throat. She pulled her hands away from Rita and, when she spoke, her voice was breathless. 'You can't ask this of me, please, Rita, you can't. You know I can't do this.'

Before he knew what he was doing, before he could think, Nick slid from the chair and knelt next to Rita, but kept his eyes averted. 'Then may *I* ask this of you, Elsa. Will you please do this for me?'

'Nick, you don't know what you're asking, please. You don't know.'

He pulled her fingers to his lips. 'I do know what I'm asking, Elsa. I know exactly what I'm asking, and there's no one else I would ask this of. Please. I'm yours. I want to be yours. I want you to do with me what you will.' He kissed her knuckles again. 'I trust you, Elsa Crane. I trust you with all of my heart.'

Chapter Twenty-two

'What should I do?' Nick asked. He had joined the Mount contingent in the living area of Elsa's office where they were all gathered around a cinema-sized screen that had been pulled down from the ceiling. Elsa had insisted that she and Nick not spend the night together before they shared the dungeon. She had kissed him tenderly and told him he would need to be well-rested, that he would need all his strength for what he would face, and so would she. Of course, he hadn't slept, and he doubted if she had either. But it didn't matter. He was ready. He would do this for Elsa.

'Don't worry, she will tell you exactly what you will do,' Leo said. He nodded to the screen. 'She has just finished preparing for you.'

Nick's stomach somersaulted as he looked at the vacant dungeon, larger than life, on the big screen. It wasn't the pain he knew he'd endure that frightened him; it was the pain he knew Elsa would have to endure. Hers was pain far beyond the physical that he would bear.

Just then, the door opened and Elsa walked in, as he had never seen her before. She wore low-slung khaki cargo pants with lots of pockets. Nick could tell some of them were heavily weighted with who knew what. The matching tank top didn't quite meet the waistband of the trousers. She wore no bra and no shoes. Her hair was pulled into a ponytail set high on the back of her head.

And Jesus, the woman wore a hunting knife belted around her waist! The skin on his scalp prickled. Her face was porcelain pale, making her eyes seem like blue fire. Everyone stepped back until only Elsa and Nick stood in the centre of the room. She studied him as though she could read him, read all that was inside him, and in that moment, he felt certain she could do just that.

With a short length of rope she unclipped from a belt loop, she bound his hands, wrist over wrist. As she bound him, the look on her face dissolved into distant neutrality that sent gooseflesh cascading down his arms; that compelled him to lower his gaze until his vision took in only her lovely bare feet, which he found himself wanting to kneel and kiss. Once he was bound, she tugged slightly on the lead end of the rope.

'Nick Chase, you'll come with me to the dungeon where you'll submit completely and wholeheartedly to me. You're not to speak unless spoken to. You're to do nothing without my permission, without my direction. For the duration of our time there, you belong totally to me. There'll be no safe word. If I decide you've had enough, I'll stop our session. If you speak when not spoken to, I'll assume you don't want to continue, so guard your tongue carefully.'

Then she gave a tug on the rope and turned. He could do nothing but follow her out of the room that Pike had led him to what now seemed like ages ago, to descend the steep stairs.

It took for ever to get there, and yet it took only a second. Nick noticed all this from somewhere outside himself. Once they arrived, Elsa led him to the centre of the dungeon, which had been strangely cleared of equipment. She guided him to stand between two concrete support pillars. There, she curled a finger beneath his chin and lifted it until he met her gaze, no longer distant, no longer neutral, but exacting, demanding, and totally present.

'I don't play like the others do, Nick, so forget everything Pike and Beetle taught you, and listen to me. Focus on me. Do as I say, pleasure me, and, if you do it well, I'll take you with me.' She removed the bindings from his wrists. 'Do you understand?'

'I understand, mistress.'

In a movement that was predator-fast, she grabbed him hard by the hair and pulled his face close. 'Don't call me mistress. My name is Elsa, and that's what I wish to be called by you.' She bruised his mouth with hers. He struggled to breathe, smothering in arousal nearly too heavy to bear. The weight of it surged through his groin like an explosion, like he'd already come and ripped himself to pieces in so doing. Then Elsa pulled away, still holding him in her gaze. 'I'm going to empty you, Nick Chase.' She gave his cock a hard grope through his trousers. 'I don't mean just the emptying of your balls; I mean the emptying of all you are. And then I'm going to take up all the space that you have, Nick; I'm going to turn you inside out and invade every cell of your body. I'm going to be the demon that possesses your soul, the tiger that devours you whole. That's what I'll do to you,' she whispered against his ear. 'And in the end, you'll give it all to me willingly, happily.'

Her words made a serpentine path into his brain, into his heart, and coiled there, so close to his centre. And God, he wanted what she wanted. More than anything, he wanted what she wanted, even as his inside turned cold with fear. He was nearly convinced that she'd already totally possessed him; that she'd already taken up residence in his emptiness when she pulled away, leaving him desolate. But surely that was just an illusion.

She selected two hanks of rope from where they hung on the wall and bound his arms outstretched – one with each hank – to metal rungs on the columns, so that each wrist trailed a long ribbon of rope which coiled to the floor. He shivered. Was she trying to recreate with him what she'd done with her husband all those years ago? Dear God, what had he got himself into? But before his imagination had time to run wild, Elsa stood to face him.

'I almost forgot. I need you naked.' She undid his jeans and, as she slid them and the boxers down, his cock sprang free. She smiled down at it. 'Always at the ready, Mr Chase. I like that about you.' Then the smile was gone, and she shimmied his jeans down and off over his feet, which were still not bound. 'As for the T-shirt – ' she unsnapped the holstered hunting knife with its wicked blade and Nick held his breath '– afraid thoughts of your nasty cock made me forget all about the T-shirt. Never mind.' She moved behind him and grabbed it by the tail, lingering to caress his bare arse. 'I'll buy you another one.' Then, with a single brisk move, she slit the shirt completely open. He sucked breath between his teeth at the feel of cool metal as the unsharpened side of the knife skimmed up his spine. Then she did the same to the front, so the shirt hung halved against his raised shoulders. She left the halves where they hung.

'Your cock enjoyed that, I can tell,' she said, cupping his balls and stroking the length of him with one hand, while the other expertly sheathed the knife. 'You like being a little bit nervous, don't you, Nick – a little bit out of control.'

With her knee, she forced his legs apart until his feet rested against the two pillars and he stood spread-eagle. 'What I want to know, Nick, is just how much control you're willing to give over to me before you get too nervous, too scared, before it hurts too much. Will you let me take you to the place I have in mind? Will you be able to?'

She was just talking, Nick told himself. Sometimes the threat of something was much worse than what was

239

being threatened, and the waiting was the hardest. Still, his pulse kicked up a notch.

Elsa moved back behind him and began to braid the two ropes down his spine in a plait of square knots. As her hands efficiently worked the rope, she stepped in close and whispered against his ear. 'You asked me once if I would hurt you, Nick Chase …'

She paused to run her tongue over the spiral of his ear, then down his neck, the humidity of her breath sending warm shivers over his belly to his cock. 'The answer is yes. I will hurt you.' Just as she said it, just as his pulse ratcheted up another notch, she tied a thick pebble of a knot and nested it tight against his anus. But before he could be fully surprised by it, she ducked under his raised arm, slid the trailing ropes up between his spread legs, and moved to stand in front of him. Then she pulled the ropes up tight to separate his arse cheeks before she crafted a cock ring of rope that settled uncomfortably close and pressed his balls upward into a heavy bulge. He bit back a curse as she guided each rope back through rings that studded the length of the posts – first at waist level, then she weaved them like a spider's web, zigzagging down each side and over and around his thighs and calves before she bound them off around each ankle. And suddenly Nick couldn't breathe.

She stood and studied him, then she lifted his head, forcing him to hold her gaze. 'Do you want me to stop?'

He shook his head.

'Then you have to relax. You have to trust me. You have to trust that I can take you where I want you to be.' She kissed him. This time gently, and his breath slowed at the touch of her, at the taste of her. 'Shall I continue?' she asked when she pulled away, still cupping his cheek.

He nodded.

'Good.' She selected a heavy leather crop from the implements displayed on the wall and ran it across her open palm. Nick pulled a deep breath and braced himself. 'You know what I'm going to do, Nick. You don't yet know why, but trust me, it'll be worth the pain.' The words were barely out of her mouth before she brought the crop down with a sharp snap against the top of his bare thighs in quick succession and frighteningly close to his erection.

The sting of it made his eyes water and caused the muscles of his shoulders to rise and knot. He forced himself to breathe through it.

'It hurts, Nick,' she said, cupping his bound balls, then bending to kiss his cock on the tip, which was already pearled with precome. 'And it'll hurt worse before I'm done. Much worse.' Then she stood and kissed him hard, her tongue dancing joyously against his, and he knew the joy of it. He felt it through his whole body, felt it through the pain of his thighs and the ache in his muscles, just as she brought the crop down hard on his left arse cheek. He hissed the pain into her mouth and she swallowed it back. Then she stepped away and trailed the crop up over his balls, over his belly, bringing the tip of it to a sharp, quick snap against each of his nipples, which were already painfully hard. Then she kissed him again.

'Oh Christ, Elsa!'

She swallowed his words and stepped back. 'Shall I stop?'

He shook his head.

'Then be quiet.' She pinched his nipples until her image became a distorted blur through his streaming eyes, and then she stepped behind him. The sting of the first few lashes felt like fire across his bare arse. She crowded in until he could feel her still-clothed breasts pressed against his back, and then she gave his balls a cupping. 'Though I'm sure you've already figured it out, I'll remind you that you're not to come until I give you

241

permission, or the punishment won't bear thinking about.' She kneaded and stroked. 'I can already feel how full you are. How badly you need relief. You see, Nick, sometimes pain isn't all that far removed from pleasure.'

She laid a crisscross of stripes over his cheeks, stopping to caress and kiss, making him wait in terrible anticipation, as she examined her work, traced the welts with her fingers, kneaded his buttocks, squeezed them together to press against the knot that dug at his anus, an act that made his breath catch and his cock surge, an act that forced him into shallow breathing and futile attempts to relax.

'And now, Nick, I need to come.' She moved back in front of him, and while he watched, she slid out of the cargo pants and kicked them to one side, but she left the sheathed knife belted at her waist. When his cock stretched toward her and his hips thrust forward as much as they could under the circumstances, she gave him a careless stroke. 'Not on your cock, not just yet. I want you to lick my pussy.'

Before Nick had time to wonder how the hell he could manage that, she stepped up onto a kneeling bench that looked as though it might have been pulled straight from an old church, gave a leap, and heaved herself up to grab a metal bar riveted to the ceiling. From there, shoulders mounded, biceps bunched, with the grace of a gymnast, she settled her legs around his neck and shifted and moved until her pussy was so close that the scent of her alone was nearly enough to make him come, and he was breathing shallowly to hold his wad. 'Lick my pussy, Nick. I'm all wet and swollen from playing with you, so lick my pussy, and make me come.'

He strained his shoulders against the rope to nose-dive into her wet depths. Her clit was diamond hard and he'd never seen her so heavy. There was a brief second of satisfaction in knowing that he was turning her on as much as she was him. Then he drew his tongue up through the pout of her, tasting her dark sweetness. He found himself wondering how the hell he could keep from shooting his wad with her literally up in his face.

She hadn't asked him to make it last, and in truth she couldn't manoeuvre much more than he could, hanging from the ceiling as she was, so he gave two long licks from her tight little arsehole all the way up her slit, lingering to slurp and nibble her labia, before he nipped her clit hard, and she came, practically smothering him in the reflexive grip of well-muscled thighs. And then he was shallow breathing again.

'Oh Nick Chase, you're a very naughty boy,' she said when she caught her breath. She dropped back onto the ground and stripped off the tank top and the belt so she stood as naked as he was. 'You hurried through my orgasm, didn't you? Because you didn't know if you could hold your load. That's cheating.' She leant in and kissed his face, wet with her juices. 'Two things. First, I can come as often as I want with or without your contribution, and second, since you were a naughty boy, I can make you watch as a part of your punishment for cheating.'

With that, she pulled a small table and a chair in front of him. Then she opened a black leather case onto the table. There in its velvet-lined interior was a large selection of dildos, butt-plugs, and anal beads. She laid the crop next to the case and selected a dildo that was about the size of Nick's cock. It looked as though it might be made of lapis lazuli. Then she settled into the chair and opened her legs wide. 'And now, Nick, my pleasure will be your punishment.' She fellated the dildo until Nick moaned, then teased it up into her grudging pussy only a little, before she pulled it out and rubbed it up, over, and around her clit. Then she pushed it back in a little farther. She repeated the process with infinite patience as though Nick weren't even there, as though his cock weren't stretching out to her in desperate empathy with the dildo. He watched breathless, mesmerized, aching. It felt like for ever, and yet it felt like a heartbeat before she finally began to thrust and squirm and ride the stone shaft, pinching first her nipples, then her clit.

Nick couldn't breathe. He didn't dare breathe. His load pressed hard at the boundary of his endurance. One breath and he knew he would come. He held it, held it tight.

'Don't you dare close your eyes, Nick. You look at me while I come,' Elsa ordered. And she did. She came, she gushed, she nearly bounced off the chair, and her juices flooded the seat. And Christ, Nick held his breath, Nick held everything. And just when the wave passed, just when he was about to congratulate himself for surviving her orgasm, quick as a cat, she grabbed the crop and brought it up with a sharp snap against his balls from underneath, and he howled with the sting of it. 'My pleasure, your pain, Nick.'

She selected another dildo, shoved it home. Once it was liberally coated with her juices, she shifted until Nick could see her anus, and she began to worry the tight O of it with the dildo. 'My pleasure, your pain' she grunted, biting her lip, 'And I promise when we're finished here you won't know the difference, nor will you care.' She gave his balls two more sharp upward smacks, and then, as she pushed the dildo home in her anus, she selected another to fill her pussy. This time when she came, she roared like a lioness and nearly fell off the chair, flicking Nick's upper thighs lightning fast with the crop. He clenched and held his breath and swore in his head.

For a split second, he closed his eyes, and when he opened them, she sat studying him. She studied him until the discomfort he felt spread upward from his heavy balls to the clutching pit of his stomach. Then she inhaled deeply as though she'd just stepped out into the fresh air. From the case, she selected a string of anal beads that matched the lapis dildo. The string began with a bead slightly larger than a pearl and graduated to one slightly smaller than a ping pong ball. She ran them across her palm, her eyes locked on his. Then, one by one, she inserted them into her mouth, before pulling them out again. Nick gulped a breath, feeling the tension move upward from his belly to clench at his chest.

It was only as she stood and moved behind him that he realised what was about to happen. As she worried the knot of rope aside to reveal his anus, for a brief second he was certain he would pass out. There was no getting his head around what she was about to do, no holding back the blush that was way more than embarrassment, the blush that was humiliation and fear as her hands competently separated his burning arse cheeks. He heard the squirt of lube, felt first her cool, slick finger and then the smallest of the beads breached his sphincter. He didn't cry out, he didn't tense, he didn't move at all, as slowly, teasingly, she inserted bead after bead, pausing in between to kiss his wounded arse cheeks, his stinging balls, the tip of his straining cock.

Christ, how could such tenderness be so closely entwined with his humiliation? Fuck if he didn't feel like a little kid about to cry. But he held it, feeling himself stretched and breached and pushed, yielding to each bead until at last Elsa leant forward, kissed the clench of his anus, and returned the knot of rope to its place.

'There, all done. And now, where were we? Oh yes, I was about to come again, wasn't I?

And fuck if she didn't! She began by smacking her clit with the crop while he clenched in empathy, then she squatted deep and open over the kneeling bench and

245

gushed her juices as she convulsed in a fierce, backbreaking orgasm.

'Oh, that was a good one, Nick. I get so turned on thinking about those beads stimulating you up inside your asshole while I play with myself. It's exquisite, isn't it?'

This time she used the crop first on his balls and then brought it down with a hard snap against his perineum. He clenched with all his might, the beads shuddering and massaging inside him. He swallowed his frustration, his desperate need, as her lashes with the crop became random, first to his thighs, then his arse, then his nipples then his balls, and then he lost track. All he could do was clench and hold and breathe when he could remember to breathe. And still the crop moved over him in a dance of pain that at some point was joined by the slide of her tongue and the press of her lips and the breeze of her breath. He felt his own need like fire in his balls, spreading upward to consume him, to swallow him whole until he was gone, Nick Chase was gone, and that he had ever existed at all seemed like a dream. The only thing that existed, the only thing that was real was Elsa Crane, controlling the world, his world. And yet he held on. He held on for her, the woman who, at this moment, he hated, the woman who he loved enough to endure this moment for and more. And he knew that he would endure whatever it took to convince her to let him into her life.

At last, she brought the crop up with a light sting against his perineum, then, with a movement that was as graceful as it was dangerous, she reached behind him and gave the string attached to the beads a hard yank. Nick's cry roared through the dungeon like something physical just before he bit it back hard and lapsed into desperate, shallow gasps for breath. Elsa slung the beads across the dungeon with a yell that sent chills up his

246

spine, her breath sounding like a windstorm raging through her chest.

'I told you I would hurt you, Nick,' she gasped. Droplets of sweat glistened between her breasts. Tendrils of auburn hair curled damp around her face, escaped from the ponytail, and her eyes held him in blue heat. And Jesus, she looked like a goddess; in spite of everything she'd done to him, she looked like heaven itself. 'I told you I would hurt you,' she repeated, her voice barely more than a whisper. 'How much more pain will you take?'

'As much as I have to,' he managed between gulps for air. 'I told you, I trust you to take me there.'

The sob that escaped her throat was wild-animal harsh. She dropped to her knees in front of him and pulled him against her, hands cupping his wounded arse, face nestled against his damp pubic curls. Then she took him in her mouth and began to suck, her tongue snaking up the underside of his penis, and he cried out and held on tight. When she pulled away, she grabbed the knife from its sheath and, in a mad flurry, sliced up through the webbing of rope in a rapid series of moves that caused him to fall forward when the bonds at his wrists were cut, caused him to fall forward into her arms. She shoved off the last of the rope along with his ruined T-shirt and helped him to the bondage bed. She must have seen the look of dread on his face because she kissed him and offered a laugh that was more like a sob.

'It's over, Nick. You've had enough.' She settled back onto the bed and gently guided him between her legs. 'You need to come now, and I want to make you feel good, so good.'

He literally fell into her. There was no finesse, just raw, jagged need that tore at him from someplace way deeper than his wounded balls, and Elsa Crane felt like home, warm and wet and waiting for him. Every part of him hurt, and yet somehow he had moved beyond it to a place where everything seemed clearer, brighter, and Elsa was there for him, like she had never been before. Her body grounded him, held him, sustained him, and he came in gut-wrenching waves, convulsing in sobs as she returned the favour. Then she reached for the red silk sheet and pulled it over them before he lost consciousness.

When he woke, she cradled his head and held a bottle of cold water to his parched lips. And when he'd drunk his fill, she wrapped him in a soft robe and led him up the stairs to a shower, where she bathed him carefully and lovingly. And though he was exhausted, the need for her still overrode even that, and he took her there against the tiles, spilling into her mindlessly with very little foreplay. Then she dried him and helped him into a bed in the adjoining room, where she gently lotioned his sore arse and all the other bits of him that hurt.

There was a soft knock at the door and someone handed in a breakfast tray, which she set for him. He ate ravenously and she watched, all the while saying nothing. As it had been when they were Leo's pets, there seemed to be little need for words and that surprised him. 'Are you all right?' she asked, when he had eaten and pushed the tray away.

'I've never experienced that level of intimacy.' He struggled to find words. 'The physical pain – well, that was just a part of what happened. The experience was so far beyond that.' He looked up into her eyes and found himself blushing. 'I didn't expect that.'

Her eyes misted and she smoothed his hair with a fingertip. 'That's why I've never wanted to return to the dungeon after that first time. Ultimately, that's why Edgar didn't pursue me, why he left everything to me. I didn't know that at the time. I thought it was The Mount making him an offer he couldn't refuse. I didn't know otherwise until last night. Pike told me.'

'I don't understand,' Nick said.

'Yes you do, Nick. What happens in the dungeon, for me, is too intimate to share with anyone else. I'm not a good sub because I can't communicate sexually from that position, and there's never been anyone I trusted enough to allow them to be my sub because it lays us both bare, and I just couldn't.' She looked down at her hands, fisted in the bedding. 'And then you came along, and I wanted you to understand. I needed you to understand.'

He pulled her into his arms and held her. 'Elsa, I don't want to lose you, and I don't want to scare you away, but you have to know that I love you, and that I'll take the pain you offer me and give it back to you the way you need it to be. You have to understand that.'

She raised her lips to his. 'Then I will hurt you, Nick, and I'll try very hard to show you how much I love you back, if you'll let me.'

Chapter Twenty-three

Nick couldn't make out where the rooftop garden in which they were all celebrating was. He'd been blindfolded when he'd been brought there. When he asked Elsa why, she said that blindfolds were sexy and he was, after all, still learning the ropes, even if he was no longer fulfilling Tanya's contract. Besides, she said, every voyeur likes blindfold scenes and initiations. What they were doing tonight was a bit of both, and it would be very well watched. Wherever he was, the night sky was clear and bright above them and the lights of Vegas twinkled like jewels below. Elsa told him that when a Mount coven convened, the place often felt as though it were somehow outside of time and space. Perhaps that was thanks to all of the sexual energy. He couldn't imagine there being a place that would have more sexual energy than a meeting of the Mount Vegas team.

When the blindfold was removed, he had eyes only for the woman in front of whom he knelt naked. Though his tender bits were well on the mend and the altered state he'd felt in the dungeon was long gone, Elsa Crane still looked like a goddess to him, standing over him in a midnight blue robe. She smiled down at him and offered him her hand. 'Nicolas Crane Chase, I welcome you into our family, now your family. I welcome you into Mount Vegas, now your home. I welcome you into The Mount, now your people. Arise and take your rightful place.'

As he rose, Pike and Beetle came forward and helped him into a robe that matched Elsa's, and Elsa Continued. 'I claim you, Nicolas Crane Chase, I claim you as our own. I claim you for this coven. I claim you for our joys, for our sorrows; I claim you for our celebrations, for our desolations; I claim you for our work and for our play. I claim you to be one of us, to be one with us on this journey.'

She took him into her arms and held him, and he returned the favour as the rest of the Mount Vegas Coven – and now it truly was a coven – gathered around to welcome their newest member.

Rita, Edward, and Leo had stayed on for the initiation, but the experience was being watched worldwide. Rita's mother, Coraline Martelli, along with the Roman Coven's High Council, watched from Rome. Also watching were representatives from the High Councils of the New York City Coven, the Paris Coven, the Buenos Aires Coven, and the Houston Coven. They had watched the raising of Mount Vegas to full coven status and the embracing of their newest member, and they now celebrated Mount Vegas' achievements vicariously from afar.

And there was a lot to celebrate. Tanya was now back in the welcoming arms of her coven family as a hero. Thanks to her and Elsa's efforts, Victor Havers and his gang of corrupt cops were jailed with the promise of very long prison sentences. Because of their efforts, Mount Vegas's position in that grey area of Vegas life was stronger than ever. In fact they were even safer and more secure under the subtle but powerful protection of The Mount. Nick was still trying to get his head around how powerful the organisation really was. But those thoughts couldn't hold his attention for long, not when Elsa stood there at his side, her fingers laced through his.

A smile flicked across her lips. 'Nick, you're looking

at me like I'm the feast.'

'I am very hungry,' he said. 'Ravenous in fact.'

She gave his ear a little nibble. 'I promise I'll do my best to satisfy that hunger –' she pulled away and held his gaze with eyes suddenly serious '– and I won't ever let you go away hungry.'

For a moment they stood wrapped in each other's arms taking in the celebration going on around them. The night was warm and crystal clear and the sounds of the city below, waking to its nightly prowling, were strangely comforting in ways Nick had never noticed before. Kandi's laugh rang bell-like through the air as Horse lifted her off the ground in a bear hug. Beetle sat next to Leo talking quietly. Tanya and Edward swayed in a tango that looked as though it could devolve into something more primal at any moment and Rita and Deb, Pagan and Pike had shed clothing and were chatting in the hot tub, champagne flutes in hand. From somewhere below, the sound of a jazz saxophone wafted in the still summer air. In the distance Nick could just make out the hulk of the mountains on the horizon. He pulled Elsa into a long, lazy kiss and, for the first time in his life, Nick Chase felt like he'd truly come home.

The Mount Series
K D Grace

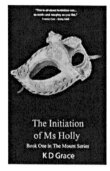  

For more information about **K D Grace**
and other **Xcite** titles
please visit our website.

www.xcitebooks.com

Lightning Source UK Ltd.
Milton Keynes UK
UKOW02f0333110215

246069UK00001B/8/P